William S. Thorburn

A Guide to the Coins of Great Britain and Ireland, in Gold, Silver,

and Copper

From the earliest period to the present time, with their value

William S. Thorburn

A Guide to the Coins of Great Britain and Ireland, in Gold, Silver, and Copper
From the earliest period to the present time, with their value

ISBN/EAN: 9783337322427

Printed in Europe, USA, Canada, Australia, Japan

Cover: Foto ©Suzi / pixelio.de

More available books at **www.hansebooks.com**

A GUIDE TO

THE

COINS

OF

GREAT BRITAIN & IRELAND,

IN

GOLD, SILVER, AND COPPER,

FROM THE EARLIEST PERIOD TO THE PRESENT TIME,

WITH THEIR VALUE.

BY THE LATE

COL. W. STEWART THORBURN,

MEMBER OF THE NUMISMATIC SOCIETY OF LONDON.

SECOND EDITION.

Illustrated with Facsimiles of Coins in Gold and Silver, and numerous other Plates in Gold, Silver, and Copper.

LONDON:

L. UPCOTT GILL, 170, STRAND, W.C.

1888.

LONDON :
PRINTED BY ALFRED BRADLEY, 170 STRAND, W.C.

In Memoriam.

LIEUT.-COLONEL WILLIAM STEWART THORBURN

Was the eldest son of the late James Thorburn, Esq., Barrister of the Inner Temple, and Mary Anne, daughter of William Stewart, Esq., of Shambellie. His paternal grandfather, the Rev. William Thorburn, was for more than fifty years Incumbent of Troqueer, Dumfries, with which district the family has been connected for many generations. Colonel Thorburn was born in 1838, and was educated at Dumfries and Edinburgh, and gave early promise of unusual abilities. He entered the Army in 1858, as Ensign in the 1st Royals, was promoted Lieutenant, and, after some years' service, joined the Army Pay Department. He served in India, and different parts of the world, and rose through the various grades of his profession until he was promoted Lieut.-Colonel, in March, 1886, and selected for the onerous and responsible post of Chief Paymaster in Ireland. He was not, however, destined long to hold a position for which his thorough knowledge of financial affairs and his abilities had peculiarly fitted him. In the beginning of August, he was suddenly struck down by the rupture of a blood vessel in the lung, and, after a painful illness of ten weeks, died on October 18th, 1886, at Dalkey, near Dublin, in the prime of his useful and active life, aged forty-eight years. He leaves a widow and two daughters to mourn their irreparable loss. By his own wish, he is interred at Malvern, beside his only son, who had died the previous year, aged fifteen.

From a very early age Colonel Thorburn had devoted much of his leisure to the study of Numismatics, having formed the nucleus of his fine collection while still a boy at school. An old friend had given him some ancient Scottish coins, which had long been treasured in the family, and this had led the lad to inquire into the subject, in which he soon became deeply interested—an interest which ended only with his existence. During his roving life of military service, and amidst the pressing duties of his profession, he never lost sight of his favourite pursuit. By degrees, here and there, as opportunity permitted, he formed his collection of English and Scottish Coins, the Stuart period especially occupying his attention.

Already a Member of the Numismatic Society, he thoroughly acquainted himself with the subject in all its branches, and compiled the "Guide to the Coins of Great Britain and Ireland," which occupied his leisure hours for more than two years, and on which he bestowed the most painstaking study and minute research. He was contemplating another and larger work on the same subject when his career was cut short by his untimely death, which was deeply mourned by his brother officers, and a large circle of friends, to whom his genial nature and high character had endeared him.

TO

JOHN EVANS, Esq., D.C.L., LL.D.,

PRESIDENT OF THE NUMISMATIC SOCIETY,

VICE-PRESIDENT OF THE ROYAL SOCIETY,

F.S.A., F.G.S., F.S.A. SCOT.,

AUTHOR OF "COINS OF THE ANCIENT BRITONS,"

ETC., ETC., ETC.,

WHOSE LABOURS AND DISCOVERIES

HAVE SO GREATLY ADVANCED

THE SCIENCE OF NUMISMATICS,

THIS VOLUME

IS

BY PERMISSION

RESPECTFULLY DEDICATED.

INTRODUCTION.

This book has been prepared with the object of supplying, in a single volume, a Guide to the Identification and Valuation of the Coins of England, Scotland, and Ireland, at once accurate, complete, and cheap. The standard works on the subject are so costly, and some are so scarce, as to be out of the reach of the majority of collectors. Ruding's "Annals of the Coinage of Great Britain and its Dependencies, from the Earliest Period of Authentic History to the Reign of Victoria," is the most comprehensive work. The last and best edition, in three quarto volumes, was published in 1840, two volumes consisting of text and one of plates. Mr. Cochran-Patrick's "Records of the Coinage of Scotland, from the Earliest Period to the Union," is the most recent work on that subject. It was published in 1875, in two quarto volumes, at £5 5s., and contains sixteen beautiful plates, printed by the autotype process from photographs of the coins themselves, but descriptions of the coins figured are not given. As their titles indicate, these works are histories of the coinage, not descriptions of the coins.

Mr. Evans' exhaustive work on "The Coins of the Ancient Britons," Hawkins's "Silver Coins of England," second edition, 1876, and its companion volume, Kenyon's "Gold Coins of England," 1884, contain minute descriptions of the coins, and are models of painstaking research. As text-books they are indispensable to the student and advanced collector of early British, Saxon, and English coins. But as regards the coins of Scotland and Ireland, the works of Lindsay* are now, in some respects, out of date, and must be read by the light of recent discoveries. Especially is this true in the case of Irish coins, forty-five years having elapsed since the publication of Lindsay's "View of the Coinage of Ireland." Dr. Aquilla Smith, of Dublin, the greatest authority on the subject, has contributed to the proceedings of various learned societies papers which contain the result of his researches. These papers have not, unfortunately, been republished in a collected form, but the information given in them has been carefully embodied in this book, and a reference made to the particular volume in which each treatise may be found. I am indebted to Dr. Smith for valuable information most kindly given to me while engaged in preparing this account of Irish coins.

---

* "A View of the Coinage of Scotland," 1 vol., 4to, 1845; "A Supplement to the Coinage of Scotland," 1 vol., 4to, 1859; "A Second Supplement to the Coinage of Scotland," 1 vol. 4to, 1865; "A View of the Coinage of Ireland," 1 vol., 4to, 1839.

In the following pages will be found a description of every denomination and issue of the coins of each reign, together with their correct weights, a knowledge of which is often most useful in identifying a coin or in determining whether a doubtful piece is genuine or not. By referring to the lists of coins here described, a collector will be able to ascertain what pieces are required to complete any particular series.

Illustrations are given of such typical coins as seemed necessary to convey a general idea of the current coin of each monarch, and an Index to the Plates is added to facilitate reference.

With regard to the valuation of coins, a few remarks may not be out of place. The late Mr. Hawkins considered it extremely difficult to give an accurate idea of the market value of coins, because the value is affected by a variety of circumstances; for example, by the rarity of the piece, the demand for it amongst collectors at the moment when offered for sale, and especially by its state of preservation. Persons residing in the country, who have not the opportunity of attending sales or examining choice collections, are liable to deceive themselves and others with respect to the pecuniary value of coins. Referring to a paragraph in a newspaper or to a priced catalogue of some distinguished collection, they find that a certain coin has been sold for a certain sum, and immediately conclude that every piece of a similar description must be worth as much or perhaps more, not adverting to, or not being aware of, the circumstance that the unusual state of its preservation, or some accidental competition between rival collectors, has carried the price beyond ordinary limits.

The prices quoted in the following pages have been actually realised at sales of coins held in London and Edinburgh during the last thirty years. It is hoped that this information may aid coin collectors in their purchases and assist possessors of coins in forming an approximate idea of the value of their collections. Many of the sale catalogues consulted were courteously lent by Messrs. Lincoln and Son, the well-known numismatists, of 69, New Oxford-street, London. A list of the more important sales, with their dates, will be found on a subsequent page.

A hint may be given to the young collector as to the arrangement and preservation of his coins. They should be kept in a cabinet of mahogany, oak, or walnut-wood, having shallow trays pierced with circular spaces or holes to contain the coins. The trays should be made of mahogany, not of cedar, as it has been found that the surface of copper coins is injured by being kept in contact with cedar-wood. Under each coin should be placed a ticket with a description of the coin, and a reference to a catalogue in which should be recorded every particular, such as the date on which the coin was acquired, the name of the person from whom purchased, and the price. A coin from a well-known collection will always bring a higher price when sold than an equally fine specimen of which the antecedents are unknown. If it be necessary to clean copper or bronze coins, a soft brush (say a very soft tooth brush) should be used, with plain soap and cold or tepid water, but no soda. Having washed the coins carefully, they should be dried by being placed in *boxwood* sawdust; then the sawdust should be brushed off with a very soft dry brush. The secret of success is not in the washing but in the drying process. The box containing the sawdust may be heated in an oven before being used, as sawdust will dry more quickly when hot than when cold.

The same sawdust, if kept free from dust and dirt, will last for several years. In the case of gold and silver coins a similar course may be followed for the removal of any adventitious dirt. It is scarcely necessary to add that on no account should coins be polished up or brightened.

These introductory remarks cannot be concluded more fittingly than in the words of the eminent author of. "The Silver Coins of England": "It is quite unnecessary here to expatiate upon the pleasure or information to be derived from the study and collecting of coins, because it is presumed that all who refer to this volume have already felt some taste or fondness for the pursuit, and only want to have their way smoothed and course directed, that they may pursue it with pleasure and success. To the utilitarian, who demands an explanation of the use of the study of coins, it is in vain to attempt a reply; the pursuit, it must be acknowledged, removes no physical necessities, supplies no animal wants; it neither clothes the naked nor feeds the hungry; its votaries are content with its affording them an agreeable and innocent occupation for their leisure hours, while at the same time it is illustrating and embellishing history, that old almanac, the contempt of modern economists, but the mine from which rich stores of wisdom and of knowledge are extracted by the sage and the philosopher."

NUMISMATIC TERMS AND ABBREVIATIONS.

Obv.—Obverse: The *head*, or principal side of a coin, usually bearing the monarch's name or bust, as distinguished from

Rev.—Reverse. The under side, or back of a coin.

m.m.—Mint mark. A private character (frequently a cross) placed upon a coin in order to distinguish the coins of each particular issue or mintage.

Weight.—The weight of coins is given in Troy grains.

The knowledge of what a coin ought to weigh is often most useful in determining whether a doubtful piece is genuine or not.

N.B.—When the bust on a coin is stated to be looking to the *right* or to the *left*, it is to be understood that it is looking to the *spectator's* right or left, not to the heraldic *dexter* or *sinister*. This is mentioned to prevent mistakes, there being no fixed rule. For example, a bust as in Plate X., Fig. 12, is described as being to the *right*.

NOTE.—The weights of the milled gold coins of Charles II., given at pages 40 and 41, are those of coins struck in and after 1670. Before that year the weights were in the proportion of $131\frac{20}{41}$ grains to the Guinea.

A GUIDE TO THE

VALUATION OF BRITISH COINS.

EARLY BRITISH COINS.

THE earliest English money (first coined between 200 and 150 B.C. is divided into two classes.

(1) **Uninscribed**, or without any lettered inscription.

(2) **Inscribed**, with lettered inscription in addition to various figures or devices.

These coins are found in gold, silver, copper, and mixed metal, chiefly tin. They vary in weight, the gold from 25 to 117 grains; silver, 40 to 93 grains; copper, 25 to 106 grains; mixed metal, 17 to 35 grains.

Some of the gold coins are of a very base standard.

Uninscribed.

GOLD.—*Obv.*, rude bust; *rev.*, triple-tailed horse to right; 12s. 6d.
   Obv., convex, plain; *rev.*, horse with pellet and crescent under; 20s. to 30s. One, extremely fine (116½ grains), £5 5s.; another (91 grains), £2 12s.

SILVER.—*Obv.*, rude bust; *rev.*, horse and emblems; 2s. 6d. to 10s.

COPPER AND MIXED METAL. From 1s.

B

Inscribed.

Note.—For convenience of reference these are arranged in alphabetical (not chronological) order.

Addedomaros.

GOLD.—*Obv.*, AD DOM, a horse to right; *rev.*, a star, with three crescents in centre (85 grains); very fine, £4; another, slightly differing (85 grains), £2 2s.; a third variety, £4 19s.

Antedrigus.

GOLD.—*Obv.*, convex, an object like a fern leaf in the field; *rev.*, ANTEDRIGV, triple-tailed horse to right, below a wheel; very fine, £7. Another similar, but unevenly struck, £3 10s. Another, with faint traces of the letters, and of rude work, 10s.

SILVER.—*Obv.*, rude head to right; *rev.*, AN with TEO above, triple-tailed horse to left; £1 1s.

Bodvo (Boadicea?).

GOLD.—*Obv.*, [B]ODVO across a convex field; *rev.*, triple-tailed horse to right, with wheel and ornaments; £5.

SILVER.—*Obv.*, BODVOC, bare head to left; *rev.*, horse galloping to right, wheel and ornaments; £21.

Cassivellaunus.

GOLD.—*Obv.*, convex, a fern leaf; *rev.*, CATTI, above, a triple-tailed horse, below, a wheel; £2 16s.

Cunobeline.

GOLD.—*Obv.*, CVNOBELIN, within a curved exergual line, two horses galloping to the left; above, a leaf, below, a wheel; *rev.*, CAMV. on a tablet, across an ornamental band; extra rare and fine, £20; others, £5 5s. to £2 2s.

SILVER.—*Obv.*, CVNO, a winged male bust to right; *rev.*, TASCIO, Sphinx squatting to left; £4 6s.; another, £2 11s.

COPPER.—*Obv.*, CVNO on a tablet, under youthful janiform heads; *rev.*, CAMV on a tablet, under a sow resting against a tree; £3 19s., £13 13s., and £40 10s.

    Obv., bust to the right, inscribed CVNOBELINVS REX; *rev.*, a bull butting, TASC beneath; £1 3s. (Fig. 160.)

    A well preserved specimen of each of the above two varieties, sold together, realised only £2 16s.

    Obv., CVNO on a tablet within a wreath; *rev.*, CAMV, horse trotting to right, fine work; £16.

    Obv.—CVNOB ELINI on two tablets, across the field; *rev.*, a Victory seated to left, holding a patera; fine and very rare, £1 9s.

    Obv., CVNO, head of Mercury to left; *rev.*, TASC, Vulcan forging a helmet; 10s.

    Other varieties, £6 6s. to £2.

Dubnovellaunus.

GOLD.—*Obv.*, D . . . OVIILLA, horse galloping to left; *rev.*, two crescents in the centre of an ornamented band; £4; others, varied, £1 1s. to £3 12s.

SILVER.—*Obv.*, DVBNO, laureate beardless head to left, wearing a tiara; *rev.*, a griffin, or Pegasus, galloping to right; a star above and below; £3 12s. 6d.

COPPER.—*Obv.*, DVBN on a tablet, beneath a lion springing to the left; *rev.*, an animal to the right; £1 1s.

Epaticcus.

GOLD.—*Obv.*, EPATICCV, horseman with javelin and shield charging to right; *rev.*, TAS. CIF divided by an ear of bearded corn; unique, £50.

SILVER.—*Obv.*, EPATI, head of Hercules to right; *rev.*, an eagle, front view, with wings expanded, standing on a serpent; £4 14s.

Eppillus.

GOLD.—*Obv.*, EPPI, horse to right, below, a flower; *rev.*, COM. F. within a circle on convex field; £3 and £6 5s.

SILVER.—*Obv.*, VIR. O., bare head to right; *rev.*, EPPI, Capricorn to left, below, COM. F.; of great rarity, £8 5s.

Tasciovanus.

GOLD.—*Obv.*, TASCIO RICON in two lines across an upright ornament composed of five lines; *rev.*, horseman to right, armed with sword and shield; extra rare and fine, £10.

Obv., TASC on a band across the field; *rev.*, Pegasus galloping to left; extra rare and fine, £2 14s., £4 1s., and £7.

SILVER.—*Obv.*, TASC on a tablet within a triple circle, the centre one beaded; *rev.*, horseman galloping to left, his body and legs protected by a diamond-shaped shield; £4. Another £3 6s.

COPPER.—*Obv.*, TASCIAVA, beardless bare head to right; *rev.*, TAS, Pegasus to left; fine and rare, £2.

Verica.

GOLD.—*Obv.*, COM. F. on a sunk tablet, across a convex field; *rev.*, horseman charging to right, above, VIR; below, REX; very fine and rare (82 grains), £9 12s., £9 17s. 6d.

Another, almost similar, realised £8.

SILVER.—*Obv.*, VERICA COMMI. F. around a circular shield; *rev.*, REX, a lion running to right, a crescent above; unique, £7.

SILVER.—*Obv.*, [C]OM.F between two crescents on a convex field, encircled by pellets; *rev.*, lion or boar, a star above; unique, £1 11s.

SAXON COINS.

The Sceatta. (The earliest coin of the Saxon period.)

SILVER.—Weight from about 8 to 20 grains.

First type, with Runic letters.
Second type, with Roman letters.
Type generally.—Obv., a rude head or figure of a bird or beast ; *rev.*, square beaded compartment.
Value varies from 5s. to 20s.

Note.—There are gold Sceattæ in the British Museum.

KINGS OF KENT.

Egcberht, 765—791.

SILVER, *Penny.— Obv.*, EGCBERHT, in outer circle, with RX, in monogram, within the circle ; *rev.*, BABBA in the angles of a cross, with a diamond-shaped centre, including four pellets ; extra rare and very fine, £37 10s. ; another, £48. (Fig. 38)

Eadbearht, or Ethelberht, surnamed Præn, 794—798.

SILVER, *Penny.—Obv.*, EADBEARHT REX in three lines across the field ; *rev.*, moneyer's name, across the field, with ornament beneath. (Fig. 39.)

Cuthred, 798–805.

SILVER, *Penny.—Obv.*, diademed bust to right, + CVDRED REX CANT ; *rev.*, +EABA. MONETA, a circle containing a cross, with a wedge in each angle ; £2 3s. ; poor, £1 7s. ; fine, £7.

Penny.—Obv., CVDRED REX, in the centre a cross and pellets ; *rev.*, EABA. within a tribrach ; £9.

Baldred, 805—823.

SILVER, *Penny.—Obv.*, +BELDRED REX CANT., bust to right : *rev.*, + SVEFNERD. MONET., and within a circle, DRVR. CITS. = *Dorovernia Civitas*, Canterbury ; of great rarity and fine ; £69 ; another, £83 10s. Weight, about 20 grains (Fig. 40.)

Penny.—Different moneyer ; £48 ; another, £44.

Penny.—Obv., + BELDRED REX CANT., in the centre a plain cross ; £20 5s.

Penny.—Obv., + BALDRED REX CN., bust to right ; *rev.*, +DVNVN MONETA, cross moline in centre ; pierced, £8 15s.

SOUTH SAXON.

(No coins of this kingdom have been discovered.)

MERCIA.

Offa, 757—796.

SILVER, *Penny.*—Weight, 18 to 20 grains. A great variety of types; from £20 10s. to £1 4s.; one, described as "fine," sold for 15s. (Figs. 41 and 42.)

Obv., bust to right, + OFFA REX; *rev.*, moneyer's name (Ciolhard) divided by a coiled serpent; £13 13s. (Fig. 41.)

Obv., king's name in the angles of a lozenge-shaped ornament, in centre, a circle and five pellets; *rev.*, ALH MVND (in two lines); £1 11s. (Fig. 42.)

Cynethryth, Queen of Offa.

SILVER, *Penny.*—very rare. *Obv.*, bust to right, EOBA; *rev.*, CYNETHRYTH REGINA round the coin, in the centre the Mercian M in a circle of pellets; £50 5s.; others, £23 10s. and £12 12s.; one, described as "doubtful," realised only 5s. Weight, 18 to 20 grains.

Coenwlf, 794—818.

SILVER, *Penny.*—Weight, 18 to 22 grains. *Obv.*, generally the king's head; *rev.*, the name of the moneyer; from 15s. to £8 2s. 6d.

Ceolwlf I., 819.

SILVER, *Penny.*—*Obv.*, + CEOLWLF REX M., diademed bust to right; *rev.*, moneyer's name, surrounding a large A in centre; £16 10s.; another, £1 2s. Weight about 21 grains.

Beornwlf, 820—824.

SILVER, *Penny.*—Weight about 18 grains. *Obv.*, bust to right; *rev.*, a cross crosslet within a circle; £29; another, £26; others, £8, £41, and £50.

Ludica, 824—825.

SILVER, *Penny.*—Weight, 19 to 22 grains. Types similar to those of Beornwlf. One, which realised £62 at the Cuff sale, is in the British Museum.

Wiglaf, 825—839.

SILVER, *Penny.*—Weight, 25½ grains. Of extreme rarity. *Obv.*, king's name surrounding a cross, with a pellet in each angle; *rev.*, moneyer's name in three lines. In British Museum, purchased in 1828, for £3 10s.

Another. *Obv.*, nude bust to right, WIGLAF REX M.; *rev.*, cross crosslet, moneyer's name in the quarters; £51.

Berhtulf, 839—852.

SILVER, *Penny.*—Weight, 17 to 20 grains. *Obv.*, generally bust to right, with name and title; *rev.*, name of moneyer; £1 6s. to £10.

Burgred, 852—874.

SILVER, *Penny.*—Common, from 5s. *Obv.*, king's head to right, surrounded by name and title; *rev.*, moneyer's name, with MONETA, in three lines. Weight, 16 to 21 grains.

Ceolwlf II., 874.

SILVER, *Penny.*—*Obv.*, diademed bust to right, with king's name: *rev.*, moneyer's name, and lozenge shaped ornament; Cuff sale, £14 5s.; same coin, Dymock sale, £27; Murchison sale, £12 12s.

Another. *Rev.*, two seated figures holding a globe, behind them a Victory with expanded wings; £81.

EAST ANGLES.

Beonna, about 750.

SILVER, *Sceatta.*—Extremely rare. *Obv.*, the king's name in Runic letters surrounding an annulet enclosing a pellet; *rev.*, + EFE in the angles of a cross; £19 5s., £23, and £52 10s. Weight, about 15 grains. (Fig. 43.)

Eadvald, 819—827.

SILVER, *Penny.*—*Obv.*, the king's name and title in three lines; *rev.*, moneyer's name in a quatrefoil, of great rarity. A specimen, broken in halves, realised £1 6s.; another, also broken, £5 5s.

Ethelstan I., 828—837.

SILVER, *Penny.*—Weight, about 18 to 21 grains. *Obv.*, rude bust to left, with king's name around; *rev.*, cross crosslet, with moneyer's name; £1 8s. to £2 14s.; one, extra rare, £17.

Ethelweard, 837—850.

SILVER, *Penny.*—Weight, about 20 grains. *Obv.*, without bust, king's name and title surrounding a cross crosslet; *rev.*, moneyer's name, in centre a cross with a pellet in each angle; 7s.; others, varied, from £1 to £3.

Beorhtric, 850—855.

SILVER, *Penny.*—Only three or four known, one in the British Museum. *Obv.*, + BEORHTRIC REX around a beaded circle enclosing the letter A; *rev.*, moneyer's name around a beaded circle enclosing a cross, with pellet in each angle. Weight, 21 to 22 grains.

Eadmund, 855 – 870.

SILVER, *Penny.*—Weight, about 20 grains. *Obv.*, king's name and title surrounding a cross; *rev.*, moneyer's name, a cross, with a wedge in each angle, 7s. ; others, varied, 12s. to 36s.

Ethelstan II. (Guthrum), 870 – 890.

SILVER, *Penny.*— *Obv.*, a small cross within the inner circle, surrounded by the king's name and title, the name being always blundered ; *rev.*, the moneyer's name in two lines ; from 13s. to £3 10s.

NORTHUMBERLAND.

The coinage of this kingdom consisted of the STYCA, the SCEATTA, and the PENNY.

The STYCA is of mixed metal, chiefly copper, weight about 19 grains, and peculiar to this kingdom.

Ecgfrith, 670 – 685.

COPPER, *Styca.*—*Obv.*, small cross surrounded by ECGFRID REX; *rev.*, an irradiated cross with the word L V X + in the angles, A few only known ; £20 and £51. (Fig. 161.)

Aldfrid, 685 – 705.

SILVER, *Sceatta.*—*Obv.*, +ALFRIDUS, surrounding a pellet within a circle; *rev.*, figure of a quadruped. Two known; one sold for £25. Weight, 20 grains.

Eadberht, 737 – 758.

SCEATTA OF BASE SILVER.—*Obv.*, king's name, variously spelt ; *rev.*, similar to that of ALDFRID ; 10s. to £2 12s. 6d., and £3 19s.

Moll Ethilwald, 759 – 765.

A Sceatta and a Styca are the only coins known.

Alchred, 765 – 774.

SILVER, *Sceatta.*—Same type as that of EADBERHT. *Obv.*, king's name ; *rev.*, animal.

Elfwald, 779 – 788.

SILVER, *Sceatta.*—Same type as preceding coin. Three specimens known ; one sold at £9 9s.

Canred, 808 – 840.

COPPER, *Styca.*—Very common, various moneyers ; 1s. to 2s.

SILVER, *Sceatta.*—Extra rare.

Æthelred II., 840 – 848.

COPPER, *Styca.*—Very common, various moneyers, 1s. to 2s. ; a rare type sold at £2 2s.

Redulf, 844.

COPPER, *Styca.*—Various moneyers ; 2s. to 5s.

Osbercht, 848—867.

COPPER, *Styca.*—Not common, 3s. to 6s.

Earl Sitric.

SILVER, *Penny.*—Only two known. One sold for £3 5s. *Obv.*, SITRIC COMES in two lines, divided by three crosses ; *rev.*, SCELDFOR, between GVNDI BERTVS, across the field.

Cnut (Cunetti), 883—900.

SILVER, *Penny and Halfpenny.*—The latter not common. *Obv.*, CNVT REX, cruciformly arranged ; *rev.*, CVNNETTI. Penny, (20 to 22 grains), 5s. to 7s. ; halfpenny (8 to 9 grains), 10s. to 15s.

Siefred, 900.

SILVER, *Penny and Halfpenny.*—Ordinary type, similar to those of CNVT ; *rev.*, EBIAICE CIVI, in four divisions, small cross. Penny, weight 20 to 22 grains ; 10s. Halfpenny, weight 8 to 10 grains.

Alwald, 901—905.

SILVER, *Penny.*—Only two known. One, *obv.*, +ALVAL DVS, a cross with a pellet in two angles, within a circle ; *rev.*, DNS DS REX in two lines ; sold for £4 2s. Weight, 23½ grains.

Sitric, 921—926.

SILVER, *Penny.*—Six known, all different. One variety has, *obv.*, SITRIC CVNVNC A, surrounding a trefoil-formed ornament ; *rev.*, ASCOL NONETRA, surrounding the Danish Standard.

Eric, 927—954.

SILVER, *Penny.*—Very rare. *Obv.*, ERIC REX in two lines, separated by a sword ; *rev.*, small cross surrounded by RADVLF MEOI ; £8 and £9 10s. ; one sold for £1 12s ; another variety, £11 and £16 5s. Weight, 18 to 19 grains.

Regnald, 912—944.

SILVER, *Pennies.*—Weight, about 20 grains. All very rare, £1 15s. ; one, extra rare and fine, £24.

Anlaf, about 941.

SILVER, *Pennies.*—Very rare. *Obv.*, ANLAF CVNVNC, in centre the Danish raven ; *rev.*, small cross in circle, and moneyer's name ; £4, £8, and £12 ; another variety, £13 10s. Weight, 14 to 22 grains. (Fig. 44.)

SAINTS.

St. Edmund, about 900.

SILVER, *Penny.*—Common. *Halfpenny*, rare. *Obv.*, the letter A, surrounded by the saint's name and title ; *rev.*, moneyer's name, with cross in centre. Penny, 4s. to 6s. ; halfpenny, 15s. to £3. A very fine Penny, with title of "Martyr," realised £2 13s.

St. Peter, 905—941.

SILVER.—*Pennies;* one *Halfpenny* (unique?) is known. *Obv.,* SCI. PETR. MO. divided by a sword; *rev.,* cross with pellet in each angle, EBRACET; 10s. to £2. Weight, 16 to 21 grains. (Fig. 45.)

St. Martin, 921—942.

SILVER, *Pennies.*—Three varieties known, one has *obv.,* SCI. MARTI. in two lines, a sword between pointing to the right; *rev.,* LINCOIA CIVIT, surrounding a large open cross enclosing a small one; £6 10s. Weight, 17 to 18 grains.

ARCHBISHOPS. ·

Jaenberht (Canterbury), 763—790.

SILVER, *Pennies.*—Weight, 18 grains. Very rare. The *obv.* has the Archbishop's name, without bust.

Obv., +IENBERHT AREP, a flower or cross, with a wedge in each angle; *rev.,* OFFA REX in two lines within ornamental compartments. Sold for £21, having previously realised £105.

Obv., IENBERHT AREP in three lines; *rev.,* OFFA REX, formed out of the curved ends of a cruciform ornament; £38.

Æthilheard (Canterbury), 790—803.

SILVER, *Pennies.*—Very rare; £15 to £36. No bust.

Obv., AEDILHARD PONT surrounding a star of six points; *rev.,* OFFA REX MERC, with star in centre. Weight, 18¾ grains.

Obv., AEDILHEARD AR. in outer circle, in centre EP: *rev.,* COENVVLF REX M.; £36 and £45.

Vulfred (Canterbury), 803—830.

SILVER, *Pennies.*—Very rare; £1 14s. to £10 10s.

Obv., front-faced portrait, + VVLFRED ARCHIEPIS.; *rev.,* SVVEFNERD MONET, with DRVR. CITS. (*Doroverniæ Civitatis*) in inner circle; £10 10s.

Obv., full-faced bust, surrounded by VVLFRED ARCHI-EPISCOPI; *rev.,* monogram in centre, SAEBERHT MONETA; £1 14s. Weight, 20½ grains. (Fig. 46.)

Ceolnoth (Canterbury), 830—870.

SILVER, *Pennies.*—Weight, 17 to 21 grains. *Obv.,* bust, usually full face (profile very rarely), name and title; *rev.,* moneyer's name; £1 5s. to £2; a rare variety, £11 7s. 6d.; another, £17 10s.

Ethered (Canterbury), 871—890.

SILVER, *Pennies.*—*Obv.,* Bust to right, with name and title; *rev.,* quatrefoil enclosing a circle over a cross.

Only three known, one purchased by the British Museum for £26 10s.; another sold for £46; weight, 22 grains.

Plegmund (Canterbury), 891—923.

SILVER, *Pennies.*—Weight, 21½ grains. Without bust; £2 10s. to £6 15s.

Eanbald (York), 796.

COPPER, *Stycæ.*—3s. to 5s. *Obv.*, name of Archbishop; *rev.*, name of moneyer.

Vigmund (York), 831—854.

COPPER, *Stycæ.*—1s. 6d. to 2s. 6d. *Obv.* and *rev.* as above.

Vulfhere (York), 854—895.

COPPER, *Stycæ.*—3s. to 4s. *Obv.* and *rev.* as before.

. WEST SAXONS.

Egbert, 800—837.

SILVER, *Pennies.*—Weight, about 22 grains. With and without bust. Very rare, £5 to £10. One fine, but pierced, sold for £1 9s.; another, cracked, sold for £1 11s.

Obv., +ECGBEORHT REX surrounding a double monogram, possibly intended for Merciorum; *rev.*, moneyer's name with a cross crosslet in the centre; a unique and extremely fine specimen, sold for £24 5s.; others, £15 10s. and £19.

Ethelwlf, 837—856.

SILVER, *Pennies.*— With and without bust. 10s. to £2; one, extra rare, £4 16s.; another, £6 2s. 6d. Weight, 22 grains.

Obv., EDELVVLF REX surrounding plain cross upon cross patonce; *rev.*, + OSMVND. MONETA, and in the centre SAXONIORVM in three lines, very fine; £3 4s.

Ethelbert, 856—866.

SILVER, *Pennies.*—Bust to right; £1 to £2.

Obv., + AEDELBEARHT REX, diademed bust; *rev.*, moneyer's name, with MONETA surrounding a floral cross. This coin realised at different sales, £7, £9 9s., and £15. Weight, 20 to 24 grains.

Ethelred I., 866—871.

SILVER, *Pennies.*—Weight, usually 18 grains. Bust to right; *rev.*, moneyer's name. 15s. to £2; one, extra rare and fine, £4 6s.

Alfred (The Great), 872—901.

SILVER, *Pennies.*—Weight, about 20 grains. With and without bust. Various types, £1 to £2; very rare varieties, £16 to £22. (Fig. 47.)

SILVER, *Halfpenny.*—Weight, 10 to 11 grains; 6s., £1 8s. to £14 5s.

Edward the Elder, 901—925.

SILVER, *Pennies* and *Halfpennies.*—Pennies, with and without head; weight about 24 grains; various types, 7s. to 15s.; extra rare varieties, £5 to £15. Halfpenny, without bust, weight, 7 to 9 grains (only three known), £2 2s. and £10; one, extra fine, realised, at different sales, £21 5s., £23, and £10 10s.

Æthelstan, 925—941.

SILVER, *Pennies.*—Weight, 22 to 24 grains. Without bust, 5s. to 15s. With bust, 10s. to £1; extra fine and rare, £2 to £6; one sold for £10 10s. (Fig. 48.)

Edmund, 941—946.

SILVER, *Pennies.*—Weight, about 24 grains. Type very similar to those of Æthelstan. Without bust, 5s. to 15s.; with bust, £1 to £2; rare variety, £6 2s. 6d. and £8.

Eadred, 946—955.

SILVER, *Pennies.*—Weight, 22 to 24 grains. Without bust, 3s. to 10s.; extra rare, £4; with bust, £1 10s. to £2 10s.; one, £5 2s. 6d.

SILVER, *Halfpenny.*—(Unique?) sold for £9 9s.

Eadwig, 955—959.

SILVER, *Pennies.*—Weight, under 24 grains. Without bust, 15s. to £1 10s.; one, extra rare, £5 2s. 6d.

SOLE MONARCHS.

Edgar, 959—975.

SILVER, *Pennies.*—Weight, 20 to 24 grains. Without bust, 4s. to 6s.; with bust, £2 to £3; one, extra rare, £8 8s.; others, £16 10s. and £25.

Edward II., the Martyr, 975—978.

SILVER, *Pennies.*—Weight, 22 to 24 grains. With bust, £1 10s. to £3 10s. One realised £7 5s.

Ethelred II., 978—1016.

SILVER, *Pennies* of several types.—Weight, 20 to 27 grains. Common varieties, 4s. to 8s.; rare typos, extra fine, 15s. to £2 2s.

Canute, 1016—1035.

SILVER, *Pennies.*—Weight, 12 to 24 grains. Bust, generally to left. Various types, 4s. to 8s.; extra rare and fine, £1 to £2. (Fig. 49.)

Harold I., 1035—1040.

SILVER, *Pennies.*—Weight, about 18 grains. With bust, £1 10s. to £2; a rare variety, £4.

Harthacnut, 1040—1042.

SILVER, *Pennies.*—Weight, about 18 grains. Very rare. Bust to right or left. £2 to £5; one, extra rare and fine, £10 5s.; another, £11 15s.

Edward the Confessor, 1042—1066.

SILVER, *Pennies.*—Weight, 15 to 28 grains. Common, 3s. 6d. to 6s.; sovereign type, 10s. to £1; a scarce variety, £2 17s.

Harold II., 1066.

SILVER, *Pennies.*—Weight, about 22 grains. Bust to right or left. 13s. to £1 10s.; one, extra rare and fine, £2 10s. (Fig. 50.)

ENGLISH COINS SINCE THE CONQUEST.

William I. (the Conqueror), 1066—1087.

SILVER, *Pennies.*—(20 to 21 grains.) *Obv.*, the king's name surrounding bust, crowned; *rev.*, an ornamented cross, encircled by the name of moneyer and mint. The names of about seventy places of mintage are known.

The principal varieties are :

1. *Obv.*, profile to left, with sceptre; 10s. to £1; one, extra fine, £3. (Fig. 51.)
2. Bonnet type. *Obv.*, front face, the crown having tassels; 10s. to £1 5s.
3. Canopy type. *Obv.*, front face, under a canopy; 10s. to £2; one, extra fine, £5 2s. 6d.
4. *Obv.*, front face, a sceptre on each side, 10s. to £1 10s.; extra fine, £1 19s.
5. *Obv* , profile to right, with sceptre; 10s. to £1 10s. ; one extra fine, £6 15s.
6. PAXS type, common ; *Obv.*, front face, with sceptre ; *rev.*, cross, the letters P A X S in the angles; 2s. to 5s.

William II. (Rufus), 1087—1100.

SILVER, *Pennies.*—(Over 21 grains.) *Obv.*, king's name and bust, crowned ; *rev.*, a cross, variously ornamented.

The principal varieties are :

1. *Obv.*, front face, a star at each side ; £1 to £2.
2. *Obv.*, profile to right, with sword; £1 to £2.
3. *Obv.*, front face, with sword; 10s. to £2.
4. *Obv.*, front face, with sceptre; a star at left side of head ; 10s. to £1 10s.
5. *Obv.*, front face, without sword, sceptre, or stars ; 15s. to £2.
6. *Obv.*, front face, an annulet at each side; £1 to £1 10s.; one, extra fine, £2 11s.

Henry I., 1100—1135.

SILVER, *Pennies.*—(Under 22¼ grains.) The types are very various and difficult to describe.

The principal varieties are :

1. *Obv.*, front face, between two annulets (resembling William II., No. 6), the king's name variously spelt ; *rev.*, cross fleury, surrounded by name of moneyer and mint; £2 to £3 10s.; one, extra fine, £7 2s. 6d.

Henry I., 1100–1135.

SILVER, *Pennies—continued.*

2. *Obv.*, front face, crowned; *rev.*, PAX across the field; £1 to £2. A variety, same *obv.*, but *rev.*, tressure of eight arches, inclosing an annulet; £2 2s.

3. *Obv.*, profile to left with sceptre; *rev.*, cross fleury; £1 to £1 10s.

4. *Obv.*, front face, or three-quarter face to left, with sceptre. The commonest variety of this king's money; 10s. to £1.

5. *Obv.*, profile to left, with sceptre; *rev.*, cross, annulet in each angle; £2 7s., £4 4s., £4 10s.

6. *Obv.*, profile to left, sceptre, head very large; *rev.*, small cross, within two concentric legends, one being the moneyer's name, the other that of the mint; £5 2s. 6d. This is the only instance of a double legend on the *rev.* of an English penny.

7. *Obv.*, front face, sceptre, at left side of neck a small cross of four pellets, or a star; £2 to £4; one, extra fine, £6 6s.

8. *Obv.*, profile to left, sceptre; *rev.*, tressure of four sides; £2 to £5; one, £7 7s.; another, £8.

9. *Obv.*, front face, sceptre at right, and a star at left side of head; *rev.*, cross voided, floret in each angle; £7 15s., £10 15s.; a very poor specimen realised only 3s.

Robert, Earl of Gloucester (illegitimate son of Henry I.).

SILVER, *Penny.—Obv.*, figure on horseback armed with a sword, conical hat, RODBERTVS .. ST . X; *rev.*, cross patée upon a cross fleury, surrounded by various ornaments in place of a legend. Only two specimens, both imperfect, are known. One (16¼ grains), is in the British Museum; the other (under 15 grains), in the Pembroke Collection, realised £11 10s.

Stephen, 1135–1154.

SILVER, *Pennies* (under 22½ grains), of several types. The king's bust and name, variously spelt, on *obv.*

The principal varieties are :

1. *Obv.*, front face, sceptre; *rev.*, voided cross, within a tressure fleury; £2 to £3.

2. *Obv.*, profile to right, sceptre; *rev.*, cross moline, the ends pierced and forming a tressure fleury. The commonest type, 5s. to £1; one, extra fine, £4. (Fig. 52.)

3. *Obv.*, same as No. 2, but flag instead of sceptre, and star in the field; £5 12s. 6d., £6 15s., £10 10s., and £13.

4. *Obv.*, very rude profile to right, sceptre; *rev.*, cross voided, martlet in each angle; WHICHELINVS DERBI; £5 12s. 2d., £7, and £7 17s. 6d.

Henry, Bishop of Winchester (illegitimate brother of Stephen).

SILVER, *Penny* (16 grains).—*Obv.*, profile to right, crozier; HENRICVS EPC.; *rev.*, STEPHANVS REX. Unique.

Stephen and Matilda, his Wife.

SILVER, *Penny* (17¼ grains).—*Obv.*, two figures, standing, holding a standard between them, extremely rare; £8, £17, £18, and £19. One, with a piece broken out, sold for £3 7s.; another, also imperfect, realised £3 16s.

Eustace, elder son of Stephen.

SILVER, *Pennies* (16 to 19 grains).—Struck while governor at York, very rare, and generally imperfect.

  1. *Obv.*, a lion passant to right, EISTACHIVS; *rev.*, ornamental cross; £4 10s., £7, £9 9s., £10 5s., and £12 10s. An imperfect specimen sold for £1 2s. One, described as fine, realised only £1.

  2. *Obv.*, half length figure to right, holding 'a sword, conical head-dress, EVSTACIVS; *rev.*, cross; £6 2s. 6d., £15, and £20 10s.

William, second son of Stephen.

SILVER, *Pennies* (15 to 16 grains).—Two known.

  1. *Obv.*, front face between two stars, LVILLEM DVO.

  2. *Obv.*, front face, no stars, WILLELMVS; *rev.*, ornamental cross.

Matilda (daughter of Henry I. and mother of Henry II.), the Empress.

SILVER, *Pennies* (14 to 16¼ grains).—Three known, supposed to have been struck by Matilda while at war with Stephen on behalf of her son.

    Obv., similar to Stephen's No. 2; IM.ERATR. = Imperatrix; *rev.*, moneyer's name and B (Bristol).

Roger, Earl of Warwick, 1123—1153.

SILVER, *Pennies* (about 22 grains). Four known. Type like Stephen's No. 2. *Obv.*, PEREKIC = Werewic; Struck in London, Lincoln, and Warwick, while an adherent of the Empress Matilda.

Henry II., 1154—1189.

SILVER, *Pennies* (about 22 grains).—Two issues.

  1. *Obv.*, king's bust nearly full faced, sceptre in right hand, with name and title; *rev.*, cross potent, a small cross in each angle name of moneyer and mint. Usually very badly struck; 2s. 6d. to 5s.; extra fine, £1 to £2 6s. and £3. (Fig. 53.)

  2. *Obv.*, king's head, front face, within inner circle, sceptre in right (rarely left) hand; *rev.*, double barred cross, small cross botone in each angle, surrounded by name of moneyer and mint; 1s. to 2s. 6d. (Fig. 54.)

Richard I., 1189—1199.

No English coins bearing the name of Richard are known. During his reign the coins struck in England were similar to those of his father, Henry II., whose name they bore.

Silver Pennies, similar to Henry II.'s second issue, were struck at the Lichfield mint during the reign of Richard I.

John, 1199—1216.

No English coins bearing the name of John are known. Silver Pennies bearing the name of his father, Henry II., were issued during John's reign. They are of neater workmanship and slightly smaller than those struck by Henry II. and Richard I.

Henry III., 1216—1272.

GOLD, *Penny* (45 grains).—*Obv.*, king enthroned; *rev.*, double cross, with a rose in each angle; extremely rare; £41 10s., £130, £140. (Fig. 1.)

SILVER, *Penny* (22½ grains).—Two issues. (1) Type of Henry II.'s second issue; (2) *rev.*, long double cross; 1s. to 2s. 6d. *with III a*

Edward I., 1272—1307.

GOLD. None.

SILVER,* Penny (22½ grains), Halfpenny, and Farthing.

> *Pennies*, struck at Berwick, Bristol, Canterbury, Chester, Durham, Exeter, Kingston (Hull), Lincoln, London, Reading, St. Edmondsbury, York, and by Robert de Hadley ; 1s. to 2s. 6d. A rare variety, *rev.*, VILLA BEREWICI, a bear's head in one of the angles; £1 3s. ; another, VILLA RADINGY, an escallop in one angle ; £1 1s. and £3.
> *Halfpennies*, struck at Berwick, Bristol, Lincoln, London, Newcastle, Reading, and York ; 1s. 6d. to 2s. 6d. ; one, struck at Berwick, two bears' heads in *rev.*, 10s. ; one of Reading, £1 1s.
> *Farthings.*—Struck at Berwick, Bristol, Lincoln, London, and York ; 2s. 6d. to 3s. 6d. ; one, of Berwick, two bears' heads on *rev.*, £1 19s. ; one, of Lincoln, fine, 14s.

PATTERN, *Groat* (86 grains).—£1 10s., £4, £5 2s. 6d., £7, £8 5s. A very poor specimen sold for 5s. (Fig. 55.)

PATTERN, *Penny* (21½ grains), showing neither shoulders nor mantle ; £5 5s. (Fig. 56.)

Edward II., 1307—1327.

GOLD.—None.

SILVER.—Penny, Halfpenny, and Farthing.

> *Penny* (22 grains).—Struck at Berwick, Bristol, Canterbury, Durham, London, Newcastle, St. Edmondsbury, and York ; 1s. to 2s. 6d.
> *Halfpenny* (11 grains).—London ; 1s. 6d. to 2s. 6d.
> *Halfpenny and Farthing* (5½ grains).—Struck at Berwick : the two 18s.

---

* The PENNIES, HALFPENNIES, and FARTHINGS of Edward I., II., III., IV. Richard II. and III., Henry IV., V., VI., and VII. (first and second issues), have on *obv.* the king's full faced bust crowned, surrounded by his name and titles, variously abbreviated, and on *rev.* a long single cross extending to edge of the coin, with usually three pellets in each angle, encircled by name of mint following CIVITAS (city) or VILLA (town)—thus, CIVITAS LONDON, VILLA BRISTOLLIE.

Edward III., 1327—1377.

GOLD.—Florin, Half Florin, Quarter Florin, Noble,* Half Noble, Quarter Noble.

Florin (108 grains).—Two known ; one sold for £113.

Quarter Florin (27 grains).—Extra rare. *Obv.*, lion, crowned, standing on a helmet ; £130, £145, £170. (Fig. 2.)

Noble (136¾ grains).—Extremely rare.

Quarter Noble (34¼ grains).—£7 5s., £9, £10, £21.

Noble (128⅛ grains).—£1 8s., £1 12s., £3 6s., £4 1s., £7 10s., £21 10s.

Quarter Noble (32 grains).—12s., £1, £1 7s.

Noble (120 grains).—£1 10s. to £2 5s. ; one, extra fine, £4 12s.

Half Noble (60 grains)—£1 to £2 ; one, extra rare and fine, £7 15s.

Quarter Noble (30 grains).—10s. to £1 ; a rare variety, £1 9s. and £2.

SILVER.—Groat,† Half Groat, Penny, Halfpenny, and Farthing.

Groat (72 grains).—London and York, 1s. 6d. to 4s. ; one, of London, with Roman M in *rev.* legend, sold for £2 11s. (Fig. 57.)

Half Groat (36 grains).—London and York, 1s. 6d. to 2s. 6d. A very thick piece (321 grains) struck from the Half Groat die, £6, and £7 2s. 6d.

Penny (20 to 22¼ grains). — Durham, London, and York, 1s. 6d. to 2s. 6d.

Halfpenny (10 to 11 grains).—London and Reading ; 1s. 6d. to 2s. 6d. ; one, Reading, with escallop, £1 1s.

Farthing (5 to 5¼ grains).—London and York ; 2s. 6d. to 3s. 6d. ; one (unique ?) of first coinage realised £1 2s.

A Groat, Half Groat, and Penny, all struck at York, and extra fine, sold for £2 15s.

A Groat, Half Groat, Penny, and Halfpenny, struck at London, realised 9s.

Richard II., 1377—1399.

GOLD.—Noble, Half Noble, Quarter Noble.

Noble (120 grains).—With and without flag ; £2 10s. to £4 ; very fine, £5 2s. 6d., £6 2s. 6d., and £9 ; others have sold for £1 5s., £2, and £2 3s.

---

* NOBLES or RIALS and HALF NOBLES have on *obv.* the figure of the king or queen crowned, in armour, standing in a ship, a sword in right hand, a shield in left, bearing the Royal Arms. The *rev.* has a tressure of eight curves, containing a cross fleury, until the second issue of Edward IV., when a sun of sixteen rays took the place of the cross.

QUARTER NOBLES have on *obv.*, the king's name and titles surrounding a shield of arms within a tressure, and on *rev.*, a tressure, with fleurs-de-lis and lions alternately in the angles, a cross fleury in centre.

† Groats and Half Groats of Edward III., IV., and V. Richard II. and III., and Henry IV., V., VI., and VII. (1st and 2nd issues) have on *obv.*, full faced bust crowned, within a tressure, encircled by the King's name and title ; and on *rev.*, a long cross extending to edge of the coin, three pellets in each angle, surrounded by two circles. In the outer circle the motto POSVI DFVM, etc. ; in the inner circle the name of mint, as on the Penny.

RICHARD II.—CONTINUED.

GOLD.—*Continued.*

Half Noble (60 grains).—£1 10s. to £4; very fine, £6, £8, £9 5s., £10 10s., £12, and £15.

Quarter Noble (30 grains).—£1 to £2; very fine, £2 11s., £3, and £3 5s.

A Noble, with flag, and Quarter Noble sold together for £1 14s.

A Half and Quarter Noble, together, sold for £1 1s.

SILVER.—Groat, Half Groat, Penny, Halfpenny, and Farthing.

Groat (72 grains).—Struck in London only; £1 to £1 10s., extra fine, £2 11s., £2 17s., and £3 5s.; others, 8s., 11s., and 16s.

Half Groat (36 grains).—Struck in London only; £1 to £1 10s.; very fine, £1 18s., £3 3s., £3 10s., and £3 15s.; poor specimens, 6s. to 10s.

Penny (18 grains).—Struck in Durham, London, and York; 4s. to 6s.; very fine, 10s. 6d.; others, £3 14s. and £4 10s.

Halfpenny (9 grains).—London only, 2s. to 3s. 6d.

Farthing (4½ grains).—London only; extra rare; £1 19s., £2 10s., and £5 10s.

A Groat, Half Groat, and two Halfpennies sold for 12s.

Two Groats, two York Pennies, and a Halfpenny sold for £1 5s.

A Groat, Half Groat, Penny (York), and Halfpenny, £1 5s.

A Half Groat, Penny (York), and two Halfpennies, £1 10s.

A Groat, Half Groat, Penny, and Halfpenny, £2 3s.

Henry IV., 1399—1413.

GOLD.—Noble, Half Noble, Quarter Noble.

Noble, first issue (120 grains).—£12 5s.

Noble, second issue (108 grains).—£11, £14 5s., and £9 5s.

Half Noble, first issue (60 grains).

Quarter Noble, first issue (30 grains).—£21 10s.; another, £1 1s.

Quarter Noble, second issue (27 grains). (Fig. 3.)

SILVER.—Groat, Half Groat, Penny, Halfpenny, and Farthing.

Groat (60 grains).—10s., 13s., £3 4s., £3 11s.; another realised only 8s.

Half Groat (33 grains).—£4 5s.; ditto (27 grains), £4 4s.

Penny (15 to 18 grains).—Durham, London, 2s., and York (18 grains), 8s., 11s., and £1.

Halfpenny (5 to 12 grains).—12s. 6d. to 21s.; London (11¼ grains), £1 6s.

A London Penny (16¼ grains) and Halfpenny (8¼ grains) together, 15s.

Farthing (3¾ grains).

Henry V., 1413—1422.

GOLD.—Noble, Half Noble, Quarter Noble.

Noble (108 grains).—£1 1s., £1 8s., £2; rare variety, £6 10s.

Half Noble (54 grains).—10s. to £1 13s.

Quarter Noble (27 grains).—10s. to £1.

C

HENRY V.—CONTINUED.

> SILVER.—Groat, Half Groat, Penny, Halfpenny, and Farthing.
>> Groat (60 grains).—London, 1s. 6d. to 3s. 6d.
>> Half Groat (30 grains).—London, 2s. to 4s.
>> Penny (15 grains)—Durham, London, and York, 2s. 6d. to 5s.
>> Halfpenny (7½ grains).—London, 1s. 6d. to 3s. 6d.
>> Farthing (3¾ grains).—2s. 6d. to 3s. 6d.

Henry VI., 1422—1461.

> GOLD.—Noble, Half Noble, Quarter Noble.
>> Noble (108 grains).—£1 10s., £2, £3 12s., £4 5s. (Fig. 4.)
>> Half Noble (54 grains).—17s., £2, £3 11s.; York, £5 2s. 6d.
>> Quarter Noble (27 grains).—10s. to 15s., £1 11s.
>> A variety (unique?): Obv., EXALTBITVR, &c.; rev., king's name and titles, £1 16s.
>
> SILVER.—Groat, Half Groat, Penny, Halfpenny, and Farthing.
>> Groat (60 grains).—London and York, 1s. 6d. to 3s. 6d.
>> Half Groat (30 grains).—London and York, 2s. to 4s.
>> Penny (15 grains).—Durham, London, and York, 1s. 6d. to 3s. 6d.
>> Halfpenny (7½ grains).—London and York; 2s. 6d. to 5s.
>> Farthing (3¾ grains).—London and York; 3s. 6d. to 5s. 6d.

Henry VI. (restored), 1470.

> GOLD.—Angel and Half Angel.*
>> Angel (80 grains).—£1, £2 5s., £3 10s., £5, £7 2s. 6d.; Bristol, £4, £5 17s. 6d., £7 15s., £10.
>> Half Angel (40 grains).—£30 10s., £31.
>
> SILVER.—Groat (48 grains), London, 12s., 15s., £1 6s.; Bristol, £1 11s., 16s., £2 11s.; York, £1 1s., 18s.; two (London and Bristol), both fine, 6s.
>> Half Groat (24 grains).—London, 6s.; York (20 grains), £0, Cuff sale, sold for £2 2s., Whitbourne sale; (19½ grains), 19s., £2 2s.; another, £5.
>> A light Groat struck at London, and one at York, and a light Half Groat, York, sold together for £3 17s.
>> Penny (12 grains).—York, 2s. to 5s.

Edward IV., 1461—1483.

> GOLD.—Noble, Half Noble, Quarter Noble, Angel, and Half Angel.
>> Noble, first issue (108 grains).
>> Noble, second issue (120 grains).—£1 to £2; Bristol, £1 2s.; Coventry, £2 14s.; Norwich, £1 19s.; York, £3 10s., £4. (Fig. 5.)
>> Half Noble (60 grains).—Bristol, £1 2s., £2 8s., £3, £3 10s., £4; London, 25s. to 35s.; Norwich, £2 6s. and £8 17s. 6d.; York, 16s., 19s., £1 11s., £2, £3 12s.
>> A Bristol Noble and Half Noble, both fine, sold for £2.

---

* Angels and Half Angels have on obr., the Archangel Michael standing on a dragon and piercing it through the mouth with a spear, surrounded by the monarch's name and titles; rev., a ship with cross for a mast, a shield of arms on the side of the ship.

EDWARD IV.—CONTINUED.

GOLD.—*Continued.*

Quarter Noble (30 grains).—10s. to £1 ; rarer types, £3 2s. and £4 4s.

Angel (80 grains).—25s. to 35s., £3 3s. ; struck at Bristol, extra fine, £12. (Fig. 6.)

Half Angel (40 grains).—15s. to 25s., £1 12s., £2 6s. ; £3 11s. ; one, extra fine, £7 15s. ; one, struck at Bristol, £4 2s.

SILVER.—Groat, Half Groat, Penny, Halfpenny, and Farthing.

Groat (60 grains).—London, 10s. to £1 ; extra fine, £2 1s.

Groat (48 grains).—Bristol, Coventry, London, Norwich, and York, 2s. to 5s.

Half Groat (30 grains).—London, very rare, £4 2s., £5; (24 grains), Bristol, Canterbury, London, Norwich, and York, 2s. to 5s.

Penny (12 grains).—Bristol, Canterbury, Durham, London (extra fine, £3 4s.), and York, 10s. to £2 4s.

A Half Groat and Penny, both of Canterbury, £2 16s. ; three York Pennies, varied, £1 13s.

Halfpenny (7½ to 8½ grains).—London, extra fine, 14s. ; (6 grains), Bristol, Canterbury, Durham, and London, 2s. to 3s. 6d.

Farthing (about 3 grains).—London. One of first issue (extra rare), and one of second issue, sold, together, for £2 11s.

Edward V., April to June, 1483.

GOLD.—*Angel* (80 grains).—*m.m.*, rose and sun united ; £7 10s., £9 15s., £10.

SILVER.—*Groat* (48 grains).—*m.m.*, rose and sun united, £1 7s., £1 10s. ; very fine, £3 4s. One, *m.m.*, rose, reading EDWARD, £1 10s. ; another, same *m.m.*, 8s. Two, *m.m.*, boar's head and rose and sun united, sold, together, for £1 6s.

Richard III., 1483—1485.

GOLD.—Angel, Half Angel or Angelet.

Angel (80 grains).—*m.m.*, boar's head ; £2, £4, £5 2s. 6d., £7 15s., £10 5s.; *m.m.*, rose and sun, £1 8s., £4 2s., £11 2s. 6d. ; *m.m.*, rose, £5 2s. 6d., £7 2s. 6d. ; *m.m.*, sun, £6 12s. 6d.

Angelet (40 grains).—*m.m.*, boar's head ; £12, £13.

SILVER.—Groat, Half Groat, Penny, and Halfpenny.

Groat (48 grains).—London and York. London, 15s. to 25s.; very fine, £2 to £3. York, £1 1s. and £1 12s.

Groat (37 grains). — London, with high arched crown (unique ?), £1 14s.

Half Groat (24 grains).—London, extremely rare. One sold for £12, £2 19s., and £13 10s., at successive sales ; another, £15 5s.

Penny (12 grains).—Durham, London, and York.

A Durham penny, poor, sold for 5s. ; fine, 17s. and £2 3s. A York penny, 9s., £2 8s., and £2 15s. ; two sold for 10s. A penny, *m.m.*, lis, realised only 2s. 6d.

RICHARD III.—CONTINUED.

SILVER.—*Continued.*

> *Halfpenny* (6 grains).— London, £1 5s. to £10 10s.; one realised, at successive sales, £6 15s., £10 10s., and £4 11s.; others, £1 5s., £3 16s., and £4.

Henry VII., 1485—1509.

GOLD.—First issue: Noble or Rial, Angel, Angelet. Second issue: Sovereign or Double Rial, Double Sovereign, Angel, Angelet.

> *Noble* (120 grains).—Extremely rare, if not unique.
>
> *Angel* (80 grains). — First issue, £5 15s.; another, £1. Second issue, 13s. to £3 3s. A variety, legend on *rev.* same as on sov., £3 12s., £4 4s.
>
> *Angelet* (40 grains).—11s. to £2 13s. A variety, roses interspersed in legend, £5.
>
> *Double Rial or Sovereign** (240 grains).—Specimens have realised at various sales, £3 1s., £11 15s., £15, £20, £26, £30, £35, £37, and £39. (Fig. 7.)
>
> *Double Sovereign* (480 grains).— Like the sovereign, but much rarer.

SILVER.—Shilling, Groat, Half Groat, Penny, Halfpenny, and Farthing.

> *Shilling* (144 grains).—*Obv.*, profile bust to right, crowned (the first instance of a true portrait on an English silver coin), HENRICVS DI. GRA. REX ANGLIE Z. FR.; *rev.*, royal arms on shield, quarterly, over a cross, POSVI, &c.
>
> A variety reads HENRIC. VII. Another, HENRIC. SEPTIM. (Fig. 58.)
>
> The prices realised at various sales were £6, £7 2s. 6d., £10, £12, and £21 5s.
>
> *Groat* (48 grains).—First issue, London, front face, with open crown, 6s. to £1 10s. Second issue, London, front face, with high arched crown, 1s. 6d. to 3s.; one, extra fine, 14s. Third issue, similar to the Shilling, profile bust to right. crowned, with, sometimes without, numerals, 2s. 6d. to 5s.; very fine, 10s. (Fig. 59.)
>
> Variety, reading SEPTIM, £2 12s. and £12.
>
> *Half Groats* (24 grains).—Types similar to the Groat. First issue, Canterbury, London, and York, very rare, £3 4s., £3 12s.; one (York) and a London Halfpenny sold, together, for £1 12s. Second issue, Canterbury, London, and York, 1s. 6d. to 2s. 6d.; very fine, 5s. Third issue, with and without numerals, none reading SEPTIM known, 2s. to 3s. 6d. A unique variety, £2 11s.
>
> *Penny* (12 grains).—First issue, Canterbury and York; *obv.*, front faced bust, open crown; *rev.*, cross and pellets, with name of town; 13s. to £1, one, extra fine, £2 2s. Second issue, Canterbury; *obv.*, front face, high arched crown; *rev.*, cross

---

* Double Rials (of Henry VII. and VIII., Edward VI., Mary, Elizabeth, and James I.) have on *obv.*, the monarch's name and titles, the king or queen enthroned; and on *rev.*, a double rose, with plain shield of arms in centre, surrounded by the motto.

HENRY VII.—CONTINUED.

SILVER.—*Penny continued.*

and pellets; extra rare: one, very fine, realised £5. Third issue, Durham, London, and York; *obv.*, king enthroned, HENRIC. DI GRA. REX ANG.; *rev.*, arms on shield; 2s. to 5s. (Fig. 60.)

Halfpenny (6 grains).—Similar to the penny of first and second issues, Canterbury, London, and York; 5s. to 7s. 6d.

A set (first issue): Groat, Half Groat, Penny, and Halfpenny, £1 1s.

A set (second issue): Groat, Half Groat, the rare Canterbury penny, and a halfpenny, all fine, sold for 18s.

Farthing (3 grains).—Second issue, only two known.

Henry VIII., 1509—1547.

GOLD.—Double Sovereign, Sovereign, Half Sovereign, Crown, Half Crown, Rose Noble or Rial, George Noble, Angel, Angelet, and Quarter Angel.

Double Sovereign (480 grains).—*Obv.*, king enthroned, a portcullis at his feet; *rev.*, a double rose. (Fig. 14.)

Sovereign, first issue (240 grains).—Similar to Double Sovereign, £2 7s., £3 11s., £4, £5 2s. 6d., £6, £7, £9 9s., £10 15s., £14, £17. Second issue (200 grains).—*Obv.*, king enthroned, a rose at his feet; *rev.*, royal shield of arms, crowned, supported by lion and dragon; £13 13s., £16, £20, £33, £34 10s. Third issue (192 grains).—Similar to second issue; £2 1s., £2 7s., £2 16s., £4 5s., £7 2s. 6d., £8, £9 10s., £11 15s.

Half Sovereign.—Similar to Sovereign; £1, £1 10s., £2 1s., £3, £3 16s., £5, £19 5s., £25.

Crown, second issue (57¼ grains).—*Obv.*, a double rose, crowned, between the letters H.K., H.A., H.I., or H.R. encircled by HENRIC. VIII. RVTILANS ROSA SINE SPINA.; £1 to £1 10s; extra fine, £2 2s. (Fig. 8.)

Crown, or Quarter Sovereign, third issue (48 grains).— *Obv.*, double rose, crowned, between H. R. surrounded by HENRIC. 8. ROSA SINE SPINA; *rev.*, shield of arms; £1 to £1 10s.

Half Crown, second issue (28¼ grains).—Almost same as Crown; £1 3s., two sold for £1 11s.; a Crown and Half Crown together, £1 4s. Third issue (24 grains).—Almost same as Crown; £3 14s.

Rose Noble, or Rial (120 grains).—Similar type to Rose Noble of Edward IV.

George Noble (71 grains).—*Obv.*, St. George on horseback spearing the dragon; *rev.*, similar to the Angel. One, very poor, £1 3s.; another, £3; others, £8, £9 5s., £14, £20 10s., £23 5s., £26, £31, and £34. (Fig. 9.)

Angel (80 grains).— First issue, similar to Angel of Henry VII, but reading HENRIC. VIII.; 15s., £1 1s., £1 3s., £2 9s., £3 6s., and £4 6s. Second issue, similar to first issue, but reading HENRIC 8.; 15s., £2 12s., £4 10s., £5 5s.

HENRY VIII.—CONTINUED.

GOLD.—*Continued.*

Angelet (40 grains).—First issue, similar to the Angel; £1 3s., £2 6s., £2 10s., £2 19s., £3 15s. Second issue, similar to the Angel; 17s., 18s., £2 6s., £2 11s.

Quarter Angel (20 grains).—Second issue only, similar to the Angel; 15s., £1 12s., £2 4s., £2 17s., £3 5s.

SILVER.*—Shilling or Testoon, Groat, Half Groat, Penny, Halfpenny, and Farthing.

Shilling (120 grains).—*Obv.*, full-faced bust, HENRIC VIII., &c.; *rev.*, a large double rose, crowned, POSVI. &c. Ordinary specimens, 10s. to £1; others, £2, £3 2s., £4, £6 2s. 6d.; finest known, £16. (Fig. 61.)

Shilling, struck at Bristol, 16s.

Groat, first issue (48 grains).—*Obv.*, profile bust of Henry VII., but with VIII.; *rev.*, shield of arms; 2s. 6d. to 5s.

Groat, second issue (42½ grains).—*Obv.*, young profile bust to right; 1s. 6d. to 2s. 6d.

Groat, third, fourth, and fifth issues (40 grains).—Bristol, Canterbury, London, and York. *Obv.*, bust, almost full-faced, crowned; 1s. 6d. to 3s. 6d.

Groat, fifth issue.—*Rev.*, REDDE CVIQVE; 11s., 17s., and £1.

Half Groat, first issue (24 grains).—Canterbury, London, and York. *Obv.*, similar to Groat of first issue; 2s. 6d. to 3s. 6d.

Groat and Half Groat, first issue, unusually fine, £1 14s.

Half Groat, second issue (21¼ grains).—Canterbury, London, and York. *Obv.*, similar to Groat of second issue; 1s. 6d. to 2s. 6d.

Groat and Half Groat, second issue, unusually fine, £1 4s.

Half Groats, third, fourth, and fifth issues (20 grains).—Bristol, Canterbury, London and York; 1s. 6d. to 2s. 6d.

Half Groat (fine silver), £2 11s.; York, 11s.

Half Groat, fifth issue. — *Rev.*, REDDE CVIQVE, &c.; £2 2s., £6 6s.

Penny, first issue (12 grains).—Canterbury, Durham, London, and York. *Obv.*, king enthroned, HENRIC. DI. GRA., &c.; *rev.*, arms, with name of mint; 1s. 6d to 3s. 6d.

Penny, second issue (10½ grains).—Durham and London. *Obv.*, king enthroned, H. D. G. ROSA SINE SPINA; *rev.*, arms and place of mintage; 1s. 6d. to 3s. 6d.

Penny, third, fourth, and fifth issues (10 grains).—Bristol, Canterbury, London, and York. *Obv.*, full faced (or three-quarter faced) bust, mantled; *rev.*, arms and place of mintage; 1s. 6d. to 3s. 6d.

Groat, Half Groat, and Penny.—Bristol, all fine, £1 16s.

---

* Many pieces were struck in base silver, some being only four parts of silver to eight parts of alloy. The pieces of fine silver are rare, but the base coins (except the Shilling) are common.

HENRY VIII.—CONTINUED.

SILVER.—*Continued.*

Halfpenny, first and second issues (5 to 6 grains).—Canterbury, London, and York. *Obv.,* front faced bust, crowned; *rev.,* cross and pellets, with place of mintage; 1s. 6d. to 3s. 6d.

A set (first issue) consisting of Shilling (fine silver), two Groats, Half Groat (Wolsey) and three others, Penny, and Halfpenny; all fine, £1 1s.

A set (second issue) comprising Shilling, Groat, four Half Groats, Penny, and Halfpenny; all fine, £1.

Halfpenny, third coinage (5 grains).—Canterbury, London, and York. *Obv.,* front faced bust, mantled, with ROSA, &c., in legend; *rev.,* cross with pellets, and name of mint; 1s. 6d. to 3s. 6d.

Farthing, first issue (3 grains).—*Obv.,* portcullis, HENRIC. DI. GRA. REX; *rev.,* a cross, with a rose upon the centre, CIVITAS LONDON; extremely rare, £15 5s.

Farthing, second issue (2½ grains). — *Obv.,* portcullis, RVTILANS ROSA; *rev.,* a rose upon the centre of a cross, HEN . . . . . AG; £4 4s., £5 2s. 6d.

Edward VI., 1547—1553.

GOLD.—Treble Sovereign, Double Sovereign, Sovereign, Half Sovereign, Crown, Half Crown, Six-Angel Piece, Angel, Angelet.

Treble Sovereign (508¼ grains). — *Obv.,* king enthroned, EDWARD VI., &c.; *rev.,* arms crowned, with supporters, IHS AVTEM, &c.

Double Sovereign (480 grains).—*Obv.,* king enthroned; *rev.,* large double rose, with arms in centre, IHESV., &c. Extremely rare, £77, £99, £165, and £175.

Sovereign, third year (169¼ grains).—Type of the Treble Sovereign, very rare; £5, £6 8s. 6d., £7 10s., £8 2s. 6d., £11, £12 10s.; the finest specimen known, £25 10s. (Fig. 11.)

Sovereign, or Double Rial, fourth year (240 grains).—Similar to the Double Sovereign, extremely rare; £7, £20, £21 10s. The finest known, £90.

Sovereign, sixth year (174¾ grains).*—*Obv.,* half-length figure of the king in armour in profile to right, crowned; *rev.,* arms, crowned, with supporters; £3 1s., £5 2s. 6d., £6, £7 10s., £8, £9 9s., £10.

Half Sovereign, first year (96 grains).—*Obv.,* king enthroned, EDWARD 6, D. G., &c.; *rev.,* arms, with supporters, IHS, AVTE, &c.; 19s., £1 9s., £2 15s., £4, £5 10s., £6, £8 15s.

Half Sovereign, third year (84¾ grains), five types.—*Obv.,* bust in profile to right, bareheaded or crowned; *rev.,* oval shield of arms. On one variety is M.D.XLVIII, the first instance of a date upon a gold coin. 18s., £1 3s., £1 6s., £2 17s., £4 12s. (Fig. 19.)

---

* Sovereigns of Edward VI. (last issue), Elizabeth, James I., Charles I., and Charles II. have on *obv.* the monarch's bust in profile to right or left, surrounded by name and titles; and on *rev.,* shield of arms crowned, usually with initial letters at sides of shield, encircled by a motto. Half Sovereign, Quarter Sovereign, and Eighth Sovereign are similar in type.

EDWARD VI.—CONTINUED.

GOLD.—*Continued.*

Half Sovereign, sixth year (87½ grains).—*Obv.*, half-length bust, crowned, in profile to right ; *rev.*, shield of arms, crowned, between the letters E. R. ; 16s., £1 2s., £2 1s., £3, £4 5s., £8 5s., £12. (Fig. 10.)

Crown, first year (48 grains).—*Obv.*, rose crowned. between the letters E. R., encircled by RVTILANS ROSA, &c. ; *rev.*, arms, crowned, between H. R., surrounded by DEI GRA., &c., unique, £50 ; another variety, also unique, £83.

Crown, third year (42½ grains).—*Obv.*, bust in profile, to right, in armour, bareheaded ; *rev.*, oval shield of arms, between the letters E. R. A variety has the bust crowned ; £1 11s., £1 17s., £2 7s., £3 14s., £5, £8 15s., £9, £10 10s.

Crown, sixth year (43½ grains).—Similar to Half Sovereign of sixth year ; *rev.*, SCVTVM FIDEI, &c. ; 14s., £1 15s., £4 4s., £5 10s., £11.

Half Crown, first year (24 grains).—*Obv.*, arms crowned, between the letters E. R., legend EDWARD 6, &c. ; *rev.*, a double rose crowned, between the letters E. R., RVTILANS, &c.

Half Crown, third year (21½ grains).— Similar to the Crowns of third year ; £2, £3 5s., £6 10s., £7 2s. 6d., £8 8s., £10 5s., £10 15s., £13.

Half Crown, sixth year (21¾ grains).—Similar to the Crown of same year ; £3 12s., £6 2s. 6d., £10 5s., £12 5s.

A Crown and Half Crown, third year (cracked), sold together for £5 2s. 6d.

Six-Angel Piece (240 grains).—Unique, and supposed to be a pattern.

Angel (80 grains).—Similar to the second issue Angel of Henry VIII. ; £21 10s., £37, £41 10s., £59.

Angelet (40 grains).—Similar to the Angel.

SILVER.—Crown, Half Crown, Testoon, Shilling, Sixpence, Groat, Threepence, Half-groat, Penny, Halfpenny, Farthing.

Crown, fifth year (480 grains), dated 1551, 1552, or 1553.— *Obv.*, king on horseback to the right, with date under the horse ; *rev.*, arms. Ordinary specimens, 15s. to £1 10s. ; in very fine condition, £2 16s., £3 11s., £4, £5.

Half Crown (240 grains).—Similar to Crown, and same dates. Ordinary specimens, 15s. to £1 10s. ; very fine, £1 16s., £2 11s., £3 11s., £5 ; the finest known, £9 5s. (Fig. 62.)

Testoon, third year (80 grains).—*Obv.*, profile, crowned, to right ; *rev.*, oval shield of arms, dated MDXLIX. or MDL., the first instance of a date upon a silver coin ; 4s. 6d. to 7s. 6d. ; very fine, £1, £1 15s., £2 2s., £3 3s. (Fig. 79.)

Shilling, fifth year (96 grains).—*Obv.*, full-faced bust, crowned, the numerals XII (for twelve pence) on right side of bust ; *rev.*, square shield of arms ; 4s. 6d. to 7s. 6d. ; extra fine, 12s., £1 2s., £1 11s. The finest known, £3 10s.

Sixpence (48 grains).—Similar to Shilling, but with VI (for sixpence) ; 3s. 6d. to 5s. 6d. ; a perfect example, £4 13s. (Fig. 80.)

EDWARD VI.—CONTINUED.

SILVER.—*Continued.*

Groat, first year (40 grains).—*Obv.*, profile, crowned, to right, EDWARD 6, &c.; *rev.*, arms, £1 to £1 10s.; a poor specimen, 7s.; fine examples, £2, £3 4s., £6 6s., £14 10s., £19, and £25 10s.

Threepence, fifth year (24 grains).—Similar to Sixpence, but with III (for 3 pence) at side of head; 10s. to £1; very fine, £1 2s., £2 10s., £3 1s.; poor specimens, 3s. 6d. to 5s.

Half Groat, first year (20 grains).—Similar to the Groat; 25s. to 35s.; very fine, £2, £2 12s.; £3 7s.; a poor specimen, 5s.

Penny, first year (10 grains).—Bristol and London. *Obv.*, Profile, crowned, to right; *rev.*, arms, with name of city; 18s., £1 10s., £2 3s., £3 4s., £4, £4 12s., £5, £6 6s.; a poor specimen, 5s.

Penny, fifth year (8 grains). — Fine silver, *obv.*, king enthroned, as on Pennies of Henry VII. and VIII., *rev.*, arms and CIVITAS LONDON; £2 12s., £6 6s., £7 12s. 6d.

Penny, base silver (8 grains).—London and York. *Obv.* full blown rose; *rev.*, arms and name of city; 3s. 6d. to 5s. 6d.; others, 8s. 6d. and 10s. 6d.

Two (London and York) very fine, together, £1 9s.

Halfpenny, first year (5¼ grains).—Bristol and London. *Obv.*, profile, crowned, to right; *rev.*, cross, with three pellets in each angle, and name of city; only three or four known, £11, £14., one, imperfect, sold for £2 1s.

A Crown, Half Crown, and Shilling, all fine, £1 9s.

A Threepence and York Rose Penny, very fine, together, 13s.

A Half Groat, Bristol Penny (bust), and a Rose Penny, together, £3 5s.

A London Groat, Canterbury Half Groat, and Bristol Penny, poor, £1 6s.

Halfpenny, fifth year (11 grains) of base metal, similar to the Penny of base metal, but the rose is single, *rev.*, CIVITAS LONDON.

Farthing, fifth year (5¼ grains) of base metal. *Obv.*, portcullis E. D. G., &c., *rev*, cross, with pellets, CIVITAS LONDON.

Mary, 1553.

GOLD.—Sovereign, Rial, Angel, and Angelet.

Sovereign, or Double Rial (240 grains).—*Obv.*, queen enthroned, legend ends with date, M.D.LIII; *rev.*, double rose, with small shield of arms in centre; £4 to £6; others £7 7s., £8 8s., £9 15s., £10 10s. Some have realised only £2 10s., £2 13s., £3, £3 3s., £3 11s. (Fig. 20.)

Rial (120 grains).—*Obv.*, queen standing in a ship; £53, £63, £68, £71, and £80; one (cracked) realised £20 10s.

Angel (80 grains).—Type similar to Edward VI.'s; £3 to £4; very fine, £5, £8, and £9 12s.; others have sold for £1 2s., £1 3s., £2 4s.

MARY.—CONTINUED.

    GOLD.—*Continued.*

        Angelet (40 grains).—Similar to Angel; £5, £5 5s., £31, £35, and £51.

    SILVER.—Groat, Half Groat, Penny.

        Groat (32 grains).—*Obv.*, profile to left, MARIA, D.G., &c.; *rev.*, arms, VERITAS TEMPORIS FILIA; 2s. 6d. to 4s. 6d.; very fine, 10s., 14s., 16s., and 21s.

        Half Groat (16 grains).—Similar to Groat; £1 11s., £3 16s., £4 2s., £6, and £10 10s.

        Penny (8 grains).—*Obv.*, bust, M. D. G. ROSA SINE SPINA; *rev.*, arms, CIVITAS LONDON; £4, £9, £13 5s.; one sold for only £1; a variety (unique), dated '53, realised £11 11s.

        Penny, base silver (10 grains).—*Obv.*, rose; 18s.

Philip and Mary, 1554—1558.

    GOLD.—Angel, Angelet.

        Angel (80 grains).—Similar to Mary's Angel, but reading PHILIP Z MARIA, &c.; £2 6s., £3 3s., £6, £7, £8 15s., and £14.

        Angelet (40 grains).—£10 5s.

    SILVER.—Shilling, Sixpence, Groat, Half Groat, and Penny.

        Shilling (96 grains).—*Obv.*, busts of the king and queen face to face, a large crown above; *rev.*, oval shield of arms; 5s. to 15s.; extra fine, £1 to £2 10s.; an exceptional specimen realised £11 11s. (Fig. 63.)

        Sixpence (48 grains).—Type similar to Shilling; 3s. 6d. to 7s. 6d.; extra fine, 15s. to 21s.; one sold for £1 13s.

        Groat (32 grains).—*Obv.*, bust of Mary, with legend PHILIP Z (or ET) MARIA. D. G. REX Z (or ET) REGINA; *rev.*, POSVIMVS, etc.; 2s. 6d. to 5s.; very fine, 7s. 6d. to 10s.; a brilliant example, £1 15s.

        Half Groat (16 grains).—Similar to the Groat, but very rare; £1 1s., £1 10s., £2 4s., £3 16s., £4 8s, £5, £6.

        Penny (8 grains).—*Obv.*, bust of Mary, with legend P. Z. M. D. G. ROSA SINE SPINA; *rev.*, arms; £1 5s., £1 10s., £3 4s., £3 15s., £5 10s., £6, £7 10s., and £8 10s.; one sold, however, for 5s. only.

        A Half Groat and Penny, together, £2 7s.

        Penny, base silver (10 grains).—*Obv.*. large double rose, with P. Z. M., etc.; *rev.*, arms; 3s. 6d. to 5s. 6d.; one extra fine, 17s.

        A·lot, consisting of Shilling, Sixpence, Groat, and Rose Penny, realised £2 18s.; a Shilling, Sixpence, and Groat, £1 4s.

Elizabeth, 1558—1603.

    GOLD.—Hammered.—Sovereign or Double Rial, Rial, Angel, Angelet, Quarter Angel, Pound Sovereign, Half Sovereign, Quarter Sovereign or Crown, One-eighth Sovereign or Half Crown. Milled—Half Sovereign, Crown, Half Crown.

ELIZABETH.—CONTINUED.

GOLD.—*Continued.*

Sovereign or Double Rial (240 grains).—£4 to £5; very fine, £6 6s., £8 10s., £9 15s.; others, £2 4s. and £3 10s.

Rial (120 grains).—*Obv.*, queen in ship; £6 6s., £8 8s., £10, £13, £17, £18, £20, £30 10s., and £32.

Angel (80 grains).—Ordinary type; £1 5s. to £1 15s. First issue, £2 18s. to £3 3s.

Angelet or Half Angel (40 grains).—15s. to £1 10s.; very fine, £1 18s. and £2 7s.

Quarter Angel (20 grains).—15s. to £1 10s.; one, very fine, £3 10s.

Angel, Angelet, and Quarter Angel, together, £2 1s.

Pound Sovereign (174$\frac{1}{2}$ grains).—*Obv.*, queen's bust to left, crowned; *rev.*, shield of arms; £3 to £4; very fine, £5 5s., £7 7s., and £10 2s. 6d. Same have sold for £1 1s., £1 8s., £2 3s., £2 10s., and £2 18s.

Half Sovereign (87$\frac{1}{2}$ grains).—£1 to £2 10s.; very fine, £3 9s., £5 12s. 6d., £8 10s., and £9 15s.

Quarter Sovereign (43$\frac{3}{4}$ grains).—£1 5s. to £2 10s.; very fine, £3, £4 4s., and £5 2s. 6d.

Eighth Sovereign (21$\frac{11}{16}$ grains).—£1 10s. to £3; very fine, £4, £4 8s., and £5 5s.

Half Sovereign, milled.—£2 to £5; extra fine, £6 15s. and £12 10s.

Crown, milled.—£4, £6 6s., £8 15s., £9 9s., £10, £11, and £15 15s.

Half Crown, milled.—£2 8s., £2 10s., £3, £6 10s., £7 5s., £9, £10 10s., and £11 2s. 6d.

SILVER.—Hammered.—Crown, Half Crown, Shilling, Sixpence, Groat, Threepenny, Half Groat, Three-halfpenny, Penny, Three-farthings, and Halfpenny. Milled—Shilling, Sixpence, Groat, Threepenny, Half Groat, and Three-farthings.

Crown (464$\frac{1}{2}$ grains).—*Obv.*, crowned bust to left; £1 10s. to £3; extra fine, £4 6s., £5 15s., and £7 2s. 6d.

Half Crown (232$\frac{1}{4}$ grains).—*Obv.*, crowned bust to left; £1 to £2; extra fine, £3, £3 11s., £4 7s., £7 2s. 6d., and £9. (Fig. 64.)

Shilling (96 and 92$\frac{3}{4}$ grains), hammered.—2s. 6d. to 5s.; one, extra fine, £1 13s. Milled—7s. 6d. to 15s.; extra fine, £1, £2 6s., and finest known, £10 5s.

Sixpence (48 and 46$\frac{1}{4}$ grains), hammered.—1s. 6d. to 3s. Milled—2s. 6d. to 5s.; extra fine, 6s. 6d., 8s., 12s., and 18s.

Groat (32 and 31 grains), hammered.—3s. to 5s. Milled—5s. to 10s.; extra fine, £1 6s., £1 15s., and £3 12s.

Threepence (24 and 23$\frac{1}{4}$ grains), hammered.—1s. to 2s. 6d. Milled—5s. to 10s.

Half Groat (16 and 15$\frac{1}{2}$ grains), hammered.—1s. to 2s. Milled—7s. 6d. to 10s. A milled set of Groat, Threepence, and Half Groat, in finest state, realised £5 2s. 6d.

Three Halfpenny (12 grains), hammered; 2s. 6d. to 5s.; very fine, 10s.

Penny (8 and 7$\frac{1}{2}$ grains); 1s. to 2s.

ELIZABETH.—CONTINUED.

SILVER.—*Continued.*

Three-Farthings (6 grains), hammered; 2s. 6d. to 5s.; milled, 10s.

Halfpenny (4 grains), hammered; 2s. to 4s.

A hammered set of eleven pieces (Half Crown to Halfpenny); sold for £1.

A hammered set of ten pieces (Shilling to Halfpenny, including Half Groat, with and without dots), in extra fine condition, realised £5; a similar set, very fine, £2 2s.; a similar set, all well preserved, 19s.

James I., 1603—1625.

GOLD.—First issue: Sovereign, Half Sovereign, Quarter Sovereign, One-eighth Sovereign. James I. Half Unit (Fig. 12).

Second issue: Unit, Double Crown, British Crown, Thistle Crown, Half Crown.

Third issue: Rose Rial, Rial or Noble, Angel, Angelet.

Fourth issue: Thirty Shilling Piece, Spur Rial or Fifteen Shilling Piece, Angel, Laurel, Half Laurel, Quarter Laurel.

Sovereign, first issue (nearly 172 grains).—*Obv.*, Bust to right, crowned; *rev.*, arms, I. R. at sides of shield; £1 10s. to £2 10s.; very fine, £3, £6 12s. 6d., and £10 10s.; one sold for only £1 7s.

Half Sovereign (nearly 86 grains).—£1 10s. to £2 10s.; extra fine, £4 8s., £5 7s. 6d., £7 12s., and £11 15s.

Quarter Sovereign (nearly 43 grains).—£1 to £1 10s.; extra fine, £2 17s., £5 2s. 6d., and £9.

One-eighth Sovereign (21¼ grains).—Very rare, £2 12s., £7 7s., and £8 8s.

Unit, second issue (nearly 155 grains).—£1 10s. to £2 5s.; extra fine, £3, £5, and £6 6s.

Double Crown (over 77 grains).—£1 5s. to £2 5s.; extra fine, £3 3s.

An Unit and Double Crown together sold for £1 19s.

A Double Crown and Half Crown realised £3 14s.

British Crown (38¼ grains).—10s. to £1; extra fine, £1 5s., £2 2s., and £2 11s.

Thistle Crown (31 grains).—*Obv.*, a double rose on its stalk, crowned, between the letters I. R., surrounded by IA. D. G. MAG. BR. F. ET. H. REX.; *rev.*, a thistle, crowned, between I. R., encircled by the motto TVEATVR VNITA DEVS; 10s. to £1; others £1 12s. and £1 14s.

Half Crown (19¼ grains).—10s. to £1; extra fine, £2 5s.

A British Crown, Thistle Crown, and Half Crown sold for only 15s.

Rose Rial, third issue (213¼ grains).—*Obv.*, King enthroned; *rev.*, large rose, with shield of arms in centre; £3 to £5; extra fine, £5 10s., £6 12s. 6d., £9 10s., and £10 15s.; others have sold for £1 17s., £2, and £2 13s.

JAMES I.—CONTINUED.

GOLD.—*Continued.*

Rial, or Noble (106½ grains).—Very rare; £2 2s., £3 12s., £5 2s. 6d., £6 5s., £8, £8 17s. 6d., £9 15s., £10, £12, £13, £15, and £25 10s.; the finest known, £32.

Angel, first issue (71½ grains).—£1 to £2; very fine, £3 5s., £3 10s., £4, £4 18s.; others have sold for 15s. and 18s.

Angelet (35½ grains).—£1 3s., £1 12s., £1 18s., £2 17s., £4 10s., £5 7s. 6d., and £6 10s.

Thirty Shilling Piece (194¼ grains).—*Obv.,* king, enthroned; *rev.,* a large shield of arms on a cross fleurée, over the shield XXX (for 30s., the value). £5 to £7; extra fine, £8 15s., £9 10s., £10 5s., £12 10s., and £15; others have sold for £2 1s., £2 6s., £2 12s., £3, £3 11s., and £4 14s.

Spur Rial, or Fifteen Shilling Piece (97⅗ grains). — *Obv.,* the Scottish lion séjant, crowned, standing behind the shield of arms; *rev.,* a sun of sixteen rays; £5 2s. 6d., £6 2s. 6d., £10 10s., £13 5s., £14, £15 10s., £20, and £27; one, pierced, sold for £4. (Fig. 13.)

Angel, second issue (64¹⁵⁄₁₆ grains). — Very rare; £1 6s., £1 12s., £2 6s., £4 9s., £9, £17; one, pierced, sold for £1 1s.

Laurel (140¼ grains). — *Obv.,* bust to left, draped and laureated, with XX (for 20s.) behind the head; £1 10s. to £2; very fine, £3 6s. and £4 18s.

Half Laurel (70¼ grains).—Similar to Laurel, but with X for value; £1 to £1 10s.

Quarter Laurel (35¼ grains).—Similar to Laurel, but with V for value; 10s. to 15s.

A Laurel, Half, and Quarter, sold together for £2, £2 12s., £3, and £5 5s.

A Half Laurel and Quarter, very fine, sold together for £4 15s.

SILVER.—First issue.—Crown, Half Crown, Shilling, Sixpence, Half Groat, Penny, Halfpenny.

Second issue.—Pieces of similar value and weight.

The motto on the *rev.* of the Crown, Half Crown, Shilling, and Sixpence of first issue is EXVRGAT DEVS, &c.; and of second issue, QVÆ DEVS CONIVNXIT, &c.

Crown, first issue (464¼ grains).—£1 to £2; extra fine, £3 11s., £3 15s., £6 2s. 6d., £7 7s., and £8 5s.

Half Crown (232¼ grains).—£1 7s., £2 2s., £2 15s., £4 4s., £9 10s., £10 15s., £12, £15 5s., and £33 10s.; the finest known, £50; a poor specimen sold for 10s. only.

Shilling (92¾ grains).—2s. 6d. to 5s.; extra fine £2 16s., £4 15s., £5 5s., and £7 5s.

Sixpence (46¼ grains).—2s. to 5s.; extra fine, 19s.; finest known, £4 11s.

Half Groat (15½ grains).—*Obv.,* bust, with II. (for 2d.) behind head; *rev.,* arms; 1s. 6d. to 3s. 6d.

Penny (7½ grains).—*Obv.,* bust, with I. (for 1d.) behind head; *rev.,* arms; 2s. to 3s. 6d.

Halfpenny (3¾ grains).—*Obv.,* portcullis; *rev.,* cross and pellets; 2s. 6d. to 3s. 6d.

JAMES I.—CONTINUED.

SILVER.—*Continued.*

> *Crown*, second issue.—£1 to £2; very fine, £2 15s., £3 10s., £4 2s., £5 2s. 6d., £5 12s. 6d., and £10.
>
> *Half Crown.*—10s. to 15s.; very fine, £1 3s., £1 12s., £2 3s., £2 10s., £4 12s., and £5 5s.
>
> *Shilling.*—2s. to 5s.; very fine, 16s., £1 7s., £1 11s., £2 2s., £3 11s., £3 15s., £4, £4 6s., and £4 17s. 6d.
>
> *Sixpence.*—2s. to 4s.; very fine, 13s. to 19s.
>
> *Half Groat.*—*Obv.*, rose crowned; *rev.*, thistle crowned, 1s. to 2s. (Fig. 65.)
>
> *Penny.*—*Obv.*, rose, *rev.*, thistle; 1s. to 2s.
>
> *Halfpenny.*—*Obv.*, rose, *rev.*, thistle, without any legend; 2s. to 3s.
>
> A Crown and Half Crown (latter poor), first issue, £3 12s.
>
> A Crown, Shilling, Sixpence, Half Groat, Penny, and Halfpenny, first issue, £1 4s.
>
> A Shilling, Sixpence, Half Groat, Penny, and Halfpenny, first issue, £1 1s.
>
> A Sixpence, Half Groat, Penny, and Halfpenny, first issue, all fine, £2 6s.
>
> A Crown, Half Crown, Shilling, and Sixpence, second issue, very fine, £4 8s.
>
> A Crown, Half Crown, and Shilling, second issue, all with plume over the arms, 15s.
>
> A Crown, Half Crown, Shilling, Sixpence, Half Groat, Penny, and Halfpenny, second issue, £1 5s.
>
> A Shilling, Sixpence, Half Groat, and Penny, second issue, 6s.
>
> A Sixpence, Half Groat, Penny, and Halfpenny, second issue, all fine, £1 5s.

Charles I., 1625—1649.

GOLD.—Three Pound Piece, Unit or Sovereign, Double Crown or Half Sovereign, Crown or Five Shilling piece, and Angel.

> OXFORD MINT.—*Three Pound Piece* (420¼ grains).—*Obv.*, half length bust to left, crowned, &c.; *rev.*, inscription, in three lines, RELIG. PROT, &c., with date (1642, 1643, or 1644) below, surrounded by the motto EXVRGAT, &c. £4 to £6; extra fine, £6 10s., £7 2s. 6d., £7 10s., £8, £9 9s., £10 5s., £11, £12 15s., £15, and £17; some have sold for £3 7s., £3 11s., and £3 16s.
>
> *Sovereign or Twenty Shilling Piece* (140½ grains). — *Obv.*, profile bust to left, crowned, XX behind head for value; *rev.*, similar to Three Pound Piece, dated 1642, 1643, 1644, 1645, or 1646; £2 to £5; others, £6 12s. 6d., £7, £7 7s., £9, and £10 10s.; some have realised only £1 3s., £1 5s., £1 7s., £1 9s., and £1 11s.
>
> *Half Sovereign or Ten Shilling Piece* (70¼ grains).—Similar to Sovereign, but X behind head for value; £2 to £3; extra fine, £5 7s. 6d., £6, £7; exceptional specimens, £40 and £43; one sold for only £1 3s.

CHARLES I.—CONTINUED.

GOLD.—*Continued.*

TOWER MINT.—Three issues, distinguished by the king's dress.

Unit, Broad, or Twenty Shilling Piece (140¼ grains).—*Obv.*, bust to left, XX behind head; *rev.*, shield of arms, square or oval, surrounded by motto FLORENT CONCORDIA REGNA.; £1 10s. to £3; extra fine, £3 12s., £4 6s., £4 11s., £5 15s., £7 5s.. and £7 15s.; exceptional specimens, £12 12s., £14, and £21; some have sold for only £1 2s. 6d. and £1 5s.

Double Crown or Ten Shilling Piece (70¼ grains).—*Obv.*, Similar to Unit, but X behind bust; *rev.*, also similar to Unit, but motto CVLTORES SVI DEVS PROTEGIT; £1 to £2; extra fine, £3, £3 11s., £4, £6 2s. 6d., and £12; one sold for 12s.

Crown or Five Shilling Piece (35¼ grains).—Similar to Double Crown, but V behind head; 10s. to £1 10s.; others, £1 16s., £3 3s., and £4 16s.; some have sold for 8s. and 8s. 6d.

Angel (nearly 65 grains).—Almost similar to Angel of James I.'s last issue, but the numeral X in the field; £2 to £4; extra fine, £4 10s., £6, £7, and £10.

BRIOT'S MINT.—*Unit or Sovereign.*—*Obv.*, profile bust to left, crowned, with a falling lace band, XX behind head; *rev.*, square garnished shield of arms with FLORENT, &c., a small B (for Briot) at end of legend on each side; £3 to £5; extra fine, £5 12s. 6d., £6, £6 6s., £7 10s,, £8 10s., £10 2s. 6d. and £11.

Half Sovereign.—*Obv.*, similar to Sovereign, but X behind bust; *rev.*, also similar, but motto CVLTORES, &c., a small B at end of legends; £2 to £4; others, £4 5s., £6 2s. 6d., £7 15s., and £8 15s.

Crown or Five Shilling Piece.—Similar to Half Sovereign, but V behind head; £27 10s.

Angel.—*Obv.*, nearly similar to the Tower Angel; *rev.*, ship larger, a small B in front of the prow.

BRISTOL MINT.—*Sovereign.*—Type similar to Oxford mint. BR, in monogram, for *m.m.*; £16 15s. and £29.

Half Sovereign.—Similar to Sovereign. *m.m.*, BR in monogram, X behind bust; £50.

A Tower Sovereign and Half Sovereign sold together for £1 9s. A Tower Half Sovereign and Crown sold together for £1 2s., £1 17s., and £3 15s. A Tower Angel and Crown sold together for 15s. and £1 1s.

SILVER.—Pound or Twenty Shilling Piece, Half Pound, Crown, Half Crown, Shilling, Sixpence, Groat, Threepenny, Half Groat, Penny, and Halfpenny.

Pound (1858 grains).—Struck at Oxford and Shrewsbury. *Obv.*, King on horseback to left; *rev.*, the declaration, RELIG. PROT. LEG. ANG. LIBER. PAR, in two lines across the field, XX with one or three plumes above, the date, usually 1642, below. Some have 1644 OX. Legend round the piece,

CHARLES I.—CONTINUED.

SILVER.—*Continued.*

EXVRGAT, &c.   £4 to £6 ; extra fine, £6 15s., £7 15s., £8, £9 7s. 6d., £10, £13, £17, £19, £20 5s. and £25. Poor specimens have sold for £1 1s., £1 8s., £2, £2 11s., £2 19s., and £3 18s.

A variety of fine work, the Declaration in three lines within a compartment, below 1644, OX. ; £10, £12 10s., £14, £15, £26 5s., £29 15s., and £37.

Half Pound (929 grains).—Similar to the Pound, but X for value.   Struck at Exeter, Oxford, and Shrewsbury.   £2 to £3 10s. ; extra fine, £4, £5 2s. 6d., £5 15s., £8, and £10 10s. ; inferior specimens, 15s., £1, £1 8s., and £1 12s.

Crown (464¼ grains).—Struck at the Tower; by Briot, at Exeter, Oxford, and Shrewsbury.   *Obv.*, king riding to left ; *rev.*, varied, according to place of mintage.

Tower.—*Rev.*, shield of arms.   15s. to £1 5s. ; very fine, £2, £3, £3 12s., £4, £4 11s., £5 2s. 6d.

Briot.—Distinguished by a small B ; £2 to £4 ; extra fine, £5, £5 10s., £6, £6 10s.

Exeter.—*Rev.*, arms, often with date 1644 or 1645 ; 15s. to £1 10s. ; extra fine, £2 2s., £5 and £7 ; others, 6s., 9s., 12s.

Oxford.—*Rev.*, Declaration, and V for value ; £1 10s. to £3 ; extra fine, £4 12s., £6 6s., and £7 7s.

Shrewsbury.—Like the Oxford ; £2 to £3 ; extra fine, £4 6s. The Oxford Crown (1644), a *Pattern* by Rawlins (Fig. 66).

Half Crown (232¼ grains).—Struck at the Tower ; by Briot, at Aberystwith, Bristol, Chester, Exeter, Oxford, Shrewsbury, Weymouth, Worcester, and York.   *Obv.*, king riding to left ; *rev.*, varied, according to place of mintage.   (Fig. 68.)

Tower.—*Rev.*, shield of arms, motto CHRISTO AVSPICE REGNO.   Ordinary specimens, 3s. 6d. to 6s. ; extra fine, 14s., £1 9s., £2, £2 13s., £3 3s., £3 12s. 6d., £4 12s., £5 7s. 6d., £5 12s. 6d., and £6 15s.   (Fig. 68.)

Briot.—Like the Crown.   Ordinary specimens, 7s. 6d. to £1 ; extra fine, £1 15s., £2, £3, £4, and £5 5s.

Aberystwith.—*Rev.*, oval shield, with plume over it ; *m.m.*, an open book or a crown, CHRISTO, &c. ; 10s. to £1 ; extra fine, £3 3s., £3 8s., and £3 11s.   A variety is known with the Declaration on *rev.*, and motto EXVRGAT, &c.

Bristol—*Rev.*, Declaration, sometimes BR in monogram. 10s. to £1 ; extra fine, £1 8s., £2 2s., £4 6s., and £6 12s.

Chester.—CHST on *obv.* under the horse ; *m.m.*, three garbs or wheat sheaves, the arms of Chester ; *rev.*, shield of arms or Declaration ; £1 to £3 ; others, £4, £4 7s. 6d., £6 7s. 6d., £7, and £17.

Exeter.—*Rev.*, arms, or sometimes the Declaration, with EX below ; *m.m.*, generally a rose ; £1 10s. to £3 ; others, £3 10s., £3 14s., £4 4s., £6, £7, £21, £22 10s., and £32.

Oxford.— *Rev.*, Declaration and date, 1642, 1643, 1644, 1645, and 1646, with or without OX. ; 10s. to £1 ; others, £1 9s., £1 16s., £2 10s., £2 15s., £3 6s., and £4 7s. 6d.

CHARLES I.—CONTINUED.

SILVER.—*Continued.*

    Shrewsbury.—Almost the same as the Oxford type.

    Weymouth.—W under the horse; 13s., £1 7s., and £3 19s.

    Worcester.—*m.m.*; three pears, the arms of Worcester; *rev.*, arms, and motto CHRISTO, &c.; £1 11s., £1 18s., £2 4s., £2 10s., £3 16s., £6 2s. 6d., and £9 10s.

    York.—*m.m.*, a lion, passant guardant, sometimes EBOR under the horse. Ordinary specimens, 7s. to £1; others, £1 12s., £2 11s., £3, £3 15s., £4 15s., £5 7s. 6d., £6 2s. 6d. and £11 12s. 6d.

    Combe-Martin.—A Half Crown, said to be of this mint, realised £5 12s.

    Shillings (92¾ grains).—Struck at the Tower, by Briot, at Aberystwith, Bristol, Exeter, Oxford, Shrewsbury, and York. *Obv.*, bust crowned to left (exceptionally to right), with XII, for value, behind the head, CAROLVS, &c.

    Tower.—*Rev.*, shield of arms. Ordinary specimens, 2s. to 5s.; extra fine, 12s., 18s., £1 1s., £1 16s., £2, £3 5s., £3 12s., and £4 8s.; perfect specimens, in proof condition, £5 5s., £7 7s., £8 5s., and £9 2s. 6d.

    Briot. — *m.m.*, anchor, small flower, and letter B; 10s. to £1.

    Aberystwith.—*m.m.*, open book; *rev.*, shield of arms; 5s. to 15s.; extra fine, £2 3s. and £3 7s.

    Bristol.—*Rev.*, Declaration and date, 1643, 1644, or 1645, BR in monogram below the date, or at the beginning of legend, EXVRGAT, &c.; 10s. to £1.

    Exeter.—*Rev.*, arms, and date 1644 or 1645 at end of legend; 5s. to 15s.; extra fine, £1 12s. and £1 16s.

    Oxford.—*Obv.*, bust to left (on two coins to right); *rev.*, Declaration with date, 1642, 1643, or 1644, sometimes OX below; 5s. to 15s.; extra fine, £1, £1 10s., and £2 13s.; one, a brilliant proof, £10 5s.

    Shrewsbury.—Like the Oxford Half Crown.

    York.—*Rev.*, arms, EBOR (for Eboraci = York) either over or under the shield; *m.m.*, a lion; 5s. to 15s.; extra fine, £1 1s., £2 6s., £2 19s., and £3 3s.

    Sixpences (46¼ grains).—Type generally like that of the Shillings. Struck at the Tower, by Briot, at Aberystwith, Bristol, Exeter, Oxford, and York.

    Tower.—Ordinary specimen, 1s. 6d. to 3s. 6d.; extra fine, 7s. 6d., 11s., 13s., £2 4s., and one (pattern?) £22.

    Briot.—3s. 6d. to 10s.; extra fine, 18s. and £1 7s.

    Aberystwith.—4s. to 10s.; one, extra fine, £3 10s.

    Bristol.—5s. to 10s.

    Exeter.—5s. to 10s.

    Oxford.—5s. to 10s.

    York.—4s. to 8s.

D

CHARLES I.—CONTINUED.

SILVER.—*Continued.*

Groats (31 grains).—Of Aberystwith, Bristol, Exeter, and Oxford; *obv.*, bust to left crowned, with IIII, for value, behind it.

Aberystwith.—A plume before the bust; *m.m.*, an open book or a crown; 3s. to 7s.

Bristol.—*m.m.*, BR in monogram; 5s. to 10s.

Exeter.—*m.m.*, a rose; the date, 1644, before CAROLVS; 5s. to 10s. A Groat and Threepence, in brilliant condition, together realised £4 4s.

Oxford.—*Rev.*, Declaration type; 4s. to 8s.: one, extra fine, £1 13s.

Threepence (22¼ grains).—Of Aberystwith, Exeter, Oxford, and York. Similar to the Groat, but with III, for value, behind the bust.

Aberystwith.—2s. 6d. to 7s. 6d.

Exeter.—5s. to 10s.

Oxford. — 3s. to 7s. A Threepence and Half Groat, together, sold for £2 19s.

York.—*m.m.*, lion, EBOR above the shield of arms; 5s. to 10s.

Half Groats (15½ grains).—Struck at the Tower, by Briot, at Aberystwith, Bristol, Exeter, and Oxford. The value is indicated by II behind the bust.

Tower.—First issue: *obv.*, rose, crowned, C. D. G. ROSA SINE SPINA; *rev.*, rose crowned, IVS. THRONVM FIRMAT, or FERMAT; 1s. to 2s.

Second issue: *obv.*, crowned bust to left, with II, for value, behind it, CAROLVS and title; *rev.*, IVSTITIA., &c., with shield of arms; 1s. to 2s.

Briot.—*m.m.*, a lozenge, a small B below the bust; 5s. to 10s. A Half Groat and Penny together realised £1 16s.

Aberystwith.—*Rev.*, plume; 3s. to 7s.; very fine, 10s. 6d., £1 7s., and £1 10s.

Bristol.—*Rev.*, Declaration, BR in monogram below; 4s. to 8s.; extra fine, £3 12s. to £3 18s.

Exeter.—*Rev.*, arms, or a large rose; 5s. to 10s.; extra fine, £1 5s., £1 10s., £2 2s., and £2 11s.

Oxford.—*Rev.*, Declaration and 1644, or 1644 with OX below it; 3s. to 7s.

Penny (7½ grains).—Struck at the Tower, by Briot, at Aberystwith, Exeter, and Oxford.

Tower.—First issue: *obv.*, rose, not crowned, C. D. G. ROSA, &c.; *rev.*, rose not crowned, IVS, &c.; 1s. to 2s.

Second issue: *obv.*, bust to left, with I, for value, behind it, CAROLVS, &c.; *rev.*, arms, IVSTITIA, &c.; 1s. to 2s.

Briot.—Similar to his Half Groat, but I, for value, behind head. A Penny and Half Groat sold together for £1 16s.

Aberystwith.—*Obv.*, bust, with I behind it; *rev.*, Prince of Wales' feathers, IVSTITIA, &c.; 5s. to 10s. A perfect specimen, £2 4s.

CHARLES I.—CONTINUED.

SILVER.—*Continued.*

Exeter.—*Obv.*, bust, with I behind, as usual; *rev.*, rose, THRO. IVS FIRMAT, 1644; £1 10s., £2, £2 11s.

Oxford.—*Obv.*, bust, with I, as usual ; *rev.*, RELIG. PRO, &c., in three lines, three fleurs-de-lis above, 1644 below, EXVRGAT, &c. Extremely rare. One sold for £5, another is said to have realised £22 10s. One (pierced) sold, together with an Oxford Crown and Half Crown, in 1869, for £2 1s.

Halfpenny (3¾ grains).—*Tower*, rose on each side ; 1s. to 2s.

Aberystwith.—*Obv.*, rose ; *rev.*, plume. 10s. and £1.

Sets of coins of the different Mints sold together have realised as under :—

Aberystwith.—Half Crown, Shilling, Sixpence, Groat, Half Groat, and Penny, £1 8s. ; Shilling, Sixpence, and Groat, £1 13s. ; Shilling, Sixpence, Groat, Threepence, and four Half Groats, £2 16s. ; Threepence, Half Groat, Penny, and Halfpenny, with a Tower Rose Penny and Halfpenny, 16s. ; three Groats, Half Groat, Half Groat (Ich Dien), Penny, Rose Penny, and Halfpenny, 17s.

Tower.—Crown, Half Crown, Shilling, Sixpence, Half Groat (rose), Half Groat (bust), Penny (rose), Penny (bust), and Halfpenny, 19s. ; Crown, Half Crown, Shilling, Sixpence, Half Groat, and Penny, 17s. ; Half Crown, Shilling, Sixpence, Half Groat, Penny, and Halfpenny, £1 10s. ; Sixpence, Half Groat, Penny, and Halfpenny, £3 12s. ; Sixpence, Half Groat, and Penny, £2 14s.

Briot.—Crown, Half Crown, Shilling, and Sixpence, £1 3s. ; Crown, Half Crown, Half Groat, and Penny, £7 ; Shilling, Sixpence, and Half Groat, 15s. and £1 3s. ; Shilling, Sixpence, Half Groat and Penny, £1 5s. and £1 15s. ; Shilling and Sixpence, £1 3s. and £3 12s. ; Shilling, Half Groat, and Penny, £2 10s. ; Sixpence, Half Groat, and Penny, 17s.

Bristol.—Half Crown, Shilling, Sixpence, Groat, and Half Groat, £1 ; Shilling and Sixpence, £1 11s., £1 19s., and £3 12s. ; a Shilling and Groat, £2 2s. ; a Shilling, Sixpence, Groat, and Penny, 17s.

Exeter.—Half Crown, Shilling, Sixpence, Groat, and Threepence, £2 11s. ; Sixpence, Groat, Threepence, and Half Groat, 11s. ; Shilling, Sixpence, Groat, and Threepence, £2 ; Shilling and Sixpence, £2 14s.

Oxford. — Shilling, Sixpence, Groat, and Threepence, £1 14s.

York.—Shilling, Sixpence, and Half Groat, 16s. ; Shilling, Sixpence, and Threepence, 19s. ; Shilling and Threepence, £1 ; Shilling and Sixpence, £1 6s.

COPPER.—*Farthing* (18 grains).—*Obv.*, CAROLVS D. G. MAG. BR. two sceptres passed through a crown ; *rev.*, FRA. ET HIB. REX, a rose crowned ; *m.m.*, star, or crescent ; 6d. to 1s. 6d. (Fig. 166.)

D 2

CHARLES I.—CONTINUED.

English Siege Pieces.

GOLD.—*Ten Shilling Piece* (66 grains). Struck at Colchester. *Obv.*, *incuse*, a castle with flag flying, and in two lines, OBS : COL. $16\frac{s}{x}48$; *rev.*, plain.

SILVER.—Struck at Beeston Castle, Carlisle, Colchester, Newark, Pontefract Castle, and Scarborough.

Beeston Castle. — *Obv.*, a castle gateway, with value below.

Two Shilling Piece (208 grains).—*Obv.*, $\frac{s}{ii}$

Sixteen-pence (130 grains).—*Obv.*, $\frac{s \ D}{i \ iiii}$; £12 12s., £20.

Fourteen-pence (99 grains).—*Obv.*, $\frac{s \ D}{i \ ii}$

Thirteen-pence (94 grains).—*Obv.*, $\frac{s \ D}{i \ i}$

Shilling (88 and 91 grains).—*Obv.*, $\frac{s}{i}$; £13 13s.

Eleven-pence (80 grains).—*Obv.*, $\frac{D}{xi}$

A piece of uncertain value, £4 2s. 6d.

Carlisle.—*Three Shillings* (246 grains).—Octagonal, nearly round. *Obv.*, under a large crown the letters C R between two anemones, below IIIs ; *rev.*, in three lines, OBS : CARL. 1645, an anemone above and below ; £3 12s., £6 12s. 6d., £6 15s., £7 7s. 6d., £7 10s., and £8 10s.

Half Crown.—*Obv.*, C R and II.VI under a crown ; *rev.*, OBs CARL. 1645, in two lines ; £2 11s. and £2 12s. 6d.

Shilling (80 grains).—*Obv.*; under a large crown, C R, with XII below ; *rev.*, as on Three Shilling Piece ; 16s., £1 1s., £2 11s., £2 12s., £4 12s., £5, £5 10s., £5 17s. 6d., £6 8s. 6d., and £8 12s. 6d.

Colchester.—*Shilling* (121 grains).—Oblong, circular, and octagonal. *Obv.*, a castle, legend *Carolj Fortuna resurgam* ; £2 3s., £2 15s., £3 12s., £4 12s., £5 2s. 6d., £7 15s., £8 5s., £9, £10, £11, and £15 10s.

Newark.—Diamond shaped, with a pearl border along the edges. (Fig. 69.)

Half Crown (128 grains).—*Obv.*, crown between C R, XXX below ; *rev.*, in three lines, OBS. NEWARK 1646 ; 10s. to £1.

Shilling (95 grains).—As above, but XII for value ; 10s. to £1.

Ninepence (70 grains).—As above, but IX for value ; 15s. to £1 5s.

Sixpence (38 grains).—As above, but VI for value ; 15s. to £1 10s.

Sets of the four pieces have realised, at different sales : £1, £1 4s., £1 17s., £2 3s., £2 4s., £2 5s., £2 7s., £3 3s., £4 4s., £4 12s. 6d., and £5 12s. 6d.

CHARLES I.—CONTINUED.

SILVER.—*Continued.*

Pontefract Castle.—Diamond shaped and octagonal.

Shillings (66 to 89 grains).—*Obv.*, C R under a crown, motto DVM SPIRO SPERO; *rev.*, the castle, at left side OBS, at right XII, with P above and C below, date 1648. Also a variety with hand issuing from side of castle, holding a sword; 16s. to £2; extra fine, £2 6s., £3 3s., £4, £4 6s., and £5 2s. 6d. (Fig. 70.)

Two Shilling Piece (152 grains).—Of similar type, £10 2s. 6d.

Scarborough.—Irregularly-shaped pieces.

Crown (292 grains).—*Obv.*, Castle, below it $\frac{s}{v}$; £12 15s. and £30.

Half Crown (219 grains).—*Obv.*, castle, with $\frac{s}{ii}\frac{D}{vi}$; *rev.*, OBS Scarborough, 1645; £7 5s. and £15 5s.

Two Shillings (208 grains).—*Obv.*, Castle, with $\frac{s}{ii}$; £7 5s. and £12 5s.

One and Ninepenny Piece (134 grains).—*Obv.*, castle, with $\frac{s}{i}\frac{D}{ix}$; £8 2s. 6d. and £15 17s. 6d.

Sixpence (43 grains).—*Obv.*, castle, with $\frac{D}{vi}$; £6 and £10.

Pieces of unknown Mints, of irregular shapes :

Crown (426 grains).—Marked $\frac{s}{v}$ under a castle.

Sevenpence (53 grains).—Marked $\frac{D}{vii}$

Sixpence (49 grains).—Marked $\frac{D}{vi}$

Fourpence (18 grains).—Marked $\frac{D}{iv}$

The Commonwealth, 1649—1660.

GOLD.—Broad or Twenty Shilling Piece, Half Broad or Ten Shilling Piece, and Five Shilling Piece.

Broad (140½ grains).—*Obv.*, a plain shield, bearing St. George's cross, motto, THE COMMONWEALTH OF ENGLAND; *rev.*, two shields conjoined, one bearing St. George's cross, the other the Irish harp, XX above, motto, GOD WITH VS, and date; £2 to £3; extra fine, £3 3s., £3 7s., £3 11s., and £4; others have sold for £1 5s., £1 8s., and £1 12s.

A Broad and a Half Broad together sold for £1 16s.

Ten Shilling Piece (70¼ grains).—Similar to the Broad, but X, for value; £2 to £3; extra fine, £3 3s., £3 8s., £4, and £4 2s.; others only 12s., 14s., and 17s.

A Ten Shilling and Five Shilling piece sold together have realised £1 2s., £1 10s., and £3 12s.

Five Shilling Piece (35¼ grains).—Also similar, but V, for value; £1 5s. to £1 15s.; extra fine, £2 2s., £2 10s., £2 16s., and £6 5s.; one sold for only 18s.

Sets of the Broad, Ten Shilling, and Five Shilling Pieces, extra fine, £4 and £5 10s.

THE COMMONWEALTH.—CONTINUED.

SILVER.—Crown, Half Crown, Shilling, Sixpence, Half Groat, Penny, and Halfpenny.

Crown (464½ grains).—*Obv.* and *rev.*, similar to Broad, but V, for value ; £1 10s. to £3 ; extra fine, £3 3s., £3 5s., £4 15s., and £5 15s. ; two exceptional specimens realised respectively £9 15s. and £15 10s.

A Crown and Shilling sold together for £2 9s., while a similar lot at another sale realised only 19s.

Half Crown (232½ grains).—Similar, but value II. VI. ; 10s. to £1 ; very fine, £1 6s., £2 2s., £2 8s., and £3 14s. ; an exceptional specimen, £7 15s.

Shilling (92¾ grains).—Similar, but value XII. ; 4s. to 10s. ; extra fine, 19s., £1 1s., £1 11s., and £2. (Fig. 71.)

A Shilling and a Sixpence sold together realised, at different sales, 7s., 13s., £1 3s., and £2 2s.

Sixpence (46¼ grains).—Similar, but value VI. ; 4s. to 10s. ; exceptional specimens, £1 and £2 12s.

Half Groat (15½ grains).—Similar, without motto or date, but value II. ; ordinary specimens, 1s. to 2s.

Penny (7½ grains).—Similar to Half Groat, but I., for value ; ordinary specimens, 1s. to 2s.

Halfpenny (3¾ grains).—*Obv.*, shield bearing St. George's cross ; *rev.*, single shield bearing the Irish harp, no legends or numeral ; 2s. to 4s.

A complete set of seven pieces (Crown to Halfpenny), in very fine condition, sold for £1 19s. and £2 2s.

An extra fine set of six coins (Half Crown to Halfpenny) realised £5.

A Half Crown, Shilling, and Sixpence sold together for £1 14s.

A Half Groat, Penny, and Halfpenny, in the finest state, sold for £2 4s.

A Sixpence, Half Groat, Penny, and Halfpenny, not so fine, realised £1.

COPPER.—*Farthings.*—Struck only as patterns.

Oliver Cromwell, Protector, 1653—1658.*

GOLD.—Fifty Shilling piece, Broad or Twenty Shilling piece, and Half Broad or Ten Shilling piece. Dates, 1656 and 1658.

Fifty Shilling Piece (351½ grains).— *Obv.*, laureated bust to left, OLIVAR D.G., &c.; *rev.*, shield of arms ; first and fourth quarters, St. George's cross ; second, cross of St. Andrew ; third, the Irish harp ; on an escutcheon of pretence, the Protector's arms, a lion rampant, motto, PAX QVÆRITVR BELLO ; edge inscribed ; £41 10s., £44, £46, £51, £70, and £77 ; a specimen,

---

* For convenience of reference the coins bearing Cromwell's name are here given, although it is disputed that they were ever current money, and the coins of the Commonwealth were being struck and circulated at the same time. Hawkins, in "The Coins of England," does not even allude to these pieces. They are beautifully executed, and were coined by machinery.

OLIVER CROMWELL.—CONTINUED.

GOLD.—*Continued.*

not fine, and which had been cracked in striking, sold for only £4 1s. in 1869.

Broad (140½ grains).—Similar, being from same die, but edge engrailed; £2 7s., £3 7s., £4, £4 12s., £4 18s., £5 2s. 6d., £5 10s., £6 5s., £6 10s., £7, £7 10s., £8 8s., and £8 15s.

Half Broad (70½ grains).—Similar to the Broad; £4 5s., £5 2s. 6d., £9 15s., £10 15s., £11, £12, £14 5s., £15, £16, £17, £20, £21, and £26 10s.

A proof, in gold (716 grains), struck from the Crown die, 1658, sold for £31.

SILVER.—Crown, Half Crown, Two Shillings, Shilling, Ninepence, and Sixpence. Dates, 1656 and 1658.

Crown (464¼ grains).—*Obv.*, laureated bust to left, OLIVAR D.G., &c.; *rev.*, arms as on the gold coin; edge inscribed; dated 1658.

There are three varieties—Simon's, Tanner's, and the Dutch Crown.

Simon's.—£2 10s., £2 12s. 6d., £2 14s., £3 5s., £3 15s., £4 4s., £5 2s. 6d., £5 12s. 6d., £7 10s., £9 9s., £11, and £28.

Tanner's.—£4 10s., £5 2s. 6d., £5 5s., £6 6s., £6 17s. 6d., £7, £7 2s. 6d., and £7 12s. 6d.

Dutch.—£2 6s., £3 10s., £4 4s., £5, £6 12s. 6d., £7 5s., £8 5s., and £8 15s.

Half Crown (232¼ grains) by Simon.—Similar to the Crown, dated 1656 and 1658; edge inscribed; £1 4s., £1 13s., £1 15s., £1 19s., £2 2s., £2 6s., £2 10s., £3 3s., £3 5s., £5 2s. 6d., and £8 10s. (Fig. 72.)

Two Shilling Piece (162 grains).—Type similar to the Crown, dated 1658; edge plain; £10, £15, £18 5s., and £25.

Shilling (92¾ grains).—Type similar to the Crown, dated 1658, edge engrailed; £1 1s., £1 6s., £1 10s., £1 14s., £2, £2 13s., £3, and £6 2s. 6d.

Ninepence (various weights, 51 to 96 grains).—Similar type, dated, edge engrailed or plain; £1 16s., £2 2s., £2 10s., £3 7s. 6d., £3 11s., £4, £4 7s., £4 11s., £5, £5 5s., £5 12s. 6d., £6 6s., £6 15s., and £7 5s.

Sixpence (46¼ grains).—The rarest of Cromwell's coins; edge engrailed; £31 and £35; a specimen, said to be a Sixpence, sold in 1869 for £5 2s. 6d.

Sets of the Crown, Half Crown, and Shilling, in fine cabinet condition, have sold for £3 18s., £4 16s., £6, £6 15s., £7 5s., and £7 17s. 6d.

A Half Crown and Shilling realised £3 5s. and £4 14s.

COPPER.—*Pattern Farthings.*

1. *Obv.*, laureated bust to left, OLIVAR PRO ENG SC IRL; *rev.*, arms as before, CHARITIE AND CHANGE; £2 12s., £3 10s., £3 16s., £5 7s. 6d., £6 5s., and £8 10s. (Fig. 162.)

2. *Obv.*, as before; *rev.*, three pillars united, THVS VNITED INVINCIBLE; £2 12s. (Fig. 163.)

OLIVER CROMWELL.—CONTINUED.

COPPER.—*Continued.*

3. *Obv.*, as before; *rev.*, a ship under sail to left, AND GOD DIRECT OVR COVRS. (Fig. 164.)
4. *Obv.*, bust as before, OLIVER PRO ENG SCO & IRE; *rev.*, arms, CONVENIENT CHANGE, 1651.

Charles II., 1660—1685.

GOLD.—Hammered.—Broad or Twenty Shilling Piece, Half Broad or Ten Shilling Piece, and Five Shilling Piece.

Milled.—Five Guinea Piece, Two Guineas, Guinea, and Half Guinea.

Hammered.—Broad (140½ grains).—*Obv.*, laureated bust to left, CAROLVS II. D.G. MAG. BRIT., &c.; *rev.*, arms, C. R. at side, FLORENT CONCORDIA REGNA.

First issue.—Without numerals, for value, behind head; £2 to £3 10s.; extra fine, £6, £6 12s. 6d., and £8 2s. 6d.; others, only £1 5s., £1 11s., and £1 16s.

Second issue.—With XX, for value, behind head; £2 to £3 10s.; extra fine, £3 17s. 6d., £5 2s. 6d., and £5 7s. 6d.; one sold for £1 9s. (Fig. 15.)

Half Broad (70¼ grains).—Similar to Broad.

First issue.—Without numerals; £2 to £3; extra fine, £8, £10 2s. 6d., and £14 10s.; others, £1 2s. and £1 6s.

Second issue.—With X behind head; £2 to £3; extra fine, £3 11s., £4 2s. 6d., and £9; one sold for £1.

Five Shillings (35⅛ grains).—Similar type.

First issue.—Without numerals; £1 10s. to £2 10s.; extra fine, £3 4s., £6 6s., £9 5s., £29 10s., and £34.

Second issue.—With V behind head; £1 10s. to £2; extra fine, £3 10s., £3 18s., and £5 2s. 6d.

A Broad and Half Broad (without numerals) sold together for £1 17s.

A Broad and Five Shilling Piece (without numerals) realised £5 10s.

A Half Broad and Five Shilling Piece (without numerals), realised £1 8s.

A Broad (with XX) and Five Shilling Piece (without V) sold for £7 7s.

Milled.*—Five Guinea Piece (647¼ grains).—*Obv.*, laureated bust to right, CAROLVS II. DEI GRATIA; *rev.*, four shields arranged in the form of a cross, &c., MAG. BR. FRA. ET. HIB. REX. and date; edge inscribed DECVS ET TVTAMEN, &c.; £6 10s. to £7 10s.; extra fine specimens have realised:

First.—Plain under bust; £8 12s., £10 12s. 6d., and £11.

---

* **FIVE GUINEA PIECES** of every reign from Charles II. to George II. have on *obv.* bust of the sovereign to right or left, with name and titles; and on *rev.*, four shields arranged crosswise, +, each crowned, a sceptre in each angle, except those of William and Mary and George II., on which the arms are placed quarterly in a single shield. DOUBLE GUINEAS, GUINEAS, and HALF GUINEAS, are similar.

CHARLES II.—CONTINUED.

GOLD.—*Continued.*

Second.—Elephant under bust; £8 2s. 6d., £3 17s. 6d., £9 15s., and £21 10s.

Some have sold for £5 6s., £5 8s., and £5 10s.

Two Guinea Piece (258½ grains).—Similar, but edge milled, and not inscribed; £3 to £4; extra fine, £4 10s., £5 7s. 6d., £6 6s., £6 12s. 6d., £7 2s. 6d., and £7 12s. 6d.

Guinea (129¾ grains).—Similar to the Two Guinea Piece; £1 10s. to £2; extra fine, £2 5s., £2 14s., £2 18s., £3 3s., and £5 2s. 6d.

Half Guinea (64⅖ grains).—Similar to the Guinea; £1 to £1 10s.; extra fine, £1 15s., £2 2s., £2 9s., and £3 5s.; others, 12s., and 16s.

A Double Guinea, Two Guineas, and Half Guinea sold for £4 18s.

SILVER.—Hammered.—Half Crown, Shilling, Sixpence, Groat, Three-pence, Half Groat, Penny.

Milled.—Crown, Half Crown, Shilling, Sixpence, and Maundy Fourpence, Threepence, Twopence, and Penny.

Hammered.—Three issues: First, without numerals for value, or inner circle; second, with numerals, but without inner circle; third, with numerals and inner circle. *Obv.*, crowned bust to left, name and title; *rev.*, CHRISTO AVSPICE REGNO, shield of arms.

Half Crown (232½ grains), first issue.—10s. to £1; extra fine, £4 4s., £5 10s., £7, £9 2s. 6d., and £19 10s. (Fig. 74.)

Second issue.—XXX behind head; 10s. to £1.

Third issue.—XXX behind head; 7s. 6d. to 15s.; extra fine, £1 7s., £9 2s. 6d., and £19 10s.

Shilling (92¾ grains), first issue.—10s. to 15s.; extra fine, £1 1s., £1 5s., £1 15s., £3, and £3 3s.

Second issue.—XII behind head; 10s. to 15s.; extra fine, £1 1s., £2 2s., and £3.

Third issue.—XII behind head; 7s. 6d. to 10s.; extra fine, £1 13s., £2 2s., and £2 16s.

Sixpence (46¼ grains), first issue.—6s. to 10s.; extra fine, £1 12s.

Second issue.—VI behind head; 6s. to 10s.; extra fine, 18s.

Third issue.—VI behind head; 6s. to 10s.; extra fine, 18s. and £2 18s.

A Shilling and Sixpence, first issue, extra fine, £3 17s. 6d.

Half Groat (15½ grains), first issue.—1s. 6d. to 2s. 6d.

Second issue.—II behind head; 1s. to 2s.

Penny (7¼ grains), first issue.—1s. 6d. to 2s. 6d.

Second issue.—I behind head; 1s. to 2s.

Groat (31 grains), third issue.—IIII behind head; 2s. to 3s. 6d.

Threepence (22¼ grains), third issue.—III behind head; 1s. 6d. to 2s. 6d.

Half Groat (15¼ grains), third issue.—II behind head; 1s. to 2s.

CHARLES II.—CONTINUED.

SILVER (Hammered).—*Continued.*

Penny (7¼ grains) third issue.—I behind head; 1s. to 2s.

A very fine set (third issue) of Groat, Threepence, Half Groat, and Penny realised £1 2s. 6d.

A set of Half Crown, Shilling, and Sixpence, first issue, £1 18s.

A set of Half Crown, Shilling, Sixpence, Groat, Threepence, Half Groat, and Penny, all of third issue, very fine, £2 7s.

Milled.—Crown (464¼ grains).*—Obv.*, laureated bust to right, CAROLVS II., &c.; *rev.*, four shields arranged in the form of a cross, MAG. BR. FRA., &c., with date (1662 to 1684), lettered edge; 7s. 6d. to 15s.; extra fine, £1 1s., £1 6s., £1 10s., £2 2s., £2 10s., £3, £4 4s., and, an exceptional specimen, £24 10s.

Half Crown (232¼ grains).—Similar to the Crown, dated from 1663 to 1684, inclusive, except 1665 and 1667, lettered edge; 5s. to 10s.; extra fine, 12s., 17s., £1 10s., £1 19s., £2 3s., and £2 11s.

Shilling (92¾ grains).—Similar to the Crown, dated 1663 to 1684 inclusive, except 1664, 1665, 1666, 1667, 1669, and 1682, edge milled with lines; 2s. 6d. to 5s.; extra fine, 7s., 14s., £1 1s., £1 9s., £2 2s., and £2 15s.

Sixpence (46¼ grains).—Similar to the Shilling, dated from 1674 to 1684, inclusive; 2s. 6d. to 5s.

A Shilling and Sixpence, extra fine, 17s.

Maundy Fourpence, Threepence, Twopence, and Penny.— *Obv.*, laureated bust to right.

First issue, by Simon, numerals of value behind head, IIII, III, II, or I. *Rev.*, arms in a shield, CHRISTO AVSPICE REGNO, 4s. 6d. to 6s. 6d. the set.

Second issue, by Roettier, dated 1670 to 1684; 3s. to 6s. the set.

Fourpence (31 grains).—*Rev.*, four C's interlinked, with crown above and date; 1s. to 2s.

Threepence (22¼ grains).—*Rev.*, three C's; 1s. to 2s.

Twopence (15¼ grains).—*Rev.*, Two C's; 1s. to 1s. 6d.

Penny (7¼ grains).—*Rev.*, one C.; 1s. to 1s. 6d.

A set, Crown, Half Crown, Shilling, and Sixpence, 13s. and £1 2s.

A Crown, Half Crown, and Shilling, elephant and castle, £1 8s.

A Crown, Half Crown, and Shilling, elephant, 1666, 10s. and 13s.

A Half Crown and Shilling, extra fine, £2 10s.

COPPER.—Halfpenny and Farthing. A pound, avoirdupois, was coined into forty halfpence or eighty farthings.

---

* The Petition Crown, 1663, a *Pattern* by Simon, is shown at Fig. 67. On some CROWNS, dated 1662, there is a *rose* below the bust. An *elephant*, or *elephant and castle*, is placed below the king's bust on certain CROWNS, HALF CROWNS, and SHILLINGS, made from silver imported by the African Company. Some HALF CROWNS, and SHILLINGS, made of silver from the Welsh mines, have a *plume* below the bust, and in centre of *rev.*

CHARLES II.—CONTINUED.

COPPER.—*Continued.*

Halfpenny (175 grains).—*Obv.*, laureated bust to left in armour, CAROLVS A CAROLO; *rev.*, Britannia seated, a palm branch in right hand, a spear in left, BRITANNIA above, the date below; 1672, 1673, or 1675; 1s. to 5s.

Farthing (87½ grains).—Similar to the Halfpenny; dated 1671—1675, and 1679; 1s. to 2s. 6d.; inferior specimens, 3d. to 6d.

TIN.—Farthing.

Farthing (87½ grains).—Similar to copper Farthing, but without date on *rev.*, in centre a stud of copper; edge lettered, NVMMORVM * FAMVLVS * 1684; or 1685; 2s. 6d. to £1.

English Siege Pieces.

GOLD.—Pontefract.

Twenty Shilling Piece.—Octagonal. *Obv.*, HANC : DEVS : DEDIT in two lines, a crown above, and 1648 below, encircled by CAROL. II. D. G. MAG. B.F. ET H. REX.; *rev.*, the castle, above it P.C. (for Pontefract Castle) on the left side OBS., a cannon issuing from right side, surrounded by POST MORTEM PATRIS PRO FILIO.

SILVER.—Pontefract.

Shilling (about 70 grains).—Octagonal, similar to the Twenty Shilling Piece described above; 10s., 17s., £1 2s., £2 2s.; and an exceptionally fine specimen, £3 10s. (Fig. 73.)

Shilling (about 70 grains).—Octagonal. *Obv.*, the castle, as described above, but the legend is CAROLVS : SECVNDVS : 1648; *rev.*, C. R. under a crown, encircled by DVM : SPIRO : SPERO; 16s., £1, £1 2s., £1 12s., and £4 8s.

The above two varieties, together, £5 5s.

James II., 1685—1688.

GOLD.—Five Guinea Piece, Two Guinea Piece, Guinea, and Half Guinea. Some pieces have an elephant and castle under the bust.

Weight.—The same as the last issue of Charles II.

Five Guinea Piece.—*Obv.*, laureated bust to left, IACOBVS II. DEI GRATIA; *rev.*, four shields arranged crosswise, edge lettered; £6 10s. to £7 10s.; extra fine, £8 5s., £11 2s. 6d., and £15 10s.; others, £5 6s., £5 10s., £5 12s. 6d., and £5 16s.

Two Guinea Piece.—Same as the Five Guinea Piece, but edge milled; £3 to £4; extra fine, £4 15s., £9, £9 17s. 6d., and £11 5s.; others, £2 4s., £2 8s., and £2 12s.

Guinea.—Similar to the Two Guinea Piece; £1 10s. to £2 2s.; extra fine, £3 6s., £3 10s., and £7 7s.; others, £1 2s. and £1 3s.

Half Guinea.—Similar to the Guinea; £1 to £1 10s.; extra fine, £1 16s., £2 4s., £2 8s., £3 3s., £3 10s., £4 6s., and £4 10s.; others, 11s. and 16s.

A Guinea and Half Guinea sold, together, for £1 13s.

JAMES II.—CONTINUED.

SILVER.—Crown, Half Crown, Shilling, Sixpence, and Maundy Fourpence, Threepence, Twopence, and Penny.

Weight.—The same as the last issue of Charles II.

Crown.—Obv., laureated bust to left, IACOBVS II. DEI
GRATIA ; *rev.*, four shields arranged crosswise, dated 1686,
1687, or 1688, edge lettered; 7s. 6d. to 15s.; extra fine, £1,
£1 5s., and £1 12s.

Half Crown.—Similar to the Crown, dated 1685 to 1688 ; 5s.
to 10s.; extra fine, £1 1s. and £1 7s.

Shilling.—Similar to the Crown, but edge milled with lines,
dated 1685 to 1688 ; 3s. to 7s.

Sixpence.—Similar to Shilling, dated 1686, 1687, or 1688 ;
4s. to 7s. 6d.

Maundy.—Obv., laureated bust to left, IACOBVS II. DEI
GRATIA ; *rev.*, the numerals IIII, III, II, or I, crowned, and
dated ; sets dated 1686, 1687, or 1688 ; 3s. 6d. to 5s. 6d.

Crown, Half Crown, Shilling, Sixpence and Maundy, the set,
15s., £2, £3 4s., and £4 7s.

Crown, Half Crown, Shilling, and Sixpence ; £1 3s., £2 8s.,
and £3 10s.

COPPER.—None.

TIN.—Halfpenny and Farthing.

Halfpenny.—Obv., laureated bust to right, IACOBVS
SECVNDVS ; *rev.*, figure of Britannia surrounded by the word
BRITANNIA, edge inscribed NVMMORVM * FAMVLVS *
1685 (or 1687): in the centre is a plug of copper; 2s. 6d. to 5s.

Farthing.—Similar to the Halfpenny, except that the bust is in
armour and not draped, dated on edge 1684 or 1685 ; 2s. 6d. to 5s.

Fine specimens of the Halfpenny and Farthing, sold together,
have realised 12s., 16s., 17s. and £1.

William and Mary, 1689—1694.

GOLD.—Five Guinea Piece, Two Guinea Piece, Guinea, and Half Guinea.

An elephant and castle is below the bust on some pieces.

Weight.—Same as the last issue of Charles II.

Five Guinea Piece.—Obv., busts of the king and queen to
right, GVLIELMVS ET MARIA DEI GRATIA ; *rev.*, arms
in a garnished shield, crowned, &c., edge lettered ; £6 10s. to
£7 10s.; extra fine, £7 15s., £8, £8 8s., £9, and £13 10s.;
others, £5 6s., £5 12s. 6d., and £5 15s.

Two Guinea Piece.—Similar to Five Guinea Piece, edge
milled ; £3 to £4 ; extra fine, £4 5s., £4 19s., £6, £7, and
£10 ; others, £2 4s. and £2 7s. (Fig. 16.)

Guinea.—Similar to Two Guinea Piece ; £1 10s. to £2; extra
fine, £2 7s., £2 11s., £3 10s., and £3 13s. ; others, £1 3s. and
£1 5s.

Half Guinea.—Similar to the Guinea ; £1 to £2 ; extra fine,
£2 6s., £2 12s., and £2 18s. ; others, 11s. and 12s.

A Guinea and Half Guinea together, sold for £1 14s., £2 1s.,
£3 6s., and £3 10s.

WILLIAM AND MARY.—CONTINUED.

SILVER.—Crown, Half Crown, Shilling, Sixpence, and Maundy Four
pence, Threepence, Twopence, and Penny.

Crown.—*Obv.*, busts to right; *rev.*, four shields in form of a
cross, in the angles W.M. in monogram; dated 1691 or 1692;
10s. to £1; extra fine, £1 7s., £1 14s., £2 8s., £2 13s., £3,
and £3 19s.

Half Crown.—*Obv.*, same as the Crown; *rev.*, three varieties.

First.—Arms, quarterly, in a square shield, crowned; dated
1689, and in one instance (unique ?) 1691; 3s. 6d. to 5s. 6d.;
extra fine, 13s. 6d.

Second.—Arms in a square shield, first and fourth quarters
having the arms of England and France quarterly; dated 1689
and 1690; 4s. to 6s.

Third.—Arms arranged crosswise, like the Crown; dated
1691, 1692, and 1693; 4s. 6d. to 7s. 6d.; extra fine, 10s. (Fig. 75.)

Shilling.—*Obv.* and *rev.*, as the Crown; dated 1692 and
1693; edge milled; 2s. 6d. to 5s.

Sixpence.—Same as Shilling; dated 1693 and 1694; edge
milled; 3s. 6d. to 6s. 6d.

Maundy Sets.—*Obv.*, busts to right; *rev.*, the figure 4, 3, 2,
or 1, crowned, and dated 1689 to 1694; 4s. to 7s.

Crown, two varieties of Half Crown, Shilling, Sixpence, and
Maundy; the set £1, £1 10s., and £2 18s.

Crown, Half Crown, Shilling, and Sixpence, £1 2s.

Half Crown, Shilling, and Sixpence, all dated 1693, extra fine,
£3 1s.

Half Crown, Shilling, Sixpence, and Maundy, 8s., £1 6s.,
and £1 17s.

TIN.—Halfpenny and Farthing, a copper plug through the centre.

Halfpenny.—*Obv.*, busts to right, GVLIELMVS ET MARIA;
rev., figure of Britannia, with the word BRITANNIA, and on
some pieces the date 1689 or 1691 below the figure; edge
lettered NVMMIORVM + FAMVLVS + 1689 +, or 1690, 1691,
1692; 2s. 6d. to 5s.

Farthing.—Like the Halfpenny, dated both on edge and in
exergue, 1690, 1691, or 1692; 2s. 6d. to 5s.

Halfpenny and Farthing, together, 16s. Two Halfpennies
and a Farthing, £1 4s.

COPPER.—Halfpenny and Farthing.

Halfpenny.—Similar to tin Halfpenny, edge plain, date under
Britannia, 1694; 1s. to 5s.

Two Halfpennies, very fine, and an Irish Halfpenny, sold for
£1 12s.

A Halfpenny, 1694, of bold work, extremely fine, realised
£7 10s. Another, 1694, of better work and brilliant condition,
sold for £2.

Farthing.—Similar to the Halfpenny, but dated 1692, 1693,
or 1694; 1s. to 5s.

A fine set, comprising a tin Halfpenny and Farthing, a copper
Halfpenny and Farthing, and a Halfpenny and Farthing of
William III., sold for £1 3s.

William III., 1694—1702.

GOLD.—Five Guinea Piece, Two Guinea Piece, Guinea, and Half Guinea.

On some pieces there is an elephant and castle below the bust.

Weight.—Same as last issue of Charles II.

Five Guinea Piece.—*Obv..* a laureated bust of the king to right, GVLIELMVS III. DEI GRA.; *rev.,* four shields, arranged crosswise, edge lettered; £6 10s. to £7 10s.; extra fine, £8 10s., £9, £9 9s., £10, and £11.

Two Guinea Piece.—Same as Five Guinea Piece, but edge milled; £3 to £4; extra fine, £5 5s., £7 2s. 6d., and £9 5s.; others, £2 5s., £2 10s., and £2 15s.

Guinea.—Similar to Two Guinea Piece; £1 10s. to £2; extra fine, £2 10s., £3 12s., and £4 10s.; others, £1 2s. and £1 6s.

Half Guinea.—Similar to Guinea; £1 to £1 10s.; extra fine, £1 17s. 6d., £2 6s., and £2 10s.; others, 12s., 14s., and 18s.

A Guinea and Half Guinea, together, realised £2 and £2 12s.

SILVER.—Crown, Half Crown, Shilling, Sixpence, and Maundy Fourpence, Threepence, Twopence, and Penny.

Crown.—*Obv.,* laureated bust to right, GVLIELMVS III. DEI GRA.; *rev.,* four shields, arranged crosswise; dated 1695, 1696, 1697, or 1700; edge lettered; 6s. to 10s.; extra fine, £1, £1 2s., £1 15s., and £1 18s.

Half Crown.*—Similar to Crown. There is a variety with elephant and castle under the bust, and another has a plume in each angle of reverse; dates, 1696, 1697, 1698, 1699, 1700, and 1701; plain, 3s. 6d. to 6s.; one, extra fine, £1.

With elephant and castle, 14s., £1, and £1 14s.

With plume, 19s., £1 10s., £2 5s., £3 4s., and £3 15s.

A set, B, C, E, N, Y, and y, £2 10s.; B, C, E, N, and y, 13s.

A set, B and E, 1696, and B, C, E, N, and Y, 1697, £3 4s.

A set, B, C, E, N, and Y, with one of Tower Mint added, £4 14s.

A brilliant specimen, Y, £3.

Shilling.—Similar to Crown, but edge milled; dates, 1695, 1696, 1697, 1698, 1699, 1700, and 1701; 2s. 6d. to 3s. 6d.

A set, B, C, E, N, Y, and y, £1 4s. and £1 8s.   Six specimens of country mints, extra fine, £5.

With plume under bust, 13s., 17s., and £1 10s.

Sixpence.—Similar to the Shilling. Dates, 1695 to 1701, inclusive; plain, 1s. to 2s. 6d.; extra fine, 11s.

With small plume under bust, £1 16s.

Country mints, 2s. 6d. to 4s. 6d.

A set (B, C, E, N, Y, and y), 6s., 8s., 12s., and 15s.

---

* HALF CROWNS, SHILLINGS, and SIXPENCES, issued at the country mints, have an initial letter under the bust: B (Bristol), C (Chester), E (Exeter), N (Norwich), and Y or y (York). These pieces are rare in fine preservation.

WILLIAM III.—CONTINUED.

SILVER.—*Continued.*

A Crown, 1696, and two complete sets of Country Sixpences, 1696 and 1697, £1 11s.

Maundy Fourpence, Threepence, Twopence, and Penny. —*Obv.*, laureated bust to right, with name; *rev.*, the figure 4, 3, 2, or 1 crowned; sets, dated 1698, 1699, 1700, and 1701. There is a Groat dated 1702.

The set of four coins, 5s. to 7s. 6d.

COPPER.—Halfpenny and Farthing.

Halfpenny.—*Obv.*, laureated bust to right, GVLIELMVS TERTIVS; *rev.*, figure of Britannia, above it the word BRITANNIA; dates, 1695 to 1701, inclusive; edge, plain; worn specimens, 6d. to 1s. 6d. One, dated 1701, extremely fine, sold for £1 11s.

Farthing.—Similar to the Halfpenny, and of the same dates. Worn specimens, 6d. to 1s. 6d.

A Halfpenny, 1699, very fine, and a Farthing, 1695, sold, together, for 17s.

Anne, 1702—1714.

GOLD*.—Two issues, before the Union and after the Union: Five Guinea Piece, Two Guinea Piece, Guinea, and Half Guinea.

Weight.—Same as the last issue of Charles II.

Five Guinea Piece.—*Obv.*, bust to left, the hair filletted, ANNA DEI GRATIA; *rev.*, four shields crosswise. A rose in centre of first issue, a star (of the Order of the Garter) in centre of second issue; edge inscribed DECVS, &c.; £7 to £8.

Before the Union.—Extra fine, £13, £14, £15, and £16; others, £5 11s., £6, £6 10s.

After the Union.—Extra fine, £7 12s. 6d., £8 10s., and £12 15s.; others, £5 10s., and £6 15s.

Two Guinea Piece, second issue only.—Like the Five Guinea Piece, but edge milled; £3 to £4; extra fine, £4 12s., £5, £5 5s., £6 7s. 6d., and £7 15s.; others, £2 5s., £2 8s., and £2 10s. (Fig. 17.)

Guinea.†—Like the Five Guinea piece of both issues, but edge milled; £1 10s. to £2.

Before the Union.—Extra fine, £2 8s., £3 7s., £3 17s., £5 7s. 6d., and £10; others, £1 3s. and £1 5s.

After the Union.—Extra fine, £2 7s. £3, and £3 6s.

Half Guinea.—Similar to the Guinea of both issues; 15s. to £1 5s.

Before the Union.—Extra fine, £1 11s., £2 3s., £3 5s., and £4.

After the Union.—Extra fine, £1 9s., £1 11s., £2 7s., and £2 14s.

---

* All the pieces dated 1703 have VIGO below the bust, the gold from which they were coined having been taken from the Spanish galleons captured in Vigo Bay, 1702.

† On some GUINEAS there is an *elephant and castle* below the bust.

ANNE.—CONTINUED.

SILVER.*—Two issues, before and after the Union : Crown, Half Crown, Shilling, Sixpence, and Maundy Fourpence, Threepence, Twopence, and Penny.

Weight.—Same as the last issue of Charles II.

Crown.—Obv., as Five Guinea Piece; *rev.*, four shields crosswise, the star of the Garter in centre; edge inscribed DECVS, &c.; dates, 1703 VIGO, 1705 plumes, 1706 or 1707 roses and plumes; after Union, 1707 and 1708 plain, 1708 plumes, 1713 roses and plumes; 7s. 6d. to 15s.; extra fine, 17s., £1 5s., £1 11s., £1 15s., £2 2s., and £3 5s.

Half Crown.—Like the Crown; dates, 1703 VIGO, 1703 plain, 1704 and 1705 plumes, 1706 and 1707 roses and plumes : after Union, 1707, 1708, 1709, and 1713 plain, 1708 plumes, 1710, 1712, 1713, and 1714 roses and plumes; 3s. 6d. to 6s.; extra fine, 8s. 6d., 10s. 6d., 13s. 6d., £1 1s., and £2 6s.

Shilling.—Like the Crown, but edge milled; dates, 1702 to 1714, inclusive, except 1706; 2s. to 3s. 6d.; extra fine, 5s., 7s., and 8s.

Sixpence.—Like the Shilling; dates, 1703, 1705, 1707, 1708, 1710, and 1711; 2s. to 4s.

Sets of Crown, Half Crown, Shilling, and Sixpence, with VIGO under bust, 11s., 15s., £1 16s., £1 18s., and £4 1s.

Similar sets, plain under bust, extra fine, plumes on *rev.*, £3 11s.; roses and plumes, £3 10s.

Maundy Fourpence, Threepence, Twopence, and Penny.—Obv., bust to left, ANNA DEI GRATIA; *rev.*, the figure 4, 3, 2, or 1 crowned, with date above.

Sets, dated 1703, 1705, 1706, 1708—1710, and 1713, 4s. to 6s.

There is no penny of 1704, and no Penny or Fourpence of 1707.

COPPER.—Farthing. Several varieties of Halfpence and Farthings were struck as patterns.

Farthing.—Obv., bust to left, ANNA DEI GRATIA; *rev.*, figure of Britannia, the word BRITANNIA above, the date, 1714, below; 15s. to £1 5s. (Fig. 165.)

George I., 1714—1727.

GOLD.—Five Guinea Piece, Two Guinea Piece, Guinea, Half Guinea, and Quarter Guinea.

Weight.—Same as the last issue of Charles II.

Five Guinea Piece.— Obv., laureated bust to right, GEORGIVS, &c.; *rev.*, four shields crosswise; edge inscribed DECVS, &c.; £7 to £8; extra fine, £8 10s., £9 10s., £10, £10 7s. 6d., and £11; others, £5 7s., £5 12s. 6d., and £6 15s.

---

* Some pieces, dated 1702 and 1703, have VIGO under the bust. Coins having *plumes* on the *rev.* were struck from Welsh silver; coins having *roses* on *rev.* were struck from silver out of English Mints; *roses and plumes*, alternately, indicate the silver as being English and Welsh combined; E, or E*, is placed below the bust on coins struck in Edinburgh.

GEORGE I.—CONTINUED.

GOLD.—*Continued.*

Two Guinea Piece.—Similar to the Five Guinea Piece, but edge milled; £3 to £4; extra fine, £4 10s., £5 5s., and £5 10s.; others, £2 5s., £2 8s., and £2 11s.

Guinea.—Similar to Two Guinea Piece; £1 10s. to £2; extra fine, £2 7s., £2 18s., and £3 3s.

The Prince Elector Guinea, £1 10s. to £2 12s.

Half Guinea—Similar to the Guinea; 15s. to £1 5s.

Quarter Guinea (32½ grains).—Similar to the Guinea, but dated only 1718; 8s. 6d. to 15s.

A Half and Quarter Guinea, together, sold for 16s., £1 15s., and £2 13s.

A Guinea, Half, and Quarter, together, £3 3s.

SILVER.*—Crown, Half Crown, Shilling, Sixpence, and Maundy Four-pence, Threepence, Twopence, and Penny.

Crown.—*Obv.*, laureated bust to right; *rev.*, four shields crosswise; edge inscribed; dates, 1716, 1718, 1720, 1723, and 1726; 12s. to £1; extra fine, £1 3s. and £1 15s. (Fig. 76.)

Half Crown.—Like the Crown; dates, 1715, 1717, 1720, and 1723; 6s. 6d. to 10s. 6d.; extra fine, 18s. and £1 4s. 6d.

Shilling.—Like the Crown, but edge milled; dates, 1715 to 1727, inclusive; 1s. 6d. to 3s. 6d.; extra fine, 6s. 6d. and 12s. 6d.

With W.C.C. below bust, dates 1723—1726, 4s. to 8s.; per-fect specimens, £1 12s. and £2 5s.

Sixpence.—Like the Crown; dates, 1717, 1720, 1723, and 1726; 1s. 6d. to 3s. 6d.

Sets: Crown, Half Crown, Shilling, and Sixpence; extra fine, 18s., £2 16s., and £2 18s.

Set: Crown, Half Crown, Shilling, Sixpence, Maundy Half-penny, and Farthing (ten pieces), £1 10s.

Maundy Fourpence, Threepence, Twopence, and Penny.—*Obv.*, bust; *rev.*, numeral, crowned.

Complete sets are dated only 1723 and 1727; odd pieces of other dates. Sets, 5s. to 6s. 6d.

COPPER.—Halfpenny and Farthing.

Halfpenny.—*Obv.*, laureated bust to right; *rev.*, same as Anne's Farthing; dates, 1717 to 1724, inclusive; 6d. to 2s. 6d.

Farthing.—Similar to Halfpenny; 6d. to 1s.

George II., 1727—1760.

GOLD.†—Two issues: (First, with young head; second, with old head).—Five Guinea Piece, Two Guinea Piece, Guinea, and Half Guinea.

Weight.—Same as last issue of Charles II.

Five Guinea Piece. — *Obv.*, laureated bust to left,

---

* The Symbols on certain coins denote the *source* of the silver from which they were struck. S.S.C. stands for South Sea Company; W.C.C. for Welsh Copper Company, as also a PLUME and two C's interlinked. PLUMES indicate Welsh silver; ROSES, English silver; and ROSES and PLUMES, English and Welsh silver combined.

† Pieces having E.I.C. below the bust were struck from gold of the East India Company those with LIMA (the capital of Peru) were struck from gold captured by privateers.

GEORGE II.—CONTINUED.

GOLD.— *Continued.*

GEORGIVS II., DEI GRATIA ; *rev.*, Arms in a single shield ; edge inscribed DECVS, &c. ; £6 10s. to £7 10s.

Young head.—Extra fine, £8 and £8 10s. ; others, £5 12s. 6d. and £6.

Old head.—Extra fine, £8 10s. and £9 5s. ; others, £5 10s. and £5 15s.

Two Guinea Piece.—Similar to the Five Guinea Piece, but edge milled ; £2 15s. to £3 15s. ; extra fine, £4. (Fig. 18.)

Guinea.—Like the Two Guinea Piece ; £1 10s. to £2 ; extra fine, £2 10s. and £2 17s. 6d.

Half Guinea.—Like the Guinea ; 15s. to £1 5s. ; extra fine, £2 11s. ; an exceptional specimen, £7.

SILVER (Two issues—young and old head).—Crown, Half Crown, Shilling, and Sixpence.

Maundy money with young head only.

Weight.—Same as last issue of Charles II.

Crown.—*Obv.*, laureated bust to left ; *rev.*, four shields crosswise ; edge inscribed. Dates, young head, Roses and Plumes, 1732, 1734, 1735, 1736 ; Roses only, 1739 and 1741. Old head, Roses, 1743 ; LIMA, 1746 ; Plain, 1746, 1750, and 1751. 10s. to 15s. (Fig. 77.)

Half Crown.—Similar to the Crown. Dates, young head, Roses and Plumes, 1731, 1732, 1734, 1735, 1736 ; Roses, 1739 and 1741. Old head, Roses, 1743, 1745 ; LIMA, 1745, 1746 ; Plain, 1750 and 1751. 3s. 6d. to 6s. ; one, extra fine, 13s.

Shilling.—Similar to the Crown, but edge milled. Dates, young head, Plumes, 1727, 1731 ; Roses and Plumes, 1727, 1728, 1729, 1731, 1732, 1734, 1735, 1736, 1737 ; Plain, 1728 ; Roses, 1739 and 1741. Old head, Roses, 1743, 1745, 1747 ; LIMA, 1745, 1746 ; Plain, 1750, 1751, and 1758. 1s. 6d. to 3s. 6d. ; one, extra fine, 10s.

Sixpence.—Similar to the Shilling. Dates, young head, Plumes, 1728 ; Roses and Plumes, 1728, 1731, 1732, 1734, 1735, 1736 ; Plain, 1728 ; Roses, 1739 and 1741. Old head, Roses, 1743, 1745 ; LIMA, 1745, 1746 ; Plain, 1750, 1751, 1757, and 1758. 1s. to 3s. ; one, extra fine, 6s. 6d.

Maundy Fourpence, Threepence, Twopence, and Penny.— *Obv.*, young head to left ; *rev.*, the figure 4, 3, 2, or 1 crowned, with date.

Sets, dated 1729, 1731, 1732, 1735, 1737, 1739, 1740, 1743, 1746, and 1760, 2s. 6d. to 4s.

A set of three Crowns, three Half Crowns, three Shillings, three Sixpences, all different, and two Maundy sets (together, twenty pieces), £2 17s.

Set : Crown, Half Crown, Shilling, and Sixpence ; Roses, old head, £2 6s. ; LIMA, £1 10s.

COPPER (Two issues, with young and old head).—Halfpenny and Farthing.

Halfpenny.—*Obv.*, laureated bust to left, GEORGIVS II. REX ; *rev.*, the usual figure of Britannia, with the word

GEORGE II.—CONTINUED.

COPPER.—*Continued.*

BRITANNIA above, and date below; dates, young head, 1729 to 1739, inclusive; old head, 1740 to 1754; 6d. to 2s.

Farthing.—Similar to the Halfpenny; 6d. to 1s.

George III., 1760—1820.

GOLD.*—Guinea, Half Guinea, Quarter Guinea, One-third Guinea or Seven Shilling Piece, Sovereign, and Half Sovereign.

Guinea (129¼ grains).—Three issues.

First issue: *Obv.*, laureated bust to right, GEORGIVS III. DEI GRATIA; *rev.*, Arms in a square garnished shield; dates, 1761 to 1786, inclusive; edge milled; £1 5s. to £1 10s.

Second issue (the Spade Guinea): *Obv.*, laureated bust to right; *rev.*, Arms in a pointed shield; dates, 1787 to 1799, inclusive; edge milled; £1 5s. to £1 10s.

Third issue: *Obv.*, laureated bust to right; *rev.*, Arms in a plain shield within the Garter; date, 1813; £1 10s. to £2.

Half Guinea (64⅝ grains).—Three issues, corresponding to the Guineas.

First issue: Dates, 1761 to 1786, inclusive; 12s. 6d. to £1.

Second issue: Dates, 1787 to 1800, inclusive; 12s. 6d. to £1.

Third issue: Dates, 1801 to 1813, inclusive; 12s. 6d. to 17s. 6d.

Quarter Guinea (32⅛ grains).—Similar to the Guinea of first issue; dated 1762 only; 7s. 6d. to 15s.

Seven Shilling Piece (43⅜ grains).—Two issues.

First issue: *Obv.*, laureated bust to right, GEORGIVS III. DEI GRATIA; *rev.*, a Crown, surrounded by MAG. BRI. FR. ET HIB. REX. and the date; dates, 1797 to 1800, inclusive; 8s. 6d. to 12s. 6d.

Second issue: *Obv.*, similar to the preceding issue; *rev.*, Crown, with date below, encircled by BRITANNIARUM REX FIDEI DEFENSOR; dates, 1801 to 1813, inclusive; 8s. 6d. to 12s. 6d.

Sovereign (123¼ grains).—*Obv.*, laureated bust to right, date below, GEORGIUS III. D.G. BRITANNIAR. REX F.D.; *rev.*, St. George and the Dragon, surrounded by the Garter; edge milled; dates, 1817, 1818, and 1820; £1 2s. to £1 5s.

Half Sovereign (61⅝ grains).—*Obv.*, bust as on Sovereign, GEORGIUS III. DEI GRATIA, date under the bust; *rev.*, shield of Arms crowned; dates, 1817, 1818, and 1820; 11s. to 12s. 6d.

SILVER.—Crown, Half Crown, Shilling, Sixpence, Maundy Fourpence, Threepence, Twopence, and Penny, and Bank of England Tokens for Five Shillings, Three Shillings, and One Shilling and Sixpence.

Crown (436¼ grains).—*Obv.*, laureated bust to right; *rev.*, St. George and the Dragon; dates, 1818, 1819, or 1820; 7s. 6d. to 15s.

---

* FIVE GUINEA PIECES, DOUBLE GUINEAS, FIVE POUND PIECES, and DOUBLE SOVEREIGNS were struck as patterns only, not for currency.

GEORGE III.—CONTINUED.

SILVER.—Continued.

Half Crown (218½ grains).—Two varieties.

First type: *Obv.*, laureated bust to right, with bare shoulders: *rev.*, Arms in a garnished shield, surrounded by the Garter and Collar of the Order ; dates, 1816 or 1817 ; 3s. 6d. to 6s.

Second type: *Obv.*, small bust, without shoulders ; *rev.*, Arms in a plain shield surrounded by the Garter, the collar being omitted ; dates, 1817 to 1820, inclusive ; 3s. 6d. to 6s.

Shilling.—Three varieties.

First type (92¼ grains):* *Obv.*, laureated youthful bust to right; *rev.*, four shields arranged crosswise, star of the Order of the Garter in the centre ; date, 1763 ; 5s. to 10s.

Second type (92¼ grains).—*Obv.*, laureated older bust to right ; *rev.*, four shields crosswise, a crown in the angles ; date, 1787 ; 2s. 6d. to 3s. 6d.

Third type (87¼ grains).—*Obv.*, laureated old head to right; *rev.*, Arms in a garnished shield ; dates, 1816 to 1820, inclusive ; 2s. to 3s.

Sixpence.—Two varieties.

First type (46¼ grains).—Similar to the Shilling of 1787, and of that date only ; 1s. 6d. to 2s. 6d.

Second type (43¾ grains).—Similar to the Shilling of last issue, and dated 1816 to 1820, inclusive ; 1s. to 2s.

Maundy Money.—Fourpence, Threepence, Twopence, and Penny. Four varieties.

First type: *Obv.*, like the Shilling of 1763 ; *rev.*, 4, 3, 2, or 1, crowned.

Sets, dated 1763, 1766, 1780, 1784, and 1786 (odd pieces of other dates, from 1762 to 1781 inclusive), 2s. 6d. to 3s. 6d.

Second type: *Obv.*, like the Shilling of 1787 ; *rev.*, the numerals 4, 3, or 2 in written form, on the Penny 1 in printed form ; date, 1792 only ; 5s. to 6s.

Third type: *Obv.*, like the Shilling of 1787 ; *rev.*, the Arabic numerals, 4, 3, 2, or 1 ; dates, 1795 and 1800 ; 3s. 6d. to 4s. 6d.

Fourth type: *Obv.*, like the Shilling of 1816, the date under the head ; *rev.*, the figures 4, 3, 2, or 1 ; dates, 1816 to 1820, inclusive ; 3s. to 4s.

Bank of England Tokens.—*Five Shillings*, or *Dollar* (415 grains): *Obv.*, laureated bust to right ; *rev.*, figure of Britannia seated, surrounded by a band inscribed FIVE SHILLINGS DOLLAR, the whole encircled by BANK OF ENGLAND, 1804 ; 6s. to 10s. (Fig. 78.)

Three Shillings (227 grains).—Two varieties ; 3s. 6d. to 4s. 6d.

First type: *Obv.*, laureated bust in armour to right, GEORGIUS III. DEI GRATIA REX ; *rev.*, within an oak wreath, inscription BANK TOKEN 3 SHILL. 1811 (or 1812) in four lines.

---

* This coin is known as the NORTHUMBERLAND SHILLING, having been struck (to the amount of £100 only) for the use of the Earl of Northumberland in Dublin, on his appointment as Lord Lieutenant of Ireland.

GEORGE III.—CONTINUED.

SILVER.—*Continued.*

Second type.—*Obv.*, laureated bust, neck bare ; *rev.*, a wreath of olive and oak leaves, with similar inscription ; dates, 1812 to 1816, inclusive.

One Shilling and Sixpence (113½ grains).—Two varieties, similar to the Three Shilling Pieces ; 2s. to 3s. 6d.

COPPER.—Twopenny Piece, Penny, Halfpenny, Farthing.

Twopenny Piece (2oz. av.).*—*Obv.*, laureated bust to right ; *rev.*, figure of Britannia. The rims are raised, the legend and date (1797) are in sunk or incuse letters ; 1s. to 5s.

Penny (1oz. av.).—Similar to the Twopenny ; date, 1797 ; 1s. to 2s. 6d.

Penny.—Dated 1806 or 1807 ; *obv.*, bust to right ; *rev.*, Britannia ; edge milled ; 1s. to 2s.

Halfpenny.—Three varieties ; 1s. to 1s. 6d. each.

First type : *Obv.*, bust to right in armour ; *rev.*, Britannia ; dates, 1770 to 1775, inclusive.

Second type : *Obv.*, bust as on the Twopence ; *rev.*, Britannia, and date, 1799.

Third type : Similar to the Penny of 1806 and 1807.

Farthing.—Three varieties ; 6d. to 1s. each.

First type : Similar to first Halfpenny ; dates, 1770 to 1775, inclusive.

Second type : Similar to second Halfpenny of 1799.

Third type : Similar to third Halfpenny, and dated 1806 and 1807.

George IV., 1820—1830.

GOLD.†—Double Sovereign, Sovereign, and Half Sovereign.

Double Sovereign (246½ grains). — *Obv.*, bust to left, GEORGIUS IIII., &c. ; *rev.*, St. George and the Dragon ; date, 1823 ; edge inscribed : £2 10s. to £3 10s.

Sovereign (123½ grains).—Two varieties ; £1 2s. to £1 5s.

First type : *Obv.*, laureated bust to left, GEORGIUS IIII., &c.; *rev.*, St. George and the Dragon ; dates, 1821 to 1825, inclusive.

Second type : *Obv.*, GEORGIUS IV., bust to left, with date (1826 to 1830, inclusive) below it ; *rev.*, arms in a garnished shield.

Half Sovereign (61½ grains).—Three varieties.

First type : *Obv.*, like first Sovereign ; *rev.*, arms in a garnished shield, ANNO 1821 ; 15s. to £1.

Second type : *Obv.*, like the first type ; *rev.*, arms in a plain shield, ANNO 1823 (1824 or 1825) ; 11s. to 12s. 6d.

Third type : *Obv.*, like second Sovereign ; dates, 1826, 1827, and 1838 ; 10s. 6d. to 12s.

---

* A broad rim HALFPENNY and FARTHING, like the Twopenny and Penny, were struck as patterns, dated 1797; also a Farthing, with broad rim, dated 1798.

† Pieces of FIVE SOVEREIGNS and TWO SOVEREIGNS, like the second type Sovereign, were struck as patterns.

GEORGE IV.—CONTINUED.

SILVER.—Crown, Half Crown, Shilling, Sixpence, and Maundy Fourpence, Threepence, Twopence, and Penny.

Crown (436¼ grains). — *Obv.*, laureated bust to left, GEORGIUS IIII. D.G., &c.; *rev.*, St. George and the Dragon; dates, 1821 and 1822 (the Crown, dated 1820, was struck as a pattern); 8s. to 15s.

Half Crown (218½ grains).—Three varieties.

First type: *Obv.*, like the Crown; *rev.*, Arms in a garnished shield, rose, shamrock, and thistle, ANNO 1820, 1821, or 1823; 4s. to 6s.

Second type: *Obv.*, like the crown; *rev.*, Arms in a plain shield, encircled by the Garter, ANNO 1823 or 1824; 4s. to 5s.

Third type*: *Obv.*, small bust, not laureated, to left, GEORGIUS IV., &c.; dates, 1825, 1826, 1828, or 1829: *rev.*, arms in a garnished shield, surmounted by a helmet; 3s. 6d. to 4s. 6d.

Shilling (87¼ grains). — Three varieties.

First type: Like the first Half Crown, 1821; 3s. to 4s. 6d.

Second type: Like the second Half Crown; dates, 1823, 1824, and 1825; 3s. to 4s.

Third type: *Obv.*, like the third Half Crown; *rev.*, a lion standing upon a crown; dates, 1825, 1826, 1827, and 1829; 2s. 6d. to 4s. 6d.

Sixpence (43⅔ grains).—Three varieties.

First type: Like the first Shilling; date, 1821; 4s. to 5s.

Second type: Like the second Shilling; dates, 1824, 1825, and 1826; 2s. 6d. to 3s. 6d.

Third type: Like the third Shilling; dates, 1826 to 1829, inclusive. 2s. 6d. to 5s.

Maundy Money. — *Obv.*, bust similar to the Crown, GEORGIUS IIII., &c.; *rev.*, the figure 4, 3, 2, or 1, crowned; dates, 1821 to 1830, inclusive; 3s. to 4s.

COPPER.†—Penny, Halfpenny, and Farthing.

Penny (291⅔ grains).—*Obv.*, bust to left; dated 1825, 1826, or 1827; *rev.*, Britannia; 1s. to 3s.

Halfpenny (146 grains).—Similar; dated, 1825, 1826, or 1827; 6d. to 1s.

Farthing (73 grains).—Two varieties; 6d. to 1s. each.

First type: *Obv.*, bust like that on the Crown; *rev.*, Britannia; dated, 1821, 1822, 1823, 1825, or 1826.

Second type: Like the Penny; dates 1826 to 1830, inclusive.

William IV., 1830—1837.

GOLD.—Sovereign and Half Sovereign. (Double Sovereigns were struck as patterns.)

Weight.—Same as those of George IV.

Sovereign.—*Obv.*, bust to right, GULIELMUS IIII., &c.;

---

* A CROWN, similar to this Half Crown, was struck as a pattern.

† A HALF FARTHING (36½ grains) and ONE-THIRD FARTHING (24½ grains) were struck for Colonial use.

WILLIAM IV.—CONTINUED.

GOLD.—*Continued.*

rev., shield of arms; below, ANNO and dates, 1831 to 1837 inclusive; £1 1s. to £1 3s.

Half Sovereign.—Similar to Sovereign; dates, 1834 to 1839, inclusive; 10s. 6d. to 12s. 6d. #

SILVER.* — Half Crown, Shilling, Sixpence, Groat, and Maundy Fourpence, Threepence, Twopence, and Penny.

Weight.—Same as those of George IV.

Half Crown.—*Obv.*, bust to right, name and title; *rev.*, shield of arms on a royal mantle; dates, 1831, 1834, 1835, and 1836; 3s. 6d. to 5s. 6d.

Shilling.—*Obv.*, similar to Half Crown; *rev.*, the words ONE SHILLING in centre of a wreath; dates, 1831 and 1834 to 1837 inclusive; 1s. 6d. to 2s. 6d.

Sixpence.—*Obv.*, like the Shilling; *rev.*, SIXPENCE within a wreath; dates as on Shilling; 1s. to 2s. 6d.

Groat (29 grains). — *Obv.*, as Sixpence; *rev.*, figure of Britannia seated, FOUR PENCE above, date (1836 or 1837) below; 9d. to 1s. 6d.

Maundy Money.—*Obv.*, bust to right, name and title; *rev.*, like that of George IV.'s Maundy money. Sets dated 1831 to 1837, inclusive, 3s. to 4s.

COPPER.†—Penny, Halfpenny, and Farthing.

Weight.—As those of George IV.

Penny. — *Obv.*, bust to right, GULIELMUS IIII. DEI GRATIA, date, below the head, 1831, 1834, 1836, or 1837; *rev.*, similar to that of George IV.; 1s. 6d. to 3s.

Halfpenny.—Similar to the Penny; 1s. to 1s. 6d.

Farthing.—Similar to the Penny; 6d. to 1s.

Victoria, 1837.

GOLD.—Sovereign and Half-Sovereign. (Five Pound Pieces were struck as patterns.)

Weight.—As those of George IV.

Sovereign.—Two varieties.

First type: *Obv.*, bust to left, the date below, VICTORIA DEI GRATIA; *rev.*, shield of arms, BRITANNIARUM REGINA FID : DEF :

Second type: *Obv.*, bust to left, VICTORIA D : G : BRITANNIAR : REG : F : D :; *rev.*, St. George and the Dragon, date below.

Half Sovereign.—Similar to the first Sovereign.

SILVER.—Crown, Half Crown, Florin, Shilling, Sixpence, Groat, and Maundy Fourpence, Threepence, Twopence, and Penny. (Three Halfpenny Pieces were struck for Colonial use.)

Weight.—As those of George IV.

Crown.‡—*Obv.*, bust to left, the date below, VICTORIA DEI

* CROWNS, dated 1831 and 1834, were struck as patterns only. Pieces of the value of THREE HALFPENCE were struck for Colonial circulation.
† A HALF FARTHING and ONE-THIRD FARTHING were struck for Colonial use
‡ A CROWN (like the Florin) was struck, as a pattern, in 1846, 1847, and 1853.

There are two varieties of the Half Sovereign. One, which is very rare, is smaller and thicker than the ordinary size, but the same weight.

VICTORIA.—CONTINUED.

SILVER.—*Continued.*

GRATIA; *rev.*, shield of Arms, BRITANNIARUM, &c.; edge inscribed; dates, 1844, 1845, 1846, 1847, and 1851; 7s. to 10s.

Half Crown.—Similar to the Crown; edge milled; dates, 1839 to 1851, inclusive, 1862, 1864, and 1874 and subsequent years; early dates, 3s. to 4s.

Florin (174¾ grains).—Two varieties.

First type (the graceless florin): *Obv.*, crowned bust to left, VICTORIA REGINA, 1849; *rev.*, four shields arranged cross-wise, ONE FLORIN, ONE TENTH OF A POUND; date 1849 only; 3s. to 4s.

Second type: Bust as on first type, legend in old English characters, Victoria d: g: Brit: reg: f: d: and the date, in letters, mdcccli.; dates 1851 and subsequent years.

Shilling.—*Obv.*, bust as on the Half Crown, name and titles; *rev.*, ONE SHILLING within a wreath; dates, 1838 and following years; early dates, 1s. 6d. to 2s.

Sixpence.—Like the Shilling, except the word SIXPENCE on *rev.*; dates, as on the Shilling; early dates, 1s. to 1s. 6d.

Groat.—*Obv.*, bust as on the Shilling; *rev.*, like the Groat of Wm. IV.; dates, 1838 to 1851, and 1853 to 1856 inclusive; 9d. to 1s. 6d.

Maundy Money. — *Obv.*, like the Groat; *rev.*, the figures, 4, 3, 2, or 1; dates, 1838 and following years; 2s. 6d. to 3s. 6d.

The Threepenny Piece has been issued in large numbers as ordinary currency.

COPPER.—Penny, Halfpenny, Farthing, and Half Farthing.*

Weight.—As those of George IV.

Penny.—*Obv.*, bust to left, date below, VICTORIA DEI GRATIA; *rev.*, figure of Britannia; dates, 1841, 1843 to 1849, 1851 to 1859, inclusive; 6d. to 2s.

Halfpenny.—Similar to the Penny; dates, 1838, 1839, 1841, 1843 to 1848, 1851 to 1860, inclusive; 6d. to 1s.

Farthing.—Similar to Halfpenny; dates, 1838 to 1860, inclusive; 6d. to 1s.

Half Farthing.—*Obv.*, bust; *rev.*, the words HALF FAR-THING in two lines, a crown above and date beneath; 6d.

BRONZE.—Penny, Halfpenny, and Farthing. (A One-third Farthing was struck for Colonial use.)

Penny.— *Obv.*, Laureated bust to left, VICTORIA D. G. BRITT. REG. F.D.; *rev.*, figure of Britannia, ONE PENNY above, date below; dates, 1860 and subsequent years.

Halfpenny.—Like the Penny, but HALF PENNY on *rev.*; dates as on Penny.

Farthing.—Like the Halfpenny, but FARTHING on *rev.*; dates as on Penny.

---

* Pieces of ONE-THIRD OF A FARTHING and A QUARTER FARTHING (18¾ grains) were struck for Colonial use.

SCOTTISH COINS.

AUTHORITIES differ as to the date of the earliest coinage of Scotland. Until the year 956 a large portion of the south of Scotland formed part of the Saxon Kingdom of Northumberland, whilst the western shores and the islands were governed by the Kings of Man and Norway. Some numismatists consider there is no reason to suppose that a Scottish coinage existed previous to the reign of David I., while others have appropriated coins to some of his predecessors.

The earliest coins connected with Scotland are stated to be three Silver Pennies (of the Crux type of Ethelred II., 978—1016), which have been attributed to Kings of the Hebrides, in the eleventh century.

KINGS OF THE HEBRIDES.

Sueno (supposed to be the father of Canute).

SILVER, *Penny* (31 grains). *Obv.*, rude head to left, with sceptre surmounted by three pearls, the legend being + EDEL REX, &c.; *rev.*, a short double cross in an inner circle, with the letters C R V + *retrograde* in the angles, surrounded by the inscription SVENO, &c. Sold for £1 9s. in 1867, and for 13s. in 1875.

Anegmund (probably intended for **Ingemund**).

SILVER, *Penny* (21½ grains). *Obv.*, ANEGMD, &c.; *rev.*, the moneyer's name and place of mintage. (See Fig. 81.) Sold for £1 1s. in 1867.

Somerled.

SILVER, *Penny* (21 grains). Same type, with king's name on *obv.* Sold for 15s. in 1867, and for 17s. in 1875.

KINGS OF SCOTLAND.

Malcolm III., 1056.

SILVER, *Penny* (23 grains). *Obv.*, king's head full face, with crown fleury, a sceptre at each side, one sceptre having a cross at the top and the other a fleur-de-lis; inscription + MA . . . . REX; *rev.*, a cross fleury, having a large pellet and a rose of annulets in the alternate angles. (See Fig. 82.) *Unique.* Sold for £7 10s. in 1859, and for £27 in 1880.

Donald VIII., 1093.

A Silver Penny has been attributed to this king, but without any degree of certainty. *Obv.*, a head with crown fleury to left, with sceptre, similar to the first coinage of William the Lion; *rev.*, a short cross with a large annulet and three dots in each angle, the legend being unintelligible.

Alexander I., 1107.

It is a matter of controversy whether any coins are known of this king, those formerly assigned to him being either blundered coins of David I. and William the Lion, or the short double-cross pennies of Alexander II.

David I., 1124—1153.

SILVER, *Pennies* (from 20 to 23 grains). Struck at Berwick and Roxburgh.

Authentic Pennies of David I. are rare. They are well executed, the king's name and title being correctly given on the *obv.*, and the name of the moneyer and mint in legible letters on the *rev.* Much more numerous are the rudely-executed coins of a similar type but with blundered legends, which some numismatists assign to the predecessors of David I., while others consider them to have been struck in imitation of the coins issued by that monarch.

Penny.—*Obv.*, king's head to right with crown fleury, and sceptre, legend DAVI . . . .; *rev.*, cross fleury with a pellet in each angle, surrounded by the inscription + HVGO ON ROCH (= Hugo of Roxburgh). (See Fig. 83.)

Pennies struck at Roxburgh have sold for 13s., £1 15s., £10, and £10 10s.; others of uncertain mints for 3s., 4s., £1 8s., and £2.

A Penny (unpublished)—*obv.*, profile to right with sceptre, + DAVID. REX.; and *rev.*, a plain cross within a tressure of eight curves, a fleur-de-lis in each angle—realised £6 2s. 6d. in 1859, and £22 in 1880.

Henry, Prince of Scotland (son of David I., created by Stephen, Earl of Northumberland).

SILVER, *Pennies* (from 22 to 24 grains).—Struck at Bamborough, or, according to some numismatists, at Berwick and Carlisle. (See Fig. 84.)

Specimens have sold for 18s., £4, £5 12s. 6d., £7 7s., and £26 10s.

A Penny of David I. and one of Henry, Earl of Northumberland, sold together for £3 2s., and a similar lot for £3 16s.

Malcolm IV., 1153.

A Penny, in type like those of David I., has been attributed to this king, but the correctness of this is disputed. It realised £1 7s. in 1867.

William the Lion, 1165—1214.

SILVER, *Pennies* (from 22 to 24 grains).—Three issues.

First issue.—Struck at Berwick, Edinburgh, Perth, and Roxburgh.

Obv., + LE REI WILAM, the king's head, with crown fleury, to left, with sceptre; *rev.*, a single cross with a crescent and pellet in each angle, surrounded by the name of the moneyer and mint. (See Fig. 85.)

Second issue.—Struck at Edinburgh, Perth, and Roxburgh.

Obv., king's head, crowned with pearls, to left, with sceptre; *rev.*, a short double cross, with a star in each angle, surrounded by name of moneyer and mint. (See Fig. 87).

Third issue.—Struck at Roxburgh only. Similar to the second issue, except that the king's head is turned to the *right*.

A specimen (unique ?) of this issue, without the sceptre, sold for £10 10s. in 1875.

The coins of the second issue are far more numerous than those of the first, while those of the third issue are very rare.

There is, in the British Museum, a unique Penny; *obv.*, + WILELMVS; *rev.*, a short single cross with a fleur-de-lis in each angle and legend + FOLPOLD . ON . RO. (= Roxburgh). (See Fig. 86.) It is doubtful whether this coin preceded the first coinage, or was struck between the first and second coinages.

Another unique coin—*rev.*, a short cross potent (as Fig. 86) with five pellets in each of the angles—realised £10 10s. in 1875.

First issue.—Four, varied, sold (1854) for 7s., and five for 9s.; nine, varied (1875), £5; ten, £5; and seven, £2 12s.

Second issue.—Ten, varied (1854), 12s. In 1875, two (unique) sold for £5; nine, varied, £6; and nine others £7 5s.

Third issue.—Nine, different (1854), 10s. In 1875 a Roxburgh Penny, fine, realised £1 2s.; and two Pennies, without place of mintage, £4 4s.

Two Pennies of David I., and three, varied, of William the Lion, sold together (1859) for £3 2s.

Six Pennies, varied, of William the Lion, sold together (1864) for 12s., and a like number for 19s.

Alexander II., 1214—1249.

SILVER, *Pennies* (about 21 grains). Struck at Roxburgh only.

The *rev.* is like that of the second and third issues of William the Lion, but there are at least five varieties of *obv.*:

1. Bare head to left, without sceptre (Fig. 88);
2. Bare head to left, with sceptre;
3. Bare head to right, with sceptre;
4. Crowned head to right, with sceptre (Fig. 89); and
5. Crowned head to left, with sceptre.

The workmanship of these coins is bold, but the letters are generally ill formed, and the legend difficult to read. They are very rare.

Fig. 88.—*Obv.*, + ALEXSANDEREX; *rev.*, + ALAIN. ANNDRV. OF RO.

ALEXANDER II.—CONTINUED.

SILVER.—*Continued.*

Fig. 89.—*Obv.*, + ALEXSANDER REX; *rev.*, + ANDRV . . . CA . . . O.

Specimens have realised £6 6s., £6 8s. 6d., £10 10s., and £11 5s.

Two, sold together (1859) for £5 5s., realised £16 in 1880.

A poor specimen sold (1864) for £1 2s. only.

Alexander III., 1249—1292.

SILVER.—Four coinages.

First coinage.—*Pennies* only (20 to 22½ grains). Struck at Berwick, Glasgow, Lanark, Markinch (?) and Perth.

Obv., bare head to right, with sceptre, ALEXANNDER REX; *rev.*, long double cross, a star of 6 points in each angle. (See Fig. 90.)

In 1867, two Pennies sold together for £1 10s.

In 1875, a Penny of Aberdeen realised £6 15s.; one of Berwick, £5 10s.; one of Lanark, £4 4s.; and one of Perth, £4.

Second coinage.—*Pennies* only (20 to 22½ grains). Struck at Aberdeen, Perth, and Roxburgh.

Obv., crowned head to right, with sceptre, ALEXANDER REX; *rev.*, long double cross, as before, R . . . NALD ON ABE. (See Fig. 91.)

In 1875, two Pennies (Aberdeen and Berwick) sold for £1 3s.; two Pennies (Aberdeen and Perth), £3 3s.; and two (Edinburgh and Perth) for £7 5s.

Third coinage.—*Pennies* only (18 to 25 grains). Struck at Aberdeen, Berwick, Dunbar, Dundee, Edinburgh, Forres, Glasgow, Inverness, Lanark, Markinch, Montrose, Perth, Roxburgh, St. Andrew's, and Stirling.

Obv., crowned head to left, with sceptre; *rev.*, as before.

In 1875, a Penny of Aberdeen sold for £3; one of St. Andrew's (or Annan?), £10 5s.; one of Dundee, £5 5s.; one of Glasgow, £10 5s., another £10 10s.; one of Inverness, £21; one of Montrose, £5 15s.; one of Stirling, £4; four, of Dunbar, Perth, and Roxburgh, £3 5s.; two (Aberdeen and Berwick). £1 3s.; and three (Berwick and Roxburgh), 14s.

In 1854, three Pennies (one of each coinage) sold together for 6s.; six Pennies, varied, for 5s.; and another lot of seven Pennies realised 4s. 6d.

In 1864, seven Pennies sold for 9s., and in 1879 two (Edinburgh and Perth) realised £12 5s.

Fourth coinage.—Penny, Halfpenny,* and Farthing of very neat workmanship, having on the *rev.* a long *single* cross.

There are no names of moneyers or mints on the long single-cross coins. The *Pennies* differ from each other chiefly in the

---

* HALFPENNIES and FARTHINGS were first coined in Scotland by Alexander III., apparently about the same date as that on which they were introduced into England, *i.e.*, about 1279.

ALEXANDER III.—CONTINUED.

SILVER.—*Continued.*

number of points contained in the mullets* or stars on the *rev.* Beginning with four mullets of 5 points each = 20 points, next three mullets of 5 points each and one of 6 points = 21 points, and so on; the number of points increases by one until the maximum of 28 points is reached, by four stars of 7 points each.

Penny (20 to 22 grains).

Obv., the king's head crowned to left, with sceptre, surrounded by ALEXANDER (sometimes ALEXSANDER) DEI GRA, or GRAC, or GCIA; *rev.*, a long single cross, having a mullet or star in each angle, and REX SCOTORVM + (see Fig. 92), or, on some coins, ESCOSSIE REX.

Ordinary specimens are worth from 1s. to 2s. each.

In 1854, six sold for 4s., sixteen for 9s., and seventeen for 8s.

In 1864, four Pennies and a Halfpenny sold for 8s., and four Pennies (one ESCOSSIE REX) realised 8s.

In 1875, eight Pennies, all different, sold for £1; three Pennies (one REX ESCOSSIE, one DEI GRAC) sold for £1 2s.; a Penny, with two stars and two mullets each of 6 points, realised £1 1s.; and a Penny, REX ESCOSSIE, extremely fine, sold for £3 17s. 6d.

Halfpenny (10 to 11 grains).

Obv., like the Penny; *rev.*, REX SCOTORVM, usually with mullets of 6 points in two of the angles of the cross, the other angles plain. Sometimes there is a star of 6 points in one angle, and a mullet of 6 points in the opposite angle.

Farthing (5 to 5½ grains).

Obv., head as on the Penny, ALEXANDER REX; *rev.*, SCOTORVM, with mullets of 6 points in all the angles of the cross.

A variety, referred to below, is stated to have on *obv.* ALEXANDER DEI GRA, and on *rev.* SCOTTORVM REX.

In 1854, a Halfpenny and three Farthings sold for 13s.

In 1859, four Pennies (one ESCOSSIE REX), a Halfpenny, and a Farthing, sold for £1 2s., and the same coins, without the Farthing, but with an additional Penny, realised £3 in 1880.

In 1861, a penny (ESCOSSIE REX), a Halfpenny, and three Farthings, sold for £2 2s.

In 1864, two Farthings, one (unpublished) having SCOTTORVM REX on *rev.*, sold for 11s., and another Farthing realised 17s. Four Pennies and a Halfpenny sold together for 8s.

In 1875, a Halfpenny sold for £4, and a Farthing for £20 10s.

John Baliol, 1292—1304.

SILVER.—Penny and Halfpenny. No Farthings are known of this reign.

---

* The difference between MULLETS and STARS is, that the former are pierced or open in the centre. Stars are shown on the *rev.* of Fig. 91, and mullets on the *rev.* of Fig. 92. Stars are sometimes termed close mullets.

JOHN BALIOL.—CONTINUED.

SILVER.—*Continued.*

Penny (about 22 grains).—Similar in type to the last coinage of Alexander III.

Obv., IOHANNES . DEI . GRA ; *rev.,* REX SCOTORVM + (see Fig. 93). Some varieties have CIVITAS SANDRE (= St. Andrew's) on *rev.* ; and some have on *obv.* I . DI . GRA . SCOTORVM . RX, with CIVITAS SANDRE on *rev.*

Ordinary specimens are worth from 4s. to 10s. each.

In 1854, seven sold for 15s., two (like those last described) for 8s., and two Pennies and a Halfpenny sold for 15s.

Halfpenny (about 9 grains).—Like the Penny. (See Fig. 94.) A variety has a mullet in each angle of the cross.

In 1859, two Pennies and two Halfpennies (both varieties) sold for 17s.

In 1864, four Pennies and a Halfpenny realised £1 3s.

In 1875, five Pennies (REX SCOTORVM), varied, sold for £4 15s. ; and three Pennies (St. Andrew's) and a Halfpenny realised £9.

Robert Bruce, 1306—1329.

SILVER.—Penny, Halfpenny, and Farthing.

Penny (19 to 21 grains).

Obv., ROBERTVS DEI GRA ; *rev.,* SCOTORVM REX. (See Fig. 95).

Halfpenny (9¼ grains).—Same type ; very rare.

Farthing (5 grains).—Same type ; extremely rare.

In 1854, five Pennies and a Farthing, very fine, sold for 16s.

In 1859, a Penny, Halfpenny, and Farthing realised only 16s.

In 1867, three Pennies and two Halfpennies sold for £2 1s.

In 1875, two Pennies sold for £2 2s. ; a Halfpenny for £9 ; and a Farthing realised £42.

David II., 1329—1371.

GOLD.—Noble.

Noble.—This is the earliest Scottish gold coin, and apparently struck in imitation of the contemporary English Nobles.

Obv., the king in a ship, DAVID . DEI . GRA . REX . SCOTORVM ; *rev.,* IHC . AVTEM . TRANCIENS . P . MEDIVM . ILLORVM . IBAT., cross fleury, within a double tressure of eight curves, a lion and crown in each angle.

Three specimens only are known, all slightly different. One is in the British Museum, and two in private collections.

One, for which Mr. Martin gave £75, sold, in 1859, for £41, and again, in 1880, for £31.

SILVER.—Groat, Half Groat, Penny, Halfpenny, and Farthing.

The earliest issue comprised the Penny, Halfpenny, and Farthing, having REX SCOTTORVM on *rev.*

The subsequent issues, with the name of the mint (Aberdeen or Edinburgh) on *rev.,* are considered by some numismatists to constitute two separate coinages distinguished by the size of the head on *obv.,* the small head pieces having preceded those

DAVID II.—CONTINUED.

SILVER.—*Continued.*

with the large head. But this view is opposed on the ground that the *weights* of these coins indicate that their issue must have been contemporaneous.

Groat (72 and 61 grains).

Obv., DAVID . DEI . GRA . REX . SCOTORVM, king's head crowned to left, with sceptre, in a tressure of 6 or 7 points; *rev.*, long single cross, with mullets of 5 points in the angles; in the outer circle, + DNS . PTECTOR . MS + LIBATOR MS. (=Dominus Protector Meus, Liberator Meus), and, in the inner circle, VILLA ABERDON, *or* VILLA EDINBVRGH.

Ordinary specimens, 3s. 6d. to 5s. 6d.

A very fine Groat, Aberdeen mint, sold for £2 2s.

Half Groat (36 and 30 grains).

Obv., as on Groat; *rev.*, +DNS . PROTECTOR . MEVS, in outer circle; and VILLA ABERDON, *or* EDINBVRGH, in inner circle. (See Fig. 96.)

Ordinary specimens, 3s. 6d. to 5s. 6d.

Penny (14 to 16 grains).

Early issue. *Obv.*, DAVID . DEI . GRACIA, crowned head to left, with sceptre (sometimes with only the head of the sceptre); *rev.*, REX . SCOTORVM + (*or* SCOTTORVM), mullets of 6 points in the angles of the cross. (See Fig. 97.) 2s. 6d. to 4s. 6d.

Penny.—Later issue. *Obv.*, similar head, with sceptre, DAVID . DEI . GRA . R . SCOTOR., *or* DAVID . DEI . GRA . REX . SC., *or* DAVID . REX . SCOTORVM; *rev.*, VILLA ABERDON, *or* VILLA EDINBVRGH, mullets of 5 points in the angles of the cross.

Ordinary specimens, 2s. 6d. to 4s. 6d.

Halfpenny.—Early issue. *Obv.*, as early Penny; *rev.*, REX . SCOTORVM (*or* SCOTTORVM), mullets of 5 points in two angles, and three pellets in the other angles of the cross.

A specimen, described as being extremely fine and rare to excess, sold for £35 in 1875.

Halfpenny.—Later issue. *Obv.*, as before; *rev.*, VILLA EDINBVRGH, mullets of 5 points in two angles, the other angles plain.

Farthing (5 grains).—*Obv.*, DAVID . DEI . GRACIA, like early issue Penny; *rev.*, REX . SCOTORVM, mullets of 5 points in the angles of the cross. *Extremely rare.*

Farthing (5 grains).—A singular variety (unique?) has, on *obv.*, + MONETA . REGIS . D., and on *rev.*, + AVID . SCOTTOR.

Sold, in 1859, for £1; and again, in 1880, together with a Groat and Half Groat of Edinburgh, for £22.

Coins of the various issues have realised the following prices:

ABERDEEN mint:

Groat and Half Groat, 4s. and £11 5s.

Groat, Half Groat, and Penny, 11s. and £6 6s.

DAVID II.—CONTINUED.

SILVER.—*Continued.*

EDINBURGH mint:

Groat, Half Groat, and Penny, 5s., 6s., £2, and £2 16s.

Half Groat and Penny, with a Penny of first issue, 5s.

Groat, Half Groat, Penny, and Halfpenny, £2 5s.

A lot, consisting of an Aberdeen and Edinburgh Groat, a Half Groat of Edinburgh, a Penny (first issue), a Penny of Edinburgh, and a Halfpenny, realised £1 1s.

A set, consisting of Groat, Half Groat, and Penny of Aberdeen, and Groat, Half Groat, and Penny, of Edinburgh, sold together for £3.

Robert II., 1371—1390.

GOLD.—St. Andrew and Lion.

St. Andrew (about 38 grains).

Obv., × ROBERTVS : DEI GRACIA REX SCOT., surrounding a shield containing the arms of Scotland, crowned; *rev.*, + DNS . PTECTOR . MS . + . LBERAT., the figure of St. Andrew, with his arms extended, between two fleurs-de-lis. (See Fig. 21.)

Specimens have realised, at various times, 12s., £1 5s. 6d., £1 12s., and £5 5s.

Lion (from 19 to 33 grains).

Obv., + ROBERTVS . DEI . G . REX . SCOTO, arms of Scotland on a shield, not crowned; *rev.*, XPC* . REGNAT . XPC . VINCT (*or* VINCIT), St. Andrew's cross, extending to the edge, between fleurs-de-lis and trefoils in opposite angles. The contractions of the legends on *obv.* and *rev.* vary somewhat in different specimens.

Specimens have sold for 7s. 6d., £1, £2, £3 4s., £3 13s. 6d., £5 5s., and £8 10s.

A Lion and St. Andrew, sold for £1 16s. in 1854, realised £5 10s. in 1880.

Two Lions and a St. Andrew, £4 15s.

SILVER.—Groat, Half Groat, Penny, and Halfpenny.

Groats (60 to 50 grains†).—Struck at Dundee, Perth, and Edinburgh.

Obv., ROBERTVS . DEI . GRA . REX . SCOTTORVM, surrounding a tressure‡ of 6 points with trefoils in the external angles; the king's head, crowned, to left, with sceptre, the letter B § behind the head; on some coins the B is omitted; *rev.*, + DNS . PTECTOR . MS . + LIBATOR . MS. in outer circle, and + VILLA × DVNDE in inner circle, a mullet of 5 points in each angle. (See Fig. 98.)

Ordinary specimens, 3s. 6d. to 5s. 6d.

---

* XPC. is a contraction of XPICTOC = Χριστός.

† In 1373, fourpence Scotch was equivalent to threepence English, and, in 1882, Scottish money was still further reduced in weight, and was received in England as bullion only.

‡ On a Half Groat of Dundee and on one of Edinburgh the tressure has 7 points; on the other Groats and Half Groats of Robert III the tressure has 6 points.

§ For BONAGIUS, the moneyer, a Florentine employed in the Scottish mint.

ROBERT II.—CONTINUED.

SILVER.—*Continued.*

Half Groats (30 to 23 grains).—Struck at Dundee, Edinburgh and Perth.

Obv., as the Groat; *rev.,* usually + DNS . PROTECTOR . MEVS in outer circle, and + VILLA DVNDE (*or* EDIN-BVRGH, *or* DE PERTH) in inner circle.

Ordinary specimens, 3s. 6d. to 5s. 6d.

Penny (16 to 14 grains).—Struck at Dundee, Edinburgh, and Perth.

Obv., + ROBERTVS . REX . SCOTOR., surrounding crowned head to left, with sceptre; *rev.,* × VILLA × DVNDE (*or* EDINBVRG, *or* DE PERTH), a mullet of 5 points in each angle of the cross.

Two Pennies and a Halfpenny of Edinburgh, and a Penny of Perth, £2 2s. A Penny and Halfpenny, Edinburgh, 11s.

Halfpenny (7 to 5½ grains).—Struck at Edinburgh and Roxburgh.

Obv., + ROBERTVS . REX., head as before; *rev.,* like the Penny.

Two Halfpennies, Edinburgh, £1 2s. One, extra fine, £2 4s.

A Groat, Half Groat, and Penny, all of Dundee mint, £1 5s.; a similar set, of Perth, 4s. 6d., £1 11s., and £2 6s.; another set of Perth, with a Groat of Edinburgh, 12s.

A Groat and Half Groat, both of Dundee, £30 10s.

A Groat, Penny, and two Halfpennies, Edinburgh, 10s.

A Groat, two Half Groats, Penny, and Halfpenny, Edinburgh, £3 5s.

A Groat, Half Groat, Penny, and Halfpenny, Edinburgh, 13s.

A Groat of Dundee, two Pennies of Perth, and two Halfpennies of Edinburgh, 6s.

A Groat and two Half Groats of Perth, two Pennies and three Halfpennies of Edinburgh, 14s.

Groats of Dundee, Edinburgh, and Perth, Half Groats, Edinburgh and Perth, a Penny and Halfpenny of Edinburgh, £2 18s.

A Groat of Dundee and Perth, 9s., and, extra fine, £4 4s.

A Groat and two Half Groats of Perth, and a Penny and Halfpenny of Edinburgh, £3 6s.

Robert III., 1390—1405.

GOLD.—St. Andrew and Half St. Andrew.

St. Andrew (59½ to 61 grains).

Obv., arms of Scotland, crowned, surrounded by + RO-BERTVS . DEI . GRACIA . REX . SCOTTORV.; *rev.,* St. Andrew extended on his cross (reaching only to the inner circle), between two fleurs-de-lis, encircled by + XPC . REGNAT . XPC . VINCIT . XPC . IMPERAT. (See Fig. 22.)

Another variety has the cross on *rev.* reaching to the edge of the coin, with the legend XPC . REGNAT . XPC . VINCT . XPC . IMP. (See figure in margin.)

F

ROBERT III.—CONTINUED.

GOLD.—*Continued.*

Specimens have sold for 17s., £1 1s., £1 10s., £2 7s. 6d., £2 12s. 6d., £3, £6 15s., and £9 9s.

Half St. Andrew (about 33 grains).

Obv., arms of Scotland, crowned, legend + ROBERTVS . DEI . GRA . REX . SCOTOR.; *rev.*, + XPC . REGNAT . XPC . VINCIT . XPC . IM., St. Andrew, with arms extended, between two fleurs-de-lis, his arms and feet extending beyond inner circle.

A specimen, sold, in 1854, for 12s., realised £8 10s. in 1880.

A variety, described as unique, £31; and another, also unique, £50.

A St. Andrew and Half St. Andrew, together, sold for £1 3s. and £5.

SILVER.—Groat, Half Groat, Penny, and Halfpenny.

Groat (40 to 46 grains).—Struck at Aberdeen, Dumbarton, Edinburgh, Glasgow, Perth, and Roxburgh.

Obv., full-faced bust, crowned, in a tressure, surrounded by + ROBERTVS DEI GRA REX SCOTOR. (see Fig. 99); *rev.*, long single cross extending to edge, in outer circle + DNS . PTECTOR . MS. + LIBATOR . MS., in inner circle VILLA EDINBVRGH (or other place of mintage), and 3 pellets in each angle of the cross. (See figure in margin.)

The legends vary somewhat in other specimens. The figure of the *Glasgow* Groat (given by Lindsay) shows the King's bust, in profile to the left, crowned, a sceptre in front and B behind the head. Its authenticity is doubted.

Ordinary specimens, 4s. to 6s.

Groat, Aberdeen, 18s., £2 7s. 6d., £3 3s., £4, and £4 15s.

Groat, Dumbarton, £6 2s. 6d.

Groat, Edinburgh, 2s. 6d.. 3s., 5s., 8s., 11s., and £1 4s.

Groat, Perth, 2s 6d. to 12s.

Groat, Roxburgh, £6 2s. 6d.

Half Groat (19 to 22 grains).—Struck at Aberdeen, Edinburgh, and Perth. Similar to the Groat.

Ordinary specimens, 4s. 6d. to 6s. 6d.

Penny (about 10 grains).—Struck at Aberdeen, Edinburgh, and Perth.

Obv., King's head, full-faced, crowned, surrounded by + ROBERTVS . DEI . GRA.; *rev.*, REX . SCOTORVM, cross with 3 pellets in each angle.

A specimen, described as unique, 12s.

Another type has on *obv.*, + ROBERTVS . DEI . G . . . . X (*or* + ROBERTVS . REX . SCOTOR); and, on *rev.*, name of mint, as VILLA . EDINBVRGH.

A fine specimen, 12s.; one of Aberdeen, £1 12s.; one of Edinburgh, £1 13s.

Halfpenny (5 to 6 grains).—Struck at Edinburgh and Perth. Of similar types to the Penny.

ROBERT III.—CONTINUED.

SILVER.—*Continued.*

First type, with REX . SCOTORVM on *rev.*

Second type, with place of mintage, as VILLA . DE . PERTH, on *rev.*

A specimen of Edinburgh, £2 2s., and one of Perth, £26.

A Groat, Half Groat, Penny, and Halfpenny, of Edinburgh, sold for 12s. in 1859, realised (with the addition of a Penny which cost 12s.) £8 8s. in 1880.

A Groat, Half Groat, and Halfpenny, of Edinburgh, 11s.

A similar set, of Perth, £1 11s.

BILLON.—Penny.

Penny (about 10 grains).—Struck at Aberdeen, Edinburgh, and Inverness.

Obv., King's head, full-faced, crowned, with name and title; *rev.*, cross and pellets, with place of mintage, as VILLA . DE . EDINBVRG, *or* VILLA . INNERNIS.

A variety is described as having on *obv.*, ROBERTVS . . EI . REX . SCO., and on *rev.*, ROB . DEI . GRA . REX.

A specimen of Aberdeen, one of Edinburgh, and a Halfpenny (?), £2 5s.

A Penny of Inverness, £3 3s.

James I., 1406—1438.

GOLD.—St. Andrew, Half St. Andrew, Lion, and Half Lion.

St. Andrew (53 to 54 grains).—Of similar type to that of Robert III., but with fleurs-de-lis in the field on *both* obv. and *rev.*; the fleurs-de-lis on the reverse crowned.

Obv., IACOBVS . DEI . GRA . REX . SCOTTORVM, the arms of Scotland crowned between two fleurs-de-lis; *rev.*, XPC . REGNAT . XPC . VINCIT . XP., St. Andrew, with nimbus on his head, extended on a cross which reaches to the edge of the coin, a fleur-de-lis crowned on each side of the Saint.

Specimens have sold for 16s., 17s., £1, £2 7s. 6d., £2 17s., £11 5s., £13 13s., and £28. One, very fine, sold for £15 in 1883.

Half St. Andrew (26½ grains).—Differs from that of Robert III. in having the Saint extended on a cross, between two crowns.

Obv., IACOBVS . D . GRA . REX . SCOTOR., arms of Scotland without crown; *rev.*, legend as on the St. Andrew, a crown on each side of the Saint.

Specimens have sold for 13s., £6, and £26.

Lion (50 to 53 grains).—See Fig. 23.

Obv., IACOBVS . DEI . GRACIA . REX . SCO., the arms of Scotland in a lozenge shield, a large crown above, fleurs-de-lis between some of the words; *rev.*, m.m. a plain cross between two fleurs-de-lis, SALVVM . FAC . POPVLVM . TVVM., a St. Andrew's cross in centre of an ornament (termed an orle of six crescents) having fleurs-de-lis at the points, with a rose between.

Specimens have realised 14s., 15s., £1 10s., £2 2s., £3 3s., £4 7s., £4 10s., and £5 5s.

F 2

JAMES I.—CONTINUED.

GOLD.—*Continued.*

Half Lion (25 to 26 grains).—Type similar to the Lion.
Obv., IACOBVS . DEI . GRACIA . R. *or* DEI . GRA . REX.;
rev., legend as on Lion.
Specimens have sold for 16s., 17s., and £2 12s.
A St. Andrew and a Lion sold together for £3 15s. and £5.
Two Lions and a Half Lion, together, realised £4 12s.
A Lion and a Half, Lion together, £1 3s. and £7.

SILVER.—Groats only; struck at Edinburgh, Linlithgow, Perth, and
Stirling.

Groat (weight 28 to 36 grains; in one instance, 41 grains).
Obv., IACOBVS . DEI . TRACIA . REX . SCOT., the King's
head full-faced, crowned, with sceptre at his right, in a tressure;
rev., in outer circle DNS . PTECOTOR MS × LIBAT, in
inner circle VILLA DE PERTH +, large cross with three
pellets and a fleur-de-lis alternately in the angles. (See
Fig. 100.)

Except in minute details the *rev.* of the Groats of James I.
is like that shown in Fig. 100, but several varieties of *obv.* are
known. For example, with the sceptre at the King's left side;
a fleur-de-lis at side of the King's neck, and with the bust
clothed. In a very rare variety the circles are formed of chain-
work or annulets.

Ordinary specimens, 4s. to 7s. Very fine, 16s. and £1 4s.
Seven, varied (4 Edinburgh, 1 Linlithgow, 1 Perth, and 1
Stirling), sold for 19s., and five for 15s.
One, with clothed bust,* realised 12s.
Two Edinburgh Groats (one without sceptre and with bust
clothed,* the other with sceptre to King's left), sold for £4 6s.
Two of Linlithgow realized £1 18s. One, very fine, £3 10s.
Two of Perth, 18s.
One of Stirling, £1 15s., and another of the same mint,
£11 10s.

BILLON.—Penny and Halfpenny.

Penny (11 to 15 grains).—Struck at Aberdeen, Edinburgh,
and Inverness.
Obv., King's head full-faced, crowned, + IACOBVS . DEI .
TRACI . RE.; *rev.*, cross and three pellets in each angle,
+ VILLA . EDINBVRGH, *or* INNERNIS., *or* DE :
AB . . . . EN.
Aberdeen, very fine and presumed to be unique, £4 4s.
Edinburgh, fine and unique, £3. One, very fine, £3 10s.
Inverness, fine, edges slightly broken, but unique, £4 4s.
Halfpenny (5¼ to 8 grains).—Struck at Edinburgh.
Obv., large head, front face, crowned, × IACOBVS . .
R . .. &c.; *rev.*, cross and pellets, VILLA E . ., &c. (See
Fig. 190.)
Five specimens sold together in 1854 for 3s.; and five, all
varied, realised £1 7s. in 1875.

---

* Groats with the bust clothed may more correctly be attributed to the first issue of
James II.

James II., 1438—1460.

GOLD.—Lion, St. Andrew, and Half St. Andrew.

Lion (46½ to 53 grains).—Type similar to the Lion of James I. There is a difficulty in assigning the Lions of James I. and II., but those which have, on *rev.*, the mint mark of a crown may be ascribed to James II. with tolerable certainty.

Specimens have realised 9s., £1 9s., £2 12s., £2 16s., £3, and £3 6s.

St. Andrew (47 to 53 grains).—Two issues.

First issue.—*Obv.*, IACOBVS . D . GRACIA . REX . SCOTOR., arms of Scotland crowned, between two crowns, m.m. crown ; *rev.*, SALVVM . FAC . POPVLVM . TVVM, St. Andrew on his cross reaching to the edge, a fleur-de-lis on each side.

Another variety reads IACOBVS . DEI . GRA . REX . SCOTTORVM, and on *rev.* there is a nimbus round the Saint's head.

Specimens have realised 18s., £1 13s., £1 16s., and £27 10s.

Second issue.—*Obv.*, IACOBVS . D . GRACIA . REX . SCO., St. Andrew, bearing his cross in his hands, to left; *rev.*, SALVVM . FAC . POPVLVM . TVV . DNE., the arms of Scotland crowned, between two fleurs-de-lis, m.m., crown. (See Fig. 24.)

Extremely rare, £26 and £30.

Half St. Andrew (21 grains).—In type, like the St. Andrew of first issue.

Obv., IACOBVS . DEI . GRACIA . REX . SCO., the arms of Scotland crowned between two fleurs-de-lis, also crowned, m.m. crown; *rev.*, SALVVIII . FAC . PPLV . TV . DN., St. Andrew on his cross between fleurs-de-lis crowned.

A specimen sold in 1859 for 17s., and another in 1875 for £51.

SILVER.—Groat and Half Groat. Three issues.

First issue.—Groats only. Struck at Edinburgh, Linlithgow, and Stirling, between 1438 and 1451.

Groat (28 to 35 grains).—Same types of *obv.* and *rev.* as on the Groats of James I., but with the bust clothed. The words are divided by two annulets, or, rarely, by two crescents.

Two Groats of Edinburgh and one of Stirling sold for 17s.

Five Groats of Edinburgh, 10s. ; and three, £1 3s.

One Groat of Edinburgh, very fine, 10s.

Second issue.—Groats and Half Groats.

Groat (52 to 57 grains).—Struck at Aberdeen,* Edinburgh, Perth, Roxburgh, and Stirling, during and after 1451.

These Groats are distinguished from the first issue by their weight, the omission of the sceptre on *obv.*, and the ornaments in the alternate angles of the cross being *crowns* instead of fleurs-de-lis. (See Fig. 101.)

Obv., IACOBVS . DEI . GRACIA . REX . SCOTORVM., m.m. crown, the King's head full-faced, crowned ; *rev.*, m.m. crown, in outer circle DNS . PTECTOR MS + LIBERATOR

---

* Lindsay mentions Berwick as a place of mintage of this issue; but the town belonged to England in the reign of James II., and was not handed over to the Scots until 1461. It was recovered by England in 1483.

JAMES II.—CONTINUED.

SILVER.—*Continued.*

MS., and in inner circle VILLA EDINBVRG, a crown and three pellets alternately in the angles of the cross. (See Fig. 101.)

Groat of Aberdeen, extremely rare, £5 5s.

Groat of Edinburgh, 6s., 14s. ; extra fine, £2 2s. and £4 14s.

Groat of Perth, fine, £6 6s. One, unpublished, £9 5s.

Groat of Roxburgh, possibly unique, very fine, £9 12s.

Groat of Stirling, 13s. ; another, extra fine, £21 10s.

Three Groats, Edinburgh, Perth, and Stirling, and a Half Groat of Edinburgh, sold together for £2 10s.

Half Groat (28½ grains).—Struck at Edinburgh only.

Obv., IACOB . DEI . GRACIA . REX . SCOTOR, m.m. cross, head like that on the Groat; *rev.*, like the Groat.

A specimen, described as fine and of excessive rarity, realised £6 12s. 6d.

Two Groats of Edinburgh, a Half Groat, and two varieties of Billon Pennies, sold together for 12s.

Third issue.*—Groat. Struck at Edinburgh only.

Groat (52 to 57 grains).

Obv., King's full-faced bust crowned and clothed, IACOBVS . DEI . GRA . REX . SCOTTORVM, words divided by crosses, m.m. cross; *rev.*, DNS . PTECTOR . ME. + LIBERATOR . ME., and in inner circle VILLA . EDINBVRG, m.m. cross before VILLA only.

Two Groats of Edinburgh sold for £8.

A Groat and a Billon Halfpenny sold together for £1 17s.

BILLON.—Penny and Halfpenny, Struck at Edinburgh. Like those of James I., but reading GRACIA instead of TRACIA.

In 1883, three Pennies sold for 7s., one for 12s., and one for £1 8s.

Halfpenny (Fig. 191) will be described under James IV.†

James III., 1460—1488.

GOLD.—Unicorn, Half Unicorn, and Rider.

Unicorn (58 to 59 grains).

Obv., IACOBVS . DEI . GRA . REX . SCOTORVM, a unicorn with crown on his neck supporting a shield of the arms of Scotland, a chain and ring under the fore feet, m.m. a cross ; *rev.*, EXVRGAT . DES . ET . DISIPENT . INIMICI . E, a flaming star on a cross fleury, m.m. cross. (See Fig. 25.)

Specimens have sold for 12s., 14s. 6d., 19s., £1 4s., £1 6s., £1 9s., £1 12s., £3 3s., £4, £4 10s., and £5.

A variety, with *rev.* legend on both sides, realised 17s., £1, £1 1s., £1 8s., £1 12s., £4 4s., and £6 15s.

Half Unicorn (28 to 30 grains).—Type similar to the Unicorn.

---

* This is Lindsay's arrangement, but its correctness has been questioned, and this type has been considered as intermediate between the first and second issues above described.

† The BILLON coins with *crowns* and *fleurs-de-lis*, originally assigned to James II., were transferred by Lindsay to James IV., under whose name they will be found described.

JAMES III.—CONTINUED.

GOLD.—*Continued.*

Obv., IACOBVS . DEI . GRACIA . REX . SCO. ; *rev.*, EXVRGAT . DS . ET . DISIPT . INIMI . E., the legends being variously contracted.

Specimens have realised £1 1s., £2, £2 2s., £2 15s., and £7 5s.

A Unicorn and Half Unicorn sold together for 17s., 19s., £1, £3 15s., £4 15s., £5 5s., and £6 6s.

A Unicorn and two Half Unicorns sold together for £21 15s.

Rider (78 to 80 grains).

Obv., IACOBVS . DEI . GRA . REX . SCOTOR., the King, with sword drawn, riding towards the right ; *rev.*, SALVVM . FAC . POPVLVM . TVVM . DNE., arms of Scotland, crowned, on a cross which extends to the *edge*. (See Fig. 26).

Specimens have sold for 15s., 17s., £1 2s., £1 5s., £1 8s., £2 10s., £3, £3 10s., £4 4s., and £5.

SILVER.—Groat, Half Groat, Penny, and Halfpenny. Six issues.

First issue.—Groat, Penny, and Halfpenny, with cross and pellets on *rev.*

Groat (40 grains).

Obv., IACOBVS . DEI . GRA . REX . SCOTORVM, m.m. a crown ; *rev.*, DNS . PTECTOR . MS. + LIBERATOR . MS., and in inner circle VILLA . EDINBVRG, m.m. a crown.

Ordinary specimens, 5s. 6d. to 7s. 6d.

Three Groats (and a Half Groat, later issue) sold for 15s.

Penny (9 to 10 grains).

Obv., IACOBVS . D . GRACIA . R., the King's bust, full-faced, crowned, m.m. a cross ; *rev.*, VILLA . EDINBVRGH., m.m. a cross. (See Fig. 103.)

Halfpenny (5 grains).—Same type as Penny.

Obv., IACOVS . DEI . GRA . REX . SC. ; *rev.*, VILLA . EDINBVRGH.; m.m. on both sides, a cross.

A specimen sold, in 1875, for £1 12s.

Second issue.—Groats only. Struck at Berwick and Edinburgh, having on *rev. large* mullets of six points, and pellets with annulets or small crosses between them. (See Fig. 102.)

Groat (40 grains).

Obv., + IACOBVS . D . GRA . REX . SCOTORVM., a small cross at each side of the head; *rev.*, + DNS . PTECTOR . MS. + LIBRTV., and in inner circle + VILLA . EDIN-BVRG.; m.m., on both sides, a cross. (See Fig. 102.)

Three Groats sold for £1 15s. One, very fine, £1 2s.

Five Groats (of second and fourth issues), £1 1s.

Third issue.—Groat, Half Groat, and Penny, having on *rev. small* mullets of six points, and pellets without annulets or small crosses ; legends as before.

Groat (38 to 40 grains).—Struck at Berwick and Edinburgh.

Obv., type and legend as on *second* issue Groat, but the King's crown is ornamented with five fleurs-de-lis of equal height.

A Groat and Half Groat of Berwick, and a Groat of Edinburgh, £6.

JAMES III.—CONTINUED.

SILVER.—*Continued.*

Three Groats (Berwick and Edinburgh), two Half Groats (Berwick and Edinburgh), two Pennies of Edinburgh, and a Halfpenny of Edinburgh, sold together for £1.

A Groat of Berwick and Edinburgh, £2 3s.

A Groat of Berwick, very fine, sold for £5 2s. 6d. in 1883.

Two Groats of Edinburgh, together, £1 11s.   One Groat, 8s.

Half Groat (20 grains).—Struck at Berwick and Edinburgh. Same type as the Groat of this issue.

A Groat and Half Groat of Edinburgh, £5 12s. 6d.

Penny (8 to 10 grains).—Struck at Edinburgh.

Obv., full-faced bust, crowned, in a circle, surrounded by IACOBVS . DEI . GRA . R.; *rev.*, mullets and annulets in alternate angles of cross, VILLA . EDEINBEVR, *or* EDEINBOVR.

Two Half Groats (Berwick and Edinburgh), four Pennies of Edinburgh, and two Billon Pennies, sold together for £1 2s.

A Groat and Half Groat of Berwick, a Silver Penny, and a Billon Penny, together, 18s.

Fourth issue.—Groat, Half Groat, and Penny, all struck at Edinburgh, having on *rev.* mullets of *five* points and pellets.

Groat (38 to 40 grains).—M.m. invariably a cross crosslet.

Obv., IACOBVS . DEI . GRA . REX . SCOTORM., full-faced bust with crown of five fleurs-de-lis of equal height ; *rev.*, legends as before.

Five Groats and a Half Groat, 13s.   Two Groats, 8s.

Half Groat (17 to 18 grains).

Of similar type to the Groat ; m.m. cross crosslet.

Penny (10 grains).

Obv., IACOBVS . DEI . GRA . REX . S., King's bust full-faced, crown with five fleurs-de-lis ; *rev.*, cross, with mullets of five points and three pellets in alternate angles, m.m. a cross.

Groat, Half Groat, and Penny, all fine, £3 4s.

Two Groats, a Half Groat, and Penny, all fine, £4 6s.

Fifth issue.—Groats only. Struck at Edinburgh, having on *rev.* a crown and three pellets in alternate angles of the cross.

Groat (40 grains).

Obv., IACOBVS . DEI . GRA . REX . SCOTOR., King's bust, full-faced, the crown having five fleurs-de-lis of equal height ; *rev.*, DNS . PTECTOR . MEVS . ET . LI, and in inner circle VILLA . EDINBVRG., m.m. cross crosslet.

Groat, with clothed bust, unpublished, extremely rare and very fine, £20.

Sixth issue.—Groats only.* Struck at Edinburgh, having on *rev.* three pellets and an annulet in two quarters of the cross, a crown and a fleur-de-lis in the other quarters. (See figure in the margin.)

---

* Lindsay wrote, "Although I consider these coins to have been struck towards the end of the reign of James III., there seems to be a possibility of their belonging to James IV., and of having been struck in his first year, or between the three-quarter face coins and those with *Salcum Fac.*"

JAMES III.—CONTINUED.

SILVER.—*Continued.*

Groat (40 grains).

Obv., IACOBVS . DEI . GRACIA . REX . SCOTO.; *rev.,* DNS . PTECT . MEVS . ET . LEBA . M., in inner circle VILLA . EDINBRG., m.m. cross crosslet.

Two Groats of this issue, and one of Berwick, £1 4s.

Fine specimens have realised £2 5s., £3 5s., and one, unpublished, £10 5s.

Five Groats, including one of this issue, sold for 18s.

BILLON.—Penny, Halfpenny, Farthing, Plack, and Half Plack.

Penny (10 to 15 grains).—Struck at Aberdeen and Edinburgh.

Obv., IACOBVS . DEI . GRACIA . REX, usual head, an annulet at each side; *rev.,* VILLA . DE . ABER., cross and pellets, an annulet in centre of cross, and after ABER.

Others are similar to the Silver Pennies of James III.

A Penny of Aberdeen, £1 11s. Three of Edinburgh, 15s.

Halfpenny (5 to 9 grains).—Struck at Edinburgh. Same type as the Penny.

Value from 2s. 6d. to 5s. each.

Farthing.—A Black Farthing is attributed to James III., having on *obv.* I R, crowned, and on *rev.* St. Andrew's cross, with a crown in the centre, and E DIN, for Edinburgh. Struck in 1466.

Plack (28 to 43½ grains).—Struck at Edinburgh.

Obv., IACOBVS . DEI . GRACIA . REX . SCOTO., in a tressure of four leaves arms of Scotland, crowned, a crown at each side ; *rev.,* VILLA + EDINBVRGH, ornaments as on Fig. 192.

Ordinary specimens, 1s. to 2s.

There is a variety, having a cross instead of a crown at each side of the arms, which has been attributed to James II.

Half Plack (15½ grains).—Struck at Edinburgh.

Type similar to the Plack.

Specimens have realised 4s. and £1 3s.

James IV., 1488—1514.

GOLD.—Unicorn, Half Unicorn, Rider, Two-thirds Rider, One-third Rider, St. Andrew, Two-thirds St. Andrew, and One-third St. Andrew; also a Six-Angel Piece.

Unicorn (60 grains).—Of similar type to that of James III., but the numeral 4 follows the King's name, or XC is found under the hind legs of the unicorn, and the legend is composed of Roman letters. They are extremely rare.

Obv., IACOBVS . 4 . DEI . GRA . REX . SCOTORVM., no ring or chain, words divided by small stars, m.m. crown ; *rev.,* EXVRGAT . DEVS . Z . DISIPENT . INIMICI . EIV., words divided by small stars, no m.m.

Another variety has the ring and chain, with XC, the words divided by three dots, m.m. crown on *obv.,* small mullet on *rev.*

Unicorn, with XC, £6 6s., and £10 10s.

Ditto, with X only, £4 15s.

Ditto, with numeral 4 after the King's name, £47.

JAMES IV.—CONTINUED.

GOLD.—*Continued.*

A Unicorn, with XC, together with a Lion of James I., and a Half Unicorn of James III., realised £5 5s.

Half Unicorn (30 grains).

Of similar type to the Unicorn, but without the numeral. Specimens have sold for £12 and £42.

Rider (60 grains).

Obv., IACOBVS . DEI . GRA . REX . SCOTTORVM, the arms of Scotland crowned; *rev.*, the King, with sword drawn in his left hand, riding to the left, SALVVM . FAC . POPVLVM . TVVM . DOMINE.

Specimens have realised £4 10s., £5 5s., and £12 10s.

Two-thirds Rider (36 to 40 grains).

Of similar type to the Rider.

Specimens have sold for £1 2s., £1 6s., £1 18s., £3 9s., £5, £5 5s., and £6 15s.

A Two-thirds Rider, with a Rider of James III., realised £5 17s. 6d.

One-third Rider (about 20 grains).

Similar to the Rider.

Specimens have sold for £10 and £26.

St. Andrew (about 78 grains).

Obv., IACOBVS . DEI . GRA . REX . SCOTTORVM . IIII., arms of Scotland, crowned, between two fleurs-de-lis, stars between some of the words, m.m. crown; *rev.*, SALVM . FAC . PPLVV . TVVM . DNE., St. Andrew, with nimbus on his head, extended on a cross reaching to the edge, a fleur-de-lis at each side, the words divided by stars, m.m. crown.

Two-thirds St. Andrew (50½ to 52 grains).

Similar to the St. Andrew.

Specimens have sold for £9 9s. and £49.

One-third St. Andrew (25 to 26 grains).

Similar to the St. Andrew.

A specimen sold for £4.

A Two-thirds Rider (bought for £1 18s.) and a One-third St. Andrew (which cost £4) sold together, in 1880, for £32.

Six Angel Piece (491 grains).

Obv., IACOBVS . 4 . DEI . GRA . REX . SCOTORVM., the archangel standing on the dragon (as on the English Angel), stars between the words; *rev.*, SALVATOR . IN . HOC . SIGNO . VICISTI., a ship with three masts, to the mainmast is attached a shield bearing the arms of Scotland, I and 4 on either side above.

Unique, and supposed to have been a pattern.

The only specimen known is in the British Museum.

SILVER.—Groat, Half Groat, and Penny.   Six issues.

First issue.—Groat (45½ grains).

Obv., the King's front-faced bust, crowned, in a tressure of twelve points, IACOBVS . DI . GRA . REX . SCOTOR, the words divided by double annulets, m.m. cross crosslet; *rev.*, m.m. cross crosslet, DNS . PROTECTOR MEVORVM,

JAMES IV.—CONTINUED.

SILVER.—*Continued.*

and in inner circle VILLA . EDINBRVG, a crown, and three pellets with an annulet, alternately in the angles of the cross.

Specimens have realised £4 4s. and £6.

Second issue.—Groat and Half Groat.

Groat (38 to 48 grains).—Struck at Aberdeen and Edinburgh.

Obv., IACOBVS . DE . GRACIA . REX . SCOTORV., the King's bust in a circle without treasure, three-quarter-faced to left; *rev.*, DNS . PROTECTOR . M . ET . LIBERAT . M., and in inner circle VILLA . EDINBVR, a crown and three pellets alternately in the angles of the cross. (See Fig. 104.)

Specimens of the Edinburgh mint, 3s. 6d. to 7s.

A Groat of Aberdeen has sold for £2 10s. and £3.

Half Groat (20 to 22 grains).—Struck at Edinburgh only. Type similar to the Groat.

A specimen sold for £1.

Three Groats and a Half Groat, £2.

A Groat and Half Groat, extremely fine, £1 8s.

A Groat of Aberdeen with a Groat and Half Groat of Edinburgh, 19s.

Two Groats and a Half Groat, Edinburgh, £1 5s.

A Groat of Aberdeen and Groat of Edinburgh, with a Groat of the fifth issue, 16s.

Third issue.—Half Groat.

Half Groat (22 grains).

Obv., IACOBVS . DI . GRA . REX . SCOTORVM . Q., the King's bust full-faced, crowned, in a treasure, m.m. cross; *rev.*, DNS . PROTECTR . MEVS., and in inner circle VILLA EDINBVG, a crown and three pellets alternately in the angles of the cross, a fleur-de-lis on centre of the cross.

A specimen, described as unique, sold for 13s. in 1859.

Fourth issue.—Groat, Half Groat, and Penny.

Groat (38 grains).

Obv., IACOBVS . DEI . GRA . REX . SCOTTORVM., words divided by trefoils, the King's full-faced bust, crowned, in a treasure, m.m. crown; *rev.*, SALVVM . FAC . POPVLV . TVV . D., and in inner circle VILLA . EDINBVRG., no m.m., a mullet of five points and three pellets alternately in the angles of the cross.

Specimens have sold for 4s. 6d. and £2 10s.

Half Groat (about 20 grains).

Type similar to the Groat. (See Fig. 105.)

A Groat and Half Groat, second issue, with a Groat of fourth, and one of fifth issue, sold together for 12s.

Penny (about 10 grains).

Obv., IACOBVS . DEI . GRA . REX . SCOTTO, m.m. crown, King's full-faced bust, crowned, in a circle; *rev.*, SALVV . FAC . PPLVV . TVV . DNE., no m.m., a mullet of five points and three pellets in alternate angles of the cross.

Specimens have sold for 12s., £2 14s., £4 4s., and £5.

JAMES IV.—CONTINUED.

SILVER.—*Continued.*

Penny.—Unique.

Obv., similar to the preceding; *rev.*, similar legend, but a crown and fleur-de-lis are in the alternate angles of the cross, as on Fig. 191.

This coin, formerly in Mr. Lindsay's cabinet, sold in 1881 for £10 15s.

Fifth issue.—Groat and Half Groat.

Groat (36 to 40 grains).

Type similar to fourth issue, but words divided by mullets, and letters QT, QRA, *or* IIII, placed at end of *obv.* legend.

A Groat, with QT, sold for £4.

A Groat, with IIII, sold for £3 10s. and £4 15s.

A Groat, with QRA, sold for £1 11s., £3 10s., and £4 5s.

Half Groat (about 20 grains).

Similar to the Groat.

A specimen, with IIII, described as extra fine and of excessive rarity, realised £30.

A Groat and Half Groat, together, sold for £1 1s. and £1 6s.

Sixth issue.—Groat.

Groat (31 grains).

Obv., the King's head bearded, full-faced, with flat crown, m.m. crown, IACOBVS 4 . DEI . GRA . REX . SCOTORV. ; *rev.*, EXVRGAT . DEVS . DISIPENI . I., and in inner circle VILLA . EDINBVRGH., a mullet of five points and three pellets in alternate angles of the cross.

A specimen was sold for £2 6s. in 1859, and for £61 in 1875.

BILLON.—Penny, Plack.

Penny (8 to 12½ grains).

Obv., IACOBVS . DEI . GRA . REX . SCOT., m.m. crown ; *rev.*, VILLA . DE . EDINBVRG, a crown alternately with a fleur-de-lis in angles of cross. (See Fig. 191, which was formerly considered by Lindsay to be a Halfpenny of James II.)

Penny (8 to 12½ grains).—Some have QT after the name of the mint.

Seven sold for 2s. 6d., and three for 10s.

Plack (24 to 29 grains).

Similar type to the Plack of James III., but *obv.* m.m. a crown. On some specimens the figure 4 follows IACOBVS, while on others without the 4 the *rev.* has crowns and saltire crosses alternately in the quarters.

Ordinary specimens, 1s. to 2s.

James V., 1514—1542.

GOLD.—Ecu or Crown, Ryal, St. Andrew, Bonnet Piece, Two-thirds Bonnet Piece, and One-third Bonnet Piece.

Some of these pieces were coined from native Scottish gold.

Ecu or *Crown* (53 grains).*

---

* A piece of similar type and legend, but weighing 873 grains and supposed to be a pattern, is in the Advocates Museum, Edinburgh.

JAMES V.—CONTINUED.

GOLD.—*Continued.*

Obv., IACOBVS . 5 . DEI . GRA . REX . SCOTORVM., the arms of Scotland crowned between two St. Andrew's crosses, m.m. a star of six points waved; *rev.*, CRVCIS . ARMA . SEQVAMVR, cross fleury, with cross in centre, a thistle-head in each angle, m.m. crown. (*Rev.* similar to Fig. 29.)

Specimens have sold for 13s., 16s., £1 4s., £1 16s., £2 4s., £2 19s., £3, £3 10s., £4 8s., £6 6s., and £9 9s.

Ryal (279 grains).—Supposed to have been a pattern.

Obv., IACOBVS . 5 . DEI . GRA . REX . SCOTOR., the King's bust crowned to right, the letters CK behind the head; *rev.*, VILLA . EDINBRVGH ×, the arms of Scotland over a cross patée. (This coin much resembles Fig. 106.)

St. Andrew.—Supposed to be unique.

Obv., IACOBVS . 5 . DEI . G . R . SCOTORV . 1539., the arms of Scotland crowned, surrounded by a collar of thistle-heads and the letters SS, m.m. cross; *rev.*, a St. Andrew's cross, encircled by a crown, between I and R, a thistle-head above the crown, and a fleur-de-lis below it, legend HONOR . REGIS . IVDICIVM . DILIGIT., m.m. crown. (See Fig. 27.)

Bonnet Piece (90 grains).—Dated 1539 and 1540.

Obv., IACOBVS . 5 . DEI . GRA . R . SCOTOR . 1.5.4.0., the King's bust, with bonnet, to right, m.m. St. Andrew's cross; *rev.*, the same legend as on the *St. Andrew*, surrounding the arms of Scotland over a cross fleury, m.m. cross. (See Fig. 28.)

Specimens have sold for 16s., £1 4s., £2, £2 7s., £2 10s., £3 5s., £3 7s., £4, £4 12s., £5 2s. 6d., £6 6s., £6 15s., £7, £7 5s., £7 7s., and £8 15s.

Two-thirds Bonnet Piece (60 grains).—Dated 1540.

Obv., similar to the Bonnet Piece, IACOBVS . D . G . R . SCOTORVM . 1.5.4.0, m.m. fleur-de-lis; *rev.*, same legend as on Bonnet Piece, the arms of Scotland crowned, between I and 5, m.m. cross.

Specimens have realised £1 4s., £1 16s., £2 4s., £4, £10 10s., £18 10s., and £21 10s.

One, which was sold in 1854 for £2 4s., realised £21 10s. in 1880.

One-third Bonnet Piece (30 grains).—Dated 1540.

Similar to the Two-thirds Bonnet Piece.

Specimens have sold for £1 2s., £3, £4 18s., and £41.

Two (one fine, the other poor) were sold together in 1854 for £4 4s., and realised, in 1880, the former £15 10s., and the latter £7.

SILVER.—Groat, Half Groat, One-third Groat. Four issues.

First issue.—Groat and Half Groat.

Groat (about 33 grains).

Obv., IACOBVS . DEI . GRA . REX . SCOTORV., the King's bust, crowned, three-quarter face to right, in a tressure, the

JAMES V.—CONTINUED.

SILVER.—*Continued.*

words divided by mullets of six points, m.m. cross, or cross crosslet; *rev.*, VILLA . EDINBVRGH, or EDINBVR, a mullet of six points and a thistle-head in alternate angles of the cross, m.m. cross, or cross crosslet.* (See figure in margin.)

7s., 14s., and £2 10s. One, very fine, £4 5s.

Another, with the Half Groat, sold for £1 5s.

Half Groat (14 to 16 grains). — Similar to the Groat.

A specimen realised 18s.

A Groat and Half Groat of this issue, together with two Groats and two One-third Groats of the second issue, sold for 16s. in 1859, and for £5 17s. 6d. in 1880.

Second issue.—Groat and One-third Groat.

Groat (38 to 43 grains).

Obv., IACOBVS . 5 . DEI . GRA . REX . SCOTORV., in a circle, without tressure, the King's bust with arched crown, in profile, to right (on some specimens there are three points ∴ behind the head), m.m. cross; *rev.*, OPPIDV . EDINBVRGI, the arms of Scotland on a shield over a cross, the words are separated by three points. (See Fig. 106.)

Specimens have realised from 3s. to 10s. each.

One-third Groat (11 to 13 grains).

Similar to the Groat. The words are separated by two points.

Specimens have sold for 4s., 14s., and £1 13s.

Third issue.—Groat only.

Groat (40 to 41 grains).

Type generally similar to second issue, but the words on *obv.* are divided by two annulets.

Specimens have sold for £1 9s., £5 5s., and £7 5s.

Fourth issue.—Groat only.

Groat (40 grains).

Type generally similar to the second issue, but the King's crown is double arched. The *rev.* has the words VILLA EDINBRVGH, which are divided by two annulets, with a St. Andrew's cross at the end of the legend.

A specimen sold for £1 and £1 9s. One, extra fine, £3 15s.

Two Groats of this issue, with a One-third Groat of second issue, sold together for 14s.

BILLON.—Penny, Plack, and Half Plack.

Penny (7 to 9 grains).

Obv., IACOBVS . DEI . GRA . REX . S., the King's head,

---

* These Groats are extremely rude and ill-struck, and generally in bad preservation. Snelling suggested their belonging to James III., to whom they have been assigned by some recent authorities. No coin of James IV. has a mullet of six points on the *rev.*, and no other coin of James V. has Saxon or old English letters in the legends. Lindsay, however (whose arrangement has been here followed), considers the correctness of the appropriation of this type of Groat to James V. is rendered nearly certain "if we regard the form of the cross, which is foliated, and the thistle-heads in the angles of the cross, in which particular they resemble many of the gold coins of James V. and billon of Francis and Mary."

JAMES V.—CONTINUED.

BILLON.—*Continued.*

full-faced, crowned, m.m. cross ; *rev.*, VILLA . EDINBVR.,
a foliated cross with trefoils in the angles, m.m. cross.

Specimens have realised 15*s.*, £1 2s., and £1 8s.

Plack (26 to 28 grains).

Obv., IACOBVS . D . G . REX . SCOTORVM, a thistle-head
crowned between I and 5, m.m. cross; *rev.*, OPPIDVM .
EDINBVRGI, St. Andrew's cross encircled by a crown, between
two fleurs-de-lis, m.m. fleur-de-lis. (See Fig. 193.)

There is a variety with an annulet over the King's initial, I.
Ordinary specimens, from 6d. to 1s. Eight sold for 2s.

Half Plack (13 to 14 grains).

Similar to the Plack.

Specimens have sold for 1s. ; extra fine, 10s., 15s., and 18s.

Mary, 1542—1567.

GOLD.—Ecu, Lion, Half Lion, Ryal, Half Ryal, Ducat, and Crown.

Ecu (53 grains).—The only gold coins of this reign without
date ; probably struck in 1542.

Obv., MARIA . DEI . GRA . REGINA . SCOTORVM,
the arms of Scotland crowned between two mullets of five
points, m.m. mullet of five points; *rev.*, CRVCIS . ARMA .
SEQVAMVR, cross fleury with a thistle-head in each angle,
m.m. a crown. (See Fig. 29.)

Specimens have realised £1 1s., £1 5s., £1 8s., £4, and £4 15s.

Lion (86 grains).—Three varieties, two being dated 1553, and
the third 1557.

First variety.—*Obv.*, MARIA . DEI . GRA . R . SCOTORVM,
arms of Scotland crowned between the letters I. and G. (which
stand for Iacobus Gubernator—James, Earl of Arran, then
Governor of Scotland), m.m. cross ; *rev.*, MARIA REGINA
in cypher, crowned, between two cinquefoils, surrounded by
DILIGITE . IVSTICIAM, 1553.

Second variety.—*Obv.*, same legend, but G for GRA, and the
arms between two mullets, no inner circle, *rev.*, as in first
variety, but I and G at side of cypher, and no inner circle.

Third variety.—*Obv.*, same legend, but SCOTOR . REGINA .
1557, and the arms between M and R ; *rev.*, same legend as in
other varieties, but MARIA R in cypher between two Maltese
crosses, no inner circle.

Specimens have realised £1 9s., £1 10s., £1 11s., £1 12s.,
£1 13s., £1 18s., £2, £4 15s., £5, £5 10s., £6, and £6 10s.

A Lion, dated 1553, *obv.*, MARIA . D . G . SCOTORVM .
REGINA., Scottish arms crowned between two cinquefoils,
described as *unique*, sold for £105 in 1875.

Half Lion (43 grains).—Two varieties, dated 1543 and 1553.

First variety. — *Obv.*, MARIA . D . G . R . SCOTORVM .
1 . 5 . 4 . 3, the arms of Scotland crowned, m.m. cross ; *rev.*,
ECCE . ANCILLA . DOMINI, surrounding the letters M R. (in
monogram) crowned, a star below, m.m. star waved. Another
variety has cinquefoils instead of stars.

MARY.—CONTINUED.

GOLD.—*Continued.*

Specimens have sold for £3 7s., £5 7s. Gd., £6 2s. Gd.,
£10 5s., and £13 13s.

Second variety.—Dated 1553. Like the Lion, first variety.

Obv., MARIA . D . G . R . SCOTORVM, the arms of Scotland crowned between I and G; *rev.*, same legend as on the
Lion with 1553, but M. R. in cypher, crowned, between two
cinquefoils.

Specimens have sold for £1, £1 13s., £1 16s., £1 19s.,
£3 5s., £4 18s., £5, £5 10s., £5 15s.. £6 15s., and £8.

Ryal (115 grains).—Dated 1555, 1557, and 1558.

Obv., MARIA . D . G . SCOTOR . REGINA, the Queen's
bust to left; *rev.*, IVSTVS . FIDE . VIVIT . 1555, the arms of
Scotland crowned.

Specimens have realised £5 7s. 6d., £5 10s., £6, £6 2s. Gd.,
£7 10s., £9, £9 5s., £13 10s., and £14.

Half Ryal (57½ grains).—Dated 1555 and 1558.

Specimens have sold for £5 13s., £6, £8 17s. 6d., £9 2s. Gd.,
£9 9s., and £24. A Dunfermline forgery, 14s.

Ducat (120 grains).—Dated 1558.

Obv., FRAN . ET . MA . D . G . R . R . SCOTOR .
DELPHIN . VIEN, busts of Francis and Mary, face to face,
with a crown over them; *rev.*, HORVM . TVTA . FIDES . 1558.,
surrounding an elaborate cruciform ornament.

This piece was considered by Lindsay to be a pattern.

Crown.—Dated 1561.

Obv., MARIA . DEI . GRA . SCOTORVM . REGINA . 1561.,
a shield bearing the arms of France half effaced by those of
Scotland, crowned; *rev.*, EXVRGAT . DEVS . ET . DISCI-
PENTVR . INIMICI . 1561., four M's crowned, with a thistle
between each, a star of eight points in the centre.

SILVER.—Testoon, Half Testoon, Nonsunt (sometimes termed a
Quarter Testoon), Ryal, Two-thirds Ryal, and One-third Ryal,
of various issues.

According to Lindsay, the coins of Queen Mary form five
distinct classes :

1. Those struck before her marriage with the Dauphin in
   1558.
2. Those struck during her marriage with that prince,
   dated 1558 to 1560.
3. Those of her first widowhood, dated 1561 and 1562.
4. Those struck during her marriage with Henry Darnley,
   dated 1565 to 1567.
5. Those struck after the murder of Darnley, dated 1567,
   and in one instance 1566.

There were also some pieces, termed Jettons, struck during
this reign, which cannot be considered as current
money.

Testoon (66 to 68 grains).—Dated 1553.

Obv., MARIA . DEI . GRA . R . SCOTORVM., in a double
circle the Queen's bust, crowned, to right; *rev.*, DA . PACEM .

MARY.—CONTINUED.

SILVER.—*Continued.*

DOMINE . 1553, the arms of Scotland crowned between two stars of five points. (See Fig. 107.)

£7, £8 8s., £21 10s., and one, extra fine, £61.

Half Testoon (33 grains).—Dated 1553.

Obv., MARIA . DEI . GRA . SCOTOR . REGINA., the Queen's bust uncrowned to left; *rev.,* IN . IVSTICIA . TVA . LIBERA . NOS . DNE . 1553, the arms of Scotland crowned between M . R. (See Fig. 108.)

A specimen (now in the British Museum) realised at different sales £14 5s. and £31.

Testoon (64 grains).—Without date.

Obv., MARIA . DEI . G . SCOTOR . REGINA., a large M crowned, between two thistle-heads also crowned (see *obv.* of Fig. 109, from which this coin differs in having a circle inside the legend and no date) ; *rev.,* DELICIE . DNI . COR . HVMILE, the arms of Scotland with a crown over the shield (see *rev.* of Fig. 109, from which this coin differs in having no cross beneath the shield of arms, in the shield being crowned, and in having a circle inside the legend).

Specimens have realised £1, £1 6s. 6d., £1 16s., £5 15s., and £15 5s. A very fine example sold for £12 10s. in 1883, and another, also very fine, realised £7 5s. at the same sale.

Testoon (115 grains).—Dated 1555.

Obv., MARIA . DEI . G . SCOTOR . REGINA., a large M crowned between two thistle-heads crowned; *rev.,* DILICI . DNI . COR . HVMILLE, the arms of Scotland, not crowned, placed above a cross potent, extending nearly to the edge. (See Fig. 109.)

14s., £1, £1 16s., £2 2s., £4 6s., £5 15s., and £6.

Half Testoon (57½ grains).—Dated 1555.

Type similar to the Testoon of same date.

Specimens have sold for £1 6s., £3 7s. 6d., and £4 15s.

A Testoon and Half Testoon sold together for 10s., £1 2s., and £1 15s.

Testoon (about 95 grains).—Dated 1556, 1557, and 1558.

Obv., MARIA . DEI . G . SCOTOR . REGINA . 1556, the arms of Scotland crowned between M . R, with (sometimes without) an annulet under each letter, m.m. cross; *rev.* a cross potent with a plain cross in each quarter, surrounded by IN . VIRTVTE . TVA . LIBERA . ME . 1556.

8s., 9s., 10s., 12s. 6d., 16s., 18s., £1, and £2.

Half Testoon (about 46 grains).—Dated 1556, 1557, and 1558. Similar to the Testoon of same date.

£1, £1 2s., £1 5s., £1 8s., and £2 7s.

Three Testoons and a Half Testoon together, 15s.

Two Testoons and three Half Testoons together, £2 6s.

Testoon (84 to 92 grains) of Francis and Mary.—Dated 1558 and 1559.

Obv., FRAN . ET . MA . D . G . R . R . SCOTOR . D . D . VIEN., the arms of the Dauphin and those of Scotland over

MARY.—CONTINUED.

SILVER.—*Continued.*

a cross potent, m.m. crown; *rev.*, FECIT . VTRAQVE . VNVM .
1558, F . M. in monogram crowned, between two double-barred
crosses, m.m. cross.

10*s.*, 13s., £1, £1 2*s.*, £1 5s., £1 8s. 6d., £1 13*s.*, and £2 15s.

Half Testoon (42 to 46 grains).—Dated 1558 and 1560.

Type similar to the above Testoon.

A specimen realised £2.

A Testoon and Half Testoon together, £2 9s.

Nonsunt (about 23 grains), sometimes styled *Quarter Testoon.*
—Dated 1558 or 1559.

Obv., FRAN . ET . MA . D . G . R . R . SCOTO . D . D .
VIEN., F . M. in monogram crowned, between a dolphin and a
thistle-head, both crowned; *rev.*, IAM . NON . SVNT . DVO .
SED . VNA . CARO. in a square compartment, between two
doubled-barred crosses, a cross over and 1559 under. (See
Fig. 196.)

From 10*s.* to 15s.

One, with a Testoon, 1558, sold for 18s.

Three, varied, realised 13s.

Testoon (92 grains).—Dated 1560 and 1561.

Obv., FRAN . ET . MA . D . G . R . R . FRANCO . SCOTOR.
B. (sometimes Q), the arms of France and Scotland crowned
between a plain cross and a saltire; *rev.*, VICIT . LEO .
DE . TRIBV . IVDA . 1560., F . M. in monogram, between a
fleur-de-lis and a thistle-head, both crowned.

Two specimens bear the extraordinary date 1565.

8*s.*, 16s., £1 5*s.*, £1 7s. 6d., £1 12*s.*, £2 3*s.*, and £4 12s. 6d.

Half Testoon (46 grains).—Similar to above. (See Fig. 110.)

A specimen, extra fine, sold for £4 10s.; others 12s. and
£3 15s.

Testoon and Half Testoon together, £1 13*s.* and £2 7*s.*

Testoon (about 92 grains).—Dated 1561 or 1562.

Obv., MARIA . DEI . GRA . SCOTORVM . REGINA, the
Queen's bust to left, in a small close cap, 1561 on a scroll
below the bust; *rev.*, SALVVM . FAC . POPVLVM . TVVM .
DOMINE, the arms of France half effaced by those of Scotland,
crowned, an M at each side, also crowned. (See Fig. 118).

£2 14*s.*, £2 15s., £3 12*s.*, £4, £4 4*s.*, £4 8*s.*, £4 10*s.*,
£4 16*s.*, £5 12s. 6d., £5 15s., £6 15*s.*, £7, £7 7*s.*, £8,
£8 10*s.*, £9, and £9 15s.

A Testoon of 1561, with a Francis and Mary VICIT LEO
Testoon, sold together for £2.

Half Testoon (46 grains).—Similar to above. (See Fig. 118.)

£1 1*s.*, £4 10*s.*, £5, £7, £8 2*s.* 6d., £9, £9 5*s.*, £10,
£11 5*s.*, £12, £15 10*s.*, and £25.

Ryal (470 grains) of Mary and Henry.—Dated 1565, 1566
and 1567.

Obv., MARIA . & HENRIC' DEI . GRA . R . & R .
SCOTORV., in a circle the arms of Scotland crowned between
two-leaved thistles; *rev.*, EXVRGAT . DEVS . & DISSIPENT*.

MARY.—CONTINUED.

SILVER.—*Continued.*

INIMICI . EI., in a circle, a palm-tree crowned with a lizard creeping up its stem, a scroll in front of the tree inscribed DAT . GLORIA . VIRES., and underneath 1565, m.m. thistle. (See Fig. 117.)

£1 1s., £1 3s., £1 5s., £1 12s. 6d., £2 2s., and £2 5s. A rubbed specimen sold for 8s. in 1883.

A Ryal and Two-thirds Ryal, together, 19s., £2 5s., and £2 19s.

Two-thirds Ryal (316½ grains).—Similar to the Ryal.

3s., 11s., £1 2s., £1 7s., £1 15s., £2 4s., and £2 6s.

One-third Ryal (151 grains).—Similar to the Ryal.

Specimens have realised 9s., 13s., and one, very fine, £1 18s.

The Two-thirds and One-third Ryal together, £3.

The set, Ryal, Two-thirds, and One-third together, £1 12s., £1 13s., and £2 9s.

Ryal (470 grains) of Mary.—Dated 1567.

Obv., MARIA . DEI . GRA . SCOTORVM . REGINA., similar type to the Ryal of Mary and Henry; *rev.,* also similar. (See Fig. 117.)

£1 5s., £2 3s., and a very fine example, £3 14s.

The Ryal and Two-thirds Ryal together, 19s., £3 3s., and £3 10s.

Two-thirds Ryal (315 grains).

Same type as the above Ryal.

A fine example, £1 16s.

The Two-thirds and One-third Ryal together, £1 7s.

One-third Ryal (157 grains).

Same type as the above.

Specimens have sold for £3 15s. and £4 4s.

The Mary and Henry Ryal, together with the Mary Ryal, £1 4s.

The set of Mary Ryal, Two-thirds, and One-third Ryal, together, £1 1s.

BILLON.—Plack, Half Plack, Penny, Hardhead or Lion, Nonsunt, and Bawbee.

Plack (23 to 31 grains).—Struck at Edinburgh and Stirling.

Obv., MARIA . D . G . REGINA . SCOTORV., a thistle-head crowned between M and R, m.m. cross; *rev.,* OPPIDVM . EDINBVRGI., a plain St. Andrew's cross through a crown, between two cinquefoils, m.m. fleur-de-lis.

Ordinary specimens, from 6d. to 1s.

The Stirling Plack differs from that of Edinburgh in having on the *rev.* a cross potent, with small crosses in the angles, and OPPIDVM . STIRLINGI, m.m. crown.

From 1s. to 2s.

Half Plack (10 to 17 grains).

Type similar to the Plack, but no cinquefoils at sides of the crown; a star in lower angle of the cross.

Three, varied, 5s.

The Plack and Half Plack together, 6s.

G 2

MARY.—CONTINUED.

BILLON.—*Continued.*

Penny (about 9 grains), with bust.

Obv., MARIA . D . G . R . SCOTORVM, the Queen's bust full-faced, crowned, m.m. cross or fleur-de-lis ; *rev.*, OPPIDVM . EDINBVR., a foliated cross, with crowns and stars (sometimes fleur-de-lis) in alternate angles.

Two sold for 16s., and two very fine specimens for £1 10s. ; also two others for £3, one for £1, and another for 10s.

Penny (8 grains), without bust.

Obv., MARIA . D . G . SCOTOR . REGINA., cross potent with small crosses in the angles, m.m. pellet or cross potent ; *rev.*, VICIT . VERITAS, 1556. (See Fig. 194.)

A very fine specimen realised 15s., and another, 18s.

Plack (32 grains).—Dated 1557.

Obv., MARIA . DEI . G . SCOTOR . REGINA . 1557, the arms of Scotland crowned between M and R ; *rev.*, SERVIO . ET . VSV . TEROR., an orle of four crescents with a crown in each and a cross in the centre, m.m. fleur-de-lis.

These Placks are frequently found countermarked with a heart and star, the badge of the Earl of Morton.

Ten, varied, sold for 11s.

Hardhead (12 to 15 grains).—Dated 1555, 1556, 1557, and 1558.

Obv., MARIA . D . G . SCOTOR . REGINA., a large M crowned, m.m. cross potent ; *rev.*, VICIT . VERITAS . 1558, lion rampant crowned. (See Fig. 195.)

Nine, varied, with a Penny, 1553, sold for £1 12s. ; one, dated 1558, with inner circle, realised 7s.

Nonsunt (21 to 24 grains) of Francis and Mary.—Dated 1558 and 1559.

Obv., FRAN . ET . MA . D . G . R . R . SCOTO . D . D . VIEN., F M in monogram crowned, between a dolphin and thistle-head, both crowned ; *rev.*, IAM . NON . SVNT . DVO . SED . VNA . CARO. (See Fig. 196.)

Ordinary specimens, 2s. 6d. to 5s.

Hardhead (10 to 17 grains) of Francis and Mary.—Dated 1558, 1559, and 1560.

Obv., FRAN . ET . MA . D . G . R . R . SCOT . D . D . VIEN., in the field F. M. in monogram, crowned, between two dolphins ; *rev.*, VICIT . VERITAS and date, a lion rampant crowned.

On some specimens, dated '58, the name FRAN. is omitted, the legend beginning ET . MA.

Many of these coins also bear the countermark of the heart and star.

Seventeen, of '58, '59, and '60, sold for 5s. ; ten for 6s. ; and five, all fine, realised 7s.

Bawbee * (very rare) of Francis and Mary.—Dated 1559.

Obv., FRAN . ET . MARIA . REX . REGINA . FRANCOR .

---

* BAWBEES, *Scottice* for *Bas Pieces.*

MARY.—CONTINUED.

BILLON.—*Continued.*

SCOT., the arms of France and Scotland on separate shields under a large crown; *rev.*, SIT . NOMEN . DNI . BENIDICTVM . 1559, a cross formed of four flower-buds, having stars of seven points waved, and thistle-heads in alternate angles, m.m. cross.

A very desirable set of the above, comprising Plack and Half Plack of Edinburgh, Plack of Stirling, Penny with bust, Penny with VICIT VERITAS, Plack of 1557, Hardhead, Nonsunt, and Hardhead of Francis and Mary (nine coins), sold for £1 1s.

James VI., 1567—1603.

GOLD.—Piece of £20 Scots, Noble, Lion, Two-thirds Lion, One-third Lion, Thistle Noble, Hat Piece, Rider, Half Rider, Sword and Sceptre Piece, and the Half Sword and Sceptre Piece.

£20 Piece (467½ grains).—Dated 1575 or 1576.

Obv., IACOBVS . 6 . DEI . GRA . REX . SCOTOR., in the exergue IN . VTRVNQVE . PARATVS . 1576., the King's bust crowned to the right, with sword in right hand and olive-branch in left; *rev.*, PARCERE . SVBIECTIS . & . DEBELLARE . SVPERBOS., the arms of Scotland crowned. (See Fig. 30.)

Specimens have sold for £5, £5 17s. 6d., £6, £6 12s. 6d., £9 10s., £11, £20, £21, £35, and £35 10s.

Noble (96 grains).—Dated 1580.

Obv., IACOBVS . DEI . GRA . REX . SCOTORVM, the King's bust with bare head to left, m.m. crown; *rev.*, EXVRGAT . DE . ET . DISSIP . INIMICI . EIVS., the arms of Scotland crowned between 15 and 80, no m.m. (See Fig. 32.)

Specimens have realised £3, £5 10s., £6 5s., £7 10s., £26, and £30.

Lion (80 grains).—Dated 1584, 1586 and 1588.

Obv., POST . 5 .& 100 . PROA . INVICTA . MANENT . HEC., a crowned lion sejant, full face, with sword in right paw and sceptre in left; *rev.*, DEVS . IVDICIVM . TVVM . REGI . DA . 1584., four crowned cyphers of I.R., forming a cross, in the centre of which the letter S. (See Fig. 33.)

Specimens have sold for £1 10s., £1 15s., £2, £2 2s., £3 2s. 6d., £17 10s., and £30.

Two-thirds Lion (52½ to 53 grains).—Dated 1585 and 1587. Type similar to the Lion.

£15 10s., £25 10s., and £201.

One-third Lion (26 grains).—Dated 1584. Type similar to the Lion.

A specimen sold in 1875 for £205.

Thistle Noble (120 grains).—Struck in 1590.

Obv., IACOBVS . 6 . DEI . GRATIA . REX . SCOTORVM., a ship with a flag at each end, one bearing the letter I, the

JAMES VI.—CONTINUED.

GOLD.—*Continued.*

other the figure 6, and on the centre of the ship the arms of
Scotland crowned, with a thistle under; *rev.*, FLORENT.
SCEPT . PIIS . REGNA . HIS . IOVA . DAT . NVMERAT . Q.
(See Fig. 31.)

£1 14s., £2 2s., £2 5s., £4, £4 8s., £5, £6 2s. 6d., £6 10s.,
£7 10s., and £8.

Hat Piece (69 grains).—Dated 1591, 1592, or 1593.

Obv., IACOBVS . 6 . D . G . R . SCOTORVM, the King's
bust with high-crowned hat to right, a thistle-head behind;
rev., TE . SOLVM . VEREOR . 1591., a lion sejant guardant
to left, holding a sceptre erect, a cloud over with the word
IEHOVAH in Hebrew letters. (See Fig. 35.)

£1 8s., £1 14s., £2 6s., £2 11s., £5, £7 7s., £8, £9 9s.,
£10, and £35.

Rider (78 grains).—Dated 1593, 1594, 1598, 1599, and 1601.

Obv., legend as on the Hat Piece, the King in armour with
sword in right hand, galloping to the right, a lion on the
horse's caparison, date under, m.m. quatrefoil; *rev.*, the
Scottish arms crowned, surrounded by SPERO . MELIORA.,
m.m. quatrefoil. (See Fig. 34.)

£1 1s., £1 8s., £1 10s., £1 16s., £1 17s., £2 10s., £2 15s.,
£3, £3 10s., £3 16s., £4, £4 2s., £4 8s., £4 10s., and £4 12s.

Half Rider (39 grains).—Dated 1593, 1594, 1595, 1599, and
1601. Type similar to the Rider.

£3 19s., £4 4s., £4 10s., £6 6s., £7, £7 15s., £8, and
£10 2s. 6d.

The Rider and Half Rider, together, £2 10s.

Sword and Sceptre Piece (77 grains).—Dated 1601, 1602,
1603, and 1604.*

Obv., legend as on the Hat Piece, the Scottish arms, crowned ;
rev., SALVS . POPVLI . SVPREMA . LEX, the sword and
sceptre in saltire, between two thistle-heads, a crown over and
the date below. (See Fig. 36.)

18s., £1, £1 1s., £1 3s., £2 10s., and £4 10s.

Half Sword and Sceptre Piece (33 grains).—Dated 1601 and
1602.

Type similar to the preceding piece.

16s. and £1 2s.

The Sword and Sceptre Piece and its Half, sold together.

£1 2s., £1 6s., £1 7s., £1 16s., £1 18s., £2 2s., £2 3s., and
£2 5s.

SILVER.—Sword Dollar, Two-thirds Sword Dollar, One-third Sword
Dollar, Noble and Half Noble, Thistle Dollar, Half Thistle
Dollar, Thistle Noble, Half Thistle Noble, Quarter Thistle
Noble, Forty Shilling, Thirty Shilling, Twenty Shilling, and Ten

---

* Lindsay gives the figure of a Sword and Sceptre Piece, dated 1611, struck in silver,
presumably as a pattern. This piece was in the possession of the late Mr. Cuff, and was
sold, at the sale of his collection in 1854, with five silver coins of this King, for 15s. (See
page 92). Another example of this pattern, with a Thistle Merk of 1605, sold for 6s.
in 1883.

JAMES VI.—CONTINUED.

SILVER.—*Continued.*

Shilling Piece, Balance Merk, Half Balance Merk, Ten Shilling Piece with bare head, Five Shilling Piece, Half Crown Piece, and One Shilling Piece Scots, Thistle Merk, Half Thistle Merk, Quarter Thistle Merk, and Eighth of Thistle Merk.

Sword Dollar (480 grains).—Dated 1567, 1568, 1569, 1570, and 1571. Current for Thirty Shillings Scots.

Obv., IACOBVS . 6 . DEI . GRATIA . REX . SCOTORVM., the arms of Scotland, crowned, between I . R , both crowned ; *rev.*, PRO . ME . SI . MEREOR . IN . ME., a sword erect, crowned, having a hand on the left of the sword pointing to the value XXX on the right side, and the date below. (See Fig. 111, *rev.* of the One-third Sword Dollar.)

Specimens have realised 12s., 13s., 14s., 16s., 17s., 18s., £1, £1 7s., and £2 6s.

Two-thirds Sword Dollar (320 grains).—Dates as above.

Type similar to the Sword Dollar, but XX. on *rev.* for value, Twenty Shillings Scots.

Specimens have sold for 14s., 15s., £1 3s., and £2 4s.

The Dollar and Two-thirds, together, 17s.

One-third Sword Dollar (160 grains).—Dates as above.

Type similar, but X for value, Ten Shillings Scots. (See Fig. 111.)

Specimens have sold for 11s., 13s., and £1 15s.

The Dollar and One-third, together, 15s. and £2 2s.

Sets of the three pieces have sold for £1, £1 10s., £2 4s., £3, £3 3s., and £3 5s.

Noble (about 103 grains).—Dated 1572 to 1577 and 1580.

Obv., same legend as on the Sword Dollar, the arms of Scotland crowned between 6—8 ; *rev.*, SALVVM . FAC . POPVLVM . DNE. and the date, an ornamented cross with a star in centre, a crown in the first and third quarters, and a thistle-head in the others, m.m. cross. (See Fig. 112.)

In some specimens, the thistle-heads are in the first and third quarters, and the crowns in the second and fourth quarters.

Ordinary specimens, from 6s. to 10s.

Half Noble (about 52 grains).—Dated 1572, 1573, 1574, 1576, 1577, and 1580.

Similar to the Noble, but 3—4 at side of the arms.

The Noble and Half, together, 6s., 8s., 9s., and £1 6s.

Two Nobles and a Half, together, 11s.

Thistle Dollar (about 343 grains).—Dated 1578 and 1579.

Obv., IACOBVS . 6 . DEI . G . REX . SCOTORVM., the Scottish arms crowned ; *rev.*, NEMO . ME . IMPVNE . LACESSET . and date, a thistle uncrowned between I and R.

Specimens have sold for £1 3s., £1 5s., £1 12s., £2, £2 6s., £3 19s., £4 5s., and an exceptional specimen £21 10s.

Half Thistle Dollar (170 grains).—Dated 1580 and 1581,

Type similar to the Thistle Dollar, but dated 1580 *or* 1581, and with a crown over the thistle on *rev.*

Specimens have realised £1 1s., £2 15s., £7, and £36.

JAMES VI.—CONTINUED.

SILVER.—*Continued.*

Thistle Noble (about 88 grains).—Dated 1581.

Type similar to the Half Thistle Dollar.

A specimen, styled a Quarter Thistle Dollar, sold in 1875 for £36.

Half Thistle Noble (about 40 grains).—Dated 1581.

Type similar to the Thistle Noble.

Quarter Thistle Noble (about 20 grains).—Dated 1581.

Type similar to the preceding.

Forty Shilling Piece (480 grains).—Dated 1582.

Obv., IACOBVS . DEI . GRATIA . REX . SCOTORVM., the King's bust in armour, crowned, to the left, with a sword in right hand; *rev.*, HONOR . REGIS . IVDICIVM . DILIGIT . 1582., Scottish arms crowned between I—R above XL—S. (See Fig. 113, *rev.* of the XXX Shilling Piece.)

Specimens have realised £13 5s., £15 15s., £20, £30 10s., £31 10s., and £85.

Thirty Shilling Piece (360 grains).—Dated 1582 to 1585.

Similar to above, but XXX—S., for value, Thirty Shillings Scots. (For *rev.* see Fig. 113.)

Specimens have sold for 10s., 13s., 14s. 6d. ; and one, dated 1585, for £4.

Two sold together for £6 10s., and three for £3 12s.

Twenty Shilling Piece (240 grains).—Dated 1582 to 1584.

Similar to above, but XX . S.

One, very fine, 18s.

Two sold together for £2 14s.

The Thirty and Twenty Shilling Pieces, together, £2 10s.

Ten Shilling Piece (120 grains).—Dated 1582 to 1584.

As above, but X . S.

Two sold together for £6 7s. 6d.

The Thirty and Ten Shilling Pieces, together, 17s.

The Twenty and Ten Shilling Pieces, together, £1 1s.

Sets (XXXs., XXs., and Xs. Pieces) have sold for £1 5s., £1 6s., £1 8s., £1 11s., £1 17s., £2 2s., and £3.

Balance Merk (72 grains).—Dated 1591, 1592, and 1593.

Obv., IACOBVS . 6 . D . G . R . SCOTORVM and date, the Scottish arms crowned between two thistle-heads ; *rev.*, HIS . DIFFERT . REGE . TYRANNVS., a sword and balance. (See Fig. 114.)

Ordinary specimens, from 7s. 6d. to 15s. One, dated 1593, sold for 4s.

Two sold together for £1 10s.; and three, with a Half Balance Merk, realised £1.

Half Balance Merk (35 grains).—Dated 1591 and 1592.

Type similar to the Balance Merk, but without the thistle-heads at side of the arms.

A specimen sold for 15s., and another, extremely fine, realised £6 5s.

The Balance Merk and its Half sold together for £1 15s. and £2 4s.

JAMES VI.—CONTINUED.

SILVER.—*Continued.*

Ten Shilling Piece, with bare head to right (98 grains).—
Dated 1593, 1594, 1595, 1598, and 1599.

Obv., IACOBVS . 6 . D . G . R . SCOTORVM, the King's
bust, bare-headed, in armour, to the right; *rev.*, NEMO . ME .
IMPVNE . LACESSIT, and the date, surrounding a thistle with
three heads crowned. (See Fig. 115.)

From 6s. 6d. to 10s.

A brilliant specimen, 1593, realised £4.

Two specimens sold together for £1, and two others for 15s.

Five Shilling Piece, with bare head (49 grains).—Dated 1593,
1594, 1595, 1598, 1599.

Similar to the preceding.

From 4s. to 8s.

Half Crown (Scots), with bare head (24½ grains).—Dated 1594,
1595, 1598, 1599, and 1601.

Similar to the preceding.

One Shilling Piece (Scots), with bare head (about 9 grains).—
Dated 1594, 1595, 1596.

Similar to the preceding.

A specimen, much finer than usually met with, sold for 12s.
in 1883.

Two Ten Shilling Pieces, the Five Shillings, Half Crown, and
Shilling, sold together for 8s.

A fine set of the four pieces realised 15s.

Thistle Merk (100 grains).—Dated 1601 to 1604.

Obv., IACOBVS . 6 . D . G . R . SCOTORVM., the arms of
Scotland crowned; *rev.*, REGEM . IOVA . PROTEGIT and the
date, a thistle with two leaves crowned. (See Fig. 116.)

From 3s. 6d. to 5s. 6d.

Two specimens sold together for £1.

Half Thistle Merk (50 grains).—Dated 1601 to 1603.

Similar to the Thistle Merk.

Ordinary specimens, 2s. 6d. to 4s. 6d.

A Thistle Merk and its Half, together, £2 10s.

Quarter Thistle Merk (25 grains).—Dated 1601 to 1604.

Similar to the preceding.

Ordinary specimens, 2s. 6d. to 4s. 6d.

A Thistle Merk, its Half, and three Quarter-Merks, sold
together for £1 16s.

A Thistle Merk, its Half and Quarter, £2.

Eighth of Thistle Merk (12½ grains).—Dated 1601 and 1602.

Similar to the preceding.

Ordinary specimens, 2s. 6d. to 4s. 6d.

A set of the Thistle Merk, Half, Quarter, and Eighth, sold
for 14s.; and a similar set, but finer, sold for £1 17s.

A Thistle Merk, two Quarter Merks, and two Eighth Merks,
together, £1 10s.

Mixed lots of some of the foregoing coins have sold as follows:

A Sword Dollar and One-third, with a Noble and Half Noble,
£1 16s.

JAMES VI.—CONTINUED.

SILVER.—*Continued.*

A Sword Dollar and One-third, with two Nobles and a Balance Merk, £1 19s.

A Sword Dollar and Ten Shilling Piece, 1582, £1 4s.

A Noble and Half Noble, a Balance and Half Balance Merk, the bare-headed Ten Shillings, Five Shillings, Half Crown, and Shilling, with a Thistle Merk, Half, Quarter, and Eighth Thistle Merk (twelve coins), £2.

A Noble and Half Noble, with the bare-headed Ten Shilling, Five Shilling, Half Crown, and Shilling Pieces, £1 8s.

BILLON.—Plack or Atkinson, Half Plack, Hardhead and Half Hardhead with lion on *rev.*, Hardhead with arms on *rev.*, and Saltire Plack.

Plack or *Atkinson* (20 to 28 grains).

Obv. IACOB . 6 . (*or* IACOBVS) D . G . R . SCO, arms of Scotland crowned; *rev.*, OPPID . EDINB, a thistle crowned. (See Fig. 197.)

Ordinary specimens, 1s. to 2s. each.

Half Plack or *Half Atkinson* (12½ grains).

Type similar to the Plack.

A good example, 7s.

Extra fine specimens have sold for £1 5s. and £2.

Hardhead (about 22 grains), with lion on *rev.*

Obv., IACOB . 6 . D . G . R . SCOTO., surrounding I . R. crowned, m.m. cross; *rev.* VINCIT . VERITAS, a lion rampant crowned, with two points.

Ordinary specimens, 9d. to 1s. 6d.

Half Hardhead (about 12 grains), with lion on *rev.*

Similar to the Hardhead, but the I . R. on *obv.* is in monogram, and there are no points behind the lion on *rev.*

A very fine specimen, 12s; another sold in 1883 for £2 5s.

Hardhead (about 22 grains).—With arms on *rev.*

Obv., IACOB . 6 . D . G . R . SCO., surrounding I . R. crowned; *rev.*, the Scottish arms crowned, VINCIT . VERITAS.

Ordinary specimens, 1s. to 1s. 6d.

Saltire Plack (about 24 grains).

Obv., IACOB . 6 . D . G . R . SCO., two sceptres in saltire, suppressed by a two-leaved thistle; *rev.*, OPPID . EDINB., in centre a lozenge with a thistle-head on each point. (See Fig. 198.)

Specimens have sold for 9s., £1 10s., and £2 2s.

A Saltire Plack and Half Hardhead, together, 7s.

A Saltire Plack and three Hardheads sold for 5s.

COPPER.—Twopence and Penny.

Twopence (55 to 60 grains).

Obv., IACOBVS . 6 . D . G . R . SCOTORVM, the King's bust, bareheaded, to the right; *rev.*, OPPIDVM . EDINBVRGI, three thistle-heads in centre.

An exceptional specimen sold for £3 in 1875.

A specimen, described as being finer than usually met with, and four Hardheads, realised only 6s. in 1883.

JAMES VI.—CONTINUED.

COPPER.—*Continued.*

Penny (about 30 grains).

Obv., legend as on the Twopence, a large pellet behind, and a small pellet in front of the King's bust; *rev.*, similar to the Twopence. (See Fig. 171.)

An exceptional specimen sold for £5 10s.

SCOTTISH COINS AFTER THE ACCESSION OF JAMES VI. TO THE THRONE OF ENGLAND.

James I., 1603—1625.

GOLD.—Unit or Sceptre, Double Crown, Crown, Half Crown, and Thistle Crown.

These coins were struck in 1605-6-11-12 and 1613, and differ from the contemporary English coins in bearing, on the escutcheon, the arms of Scotland in the first and fourth quarters, the arms of France and England quarterly in the second quarter, and the harp of Ireland in the third quarter.

The weights of these pieces are the same as of James I.'s *second* English gold issue.

Specimens have realised the following prices :

Unit, £1 7s., £1 16s., and £15 15s.

Double Crown, £5 17s. 6d. and £30.

Crown, £4 6s. and £12.

Half Crown, £12.

A Half Crown and Thistle Crown, together, £1 15s.

Thistle Crown. (See Fig. 37.)

Specimens have sold for 8s. and 17s.

It was intended that the coins of the two kingdoms should circulate in either country indiscriminately, but the proportionate value of the Scottish coins to the English was nominally as one to twelve, the gold piece worth 20s. in England passing in Scotland for £12 Scots.

SILVER.—Crown, Half Crown, Shilling, Sixpence, Twopence, and Penny.

First coinage.—Struck between 1605 and 1610.

These coins are very like the English issue, and were until recently classed as English coins. The Crown and Half Crown have m.m. thistle, " & " instead of ET in the legend, and a *thistle* in place of a *rose* upon the housings of the horse, although the arms on *rev.* are placed as on the English issue.

Crown (464¼ grains).—Named in Scots money *The £3 Piece.*

A very fine example, £3 14s.

Half Crown (232¼ grains) or *Thirty Shillings Scots.*

The Crown and Half Crown, together, £2 3s.

Shilling (92¾ grains) or *Twelve Shillings Scots.*

The King's crown is ornamented by a lis between two crosses, whereas on the English Shilling the crown has a cross between two lis.

JAMES I.—CONTINUED.

SILVER.—*Continued.*

Sixpence.—Any with m.m. thistle and having the crown ornamented as on the Shilling just described, and dated between 1605 and 1610, are Scottish.

Second coinage.—After 1610.

Crown.—*Obv.*, IACOBVS.D.G.MAG.BRIT.FRAN.&.HIB. REX., a thistle-head crowned on the caparison of the horse, m.m. thistle-head; *rev.*, QVÆ.DEVS.CONIVNXIT.NEMO. SEPARET., on an escutcheon garnished the arms of Scotland in the first and fourth quarters, those of England quarterly with France in the second, and those of Ireland in the third; m.m. thistle-head.

From £1 5s. to £2 10s.

Half Crown.—Similar to the Crown.

From 8s. 6d. to 15s.; one, extra fine, £1 11s.

The Crown and Half Crown, together, £1 11s.

Shilling.—Legend as on the Crown.

Obv., the King's bust crowned to the right, XII behind, m.m. thistle-head; *rev.*, similar to the Crown, but the shield plain.

From 3s. 6d. to 5s. 6d.

Specimens sold in 1883 for 8s. and 13s.

Sixpence.—Similar to the Shilling, but VI behind the bust, and the date over the shield. Sixpences only are dated.

A Sixpence, dated 1619, supposed to be unique, sold for £4 6s.

Twopence.—Current for Two Shillings Scots.

Similar to Fig. 65, but m.m. thistle on both sides.

Penny.—Current for One Shilling Scots.

As the Twopence, but no crown over the rose or thistle, m.m. thistle-head on both sides.

The following prices have been realised for lots of the above coins, sold together:

Two Half Crowns (of the *second issue*), a Shilling, Twopence, and Penny, together with the silver pattern of the Sword and Sceptre Piece, 1611 (referred to in the foot note on page 86), realised 15s.

A Half Crown, Shilling, Penny and Halfpenny, £1 4s.

A Crown, Half Crown, Shilling, and Sixpence, £1 11s.

A Crown, Half Crown, Shilling, Twopence, and Penny, £5 7s. 6d.

COPPER.—Hardhead or Bodle, and Half Hardhead.

Hardhead (about 30 grains).

Obv., IACOBVS . D . G . MAG . BRIT., a three-headed thistle; *rev.*, FRAN. & HIB . REX, lion rampant crowned, two points behind. (See Fig. 167, from which the points have been inadvertently omitted.)

Some specimens read DEI . GRA. and FRANCIE . ET HIBERNIE . REX.

Ordinary specimens, from 1s. to 2s.

An exceptional specimen, 4s.

JAMES I.—CONTINUED.

COPPER.—*Continued.*

Half Hardhead (about 15 grains).

Similar to the Hardhead, but only one point behind the lion.

An extra fine specimen realised £7 in 1875; one sold for £9 5s.; one, described as being probably the finest known, sold for £3 5s. in 1883; and another, well preserved, realised only 17s. at the same sale.

Charles I., 1625—1649.

GOLD.—*First coinage.*—Sceptre *or* Unit, Half Unit, and Quarter Unit or Crown.

Second coinage, by Briot.—Unit or Sovereign, Half Unit, Quarter Unit, and Eighth of the Unit.

Sceptre or *Unit,* first coinage (154 grains).

Similar to the Unit of James I., except that CAROLVS is substituted for JACOBVS.

Specimens have sold for £1 15s., £3 4s., and £6 6s.

Half Unit.—As above.

Specimens have sold for 16s. and £11 15s.

Crown.—As above.

A Half Unit and Crown sold for £2 5s.

Briot's Unit or *Sovereign* (155 grains).

Obv., CAROLVS . D . G . MAG . BRITAN . FRAN . ET . HIB . REX., King's bust in armour, crowned, to the right, with sceptre in right hand and orb in left, thistle-head after the legend, a small B over the crown; *rev.,* HIS . PRÆSVM . VT . PROSIM., Royal arms crowned between C and R, both crowned.

This is one of the finest coins ever struck.

Specimens have sold for £1 11s., £1 13s., £2 6s., £2 12s., £2 14s., £2 15s., £3 1s., £3 3s., £3 5s., £3 10s., £4, £4 4s., £4 12s. 6d., £4 16s., £6 and £3 3s.

Briot's Half Unit (77 grains).

Obv., CAR . D . G . MAG . BRIT . FRAN . ET . HIB . REX., the King's bust with flowing hair, crowned, to the left, and extending below the inner circle, small B under the bust; *rev.,* VNITA . TVEMVR, arms, &c., as on the Unit. Some specimens have a lozenge under the C and R.

Specimens have realised 14s., £1 9s., £2 2s., £3 7s. 6d., £4, £4 14s., and £5 10s.

Briot's Quarter Unit (38½ grains).

Type similar to the preceding.

Specimens have sold for 11s., £1 10s., £2 11s., £4 8s., and £5 10s.

Briot's Eighth of the Unit (19 grains).

Type similar to preceding, but some specimens are without the C and R, and on others the C and R are not crowned.

Specimens have realised £1, £1 1s., £2 17s., £4 15s., £5, and £6 10s.

The Half, Quarter, and Eighth, together, £18.

CHARLES I.—CONTINUED.

SILVER.—Crown, Half Crown, Shilling, Sixpence, Twopence, and Penny, Noble, Half Noble, Quarter Noble, and Piece of Two Shillings Scots.

Crown, first coinage.

Exactly similar to the second coinage Crown of James I., but CAROLVS for IACOBVS.

Specimens have sold for 17s., £1 8s., and £4 15s.

Half Crown, first coinage.—As above.

Specimens have sold for 4s., 8s. 6d., 12s., 15s., 19s., and £1 5s.

Crown and Half Crown, together, £5 2s. 6d.

Shilling, first coinage.—As above.

From 4s. 6d. to 7s. 6d.

Crown, Half Crown, and Shilling, together, £2 14s.

Sixpence, first coinage.—Dated 1625, 1632, 1633. As above.

Shilling and Sixpence, together, £5 15s.

Half Crown, Shilling, and Sixpence, 11s.

Crown, Half Crown, Shilling, and Sixpence, £1 12s.

Twopence.

Obv., C . D . G . ROSA . SINE . SPINA, a rose crowned, m.m. thistle; *rev.*, TVEATVR . VNITA . DEVS., a thistle crowned, m.m. thistle.

A specimen sold for 17s. in 1883.

Penny.—Similar to the above, but no crown over the rose and thistle.

Crown, by Briot.—Issued 1637.

Obv., CAROLVS . D . G . MAGN . BRITANN . FRANC . ET HIBERN . REX., the King on horseback riding to the left, m.m. thistle; *rev.*, legend and type as those of the first Crown, but the arms crowned, m.m. thistle-head and small B at end of the legend.

Specimens have realised £1 2s., £1 7s., £2, £3 3s., £3 7s., £4, and £4 4s.

Half Crown, by Briot.

Type similar to the Crown.

Specimens have realised 4s., 10s., 12s., 15s., 16s., 19s., £1 8s., £1 12s., £1 17s. 6d., £2 11s., and £3 3s.

Crown and Half Crown, together, £1 6s., £1 8s., and £1 10s.

Half Crown, by Falconer.*

Type similar to Briot's Crown, but in some specimens a small F is under the horse's feet.

Specimens have sold for 8s., 9s., £1 2s., and £2.

Shilling, by Briot.

Obv., CAR . D . G . MAG . BRIT . FRAN . ET . HIB . REX., the King's bust to left, extending to edge of the piece below, XII behind, a small B at the end of the legend; *rev.*, arms on a plain shield crowned between C and R both crowned, a small B at the end of the legend.

From 5s. to £1.

---

* FALCONER, of the Edinburgh mint, was Briot's son-in-law.

CHARLES I.—CONTINUED.

    SILVER.—*Continued.*

Shilling, by Falconer.

Type similar to Briot's Shilling, but the bust is within the inner circle, and instead of the small B there is a small F either on *obv.* or on *rev.* over the crown.

From 5s. to 10s.

A Half Crown and Shilling, together, £1 1s.

Sixpence, by Briot, and also by Falconer.

Type similar to the Shilling.

Briot's Shilling and Sixpence, together, £1 16s. and £2 2s.

Two Sixpences by Briot, with a Shilling by Falconer, sold for 8s. in 1883.

Noble (48 to 55 grains), by Briot.—Six Shillings and Eightpence Scots = $6\frac{3}{4}$d. English.

Obv., CAR . D . G . SCOT . ANG . FR . ET . HIB . R., the King's bust crowned to the left, extending to edge of coin below, VI . 8 behind the bust, a small B under the bust; *rev.*, CHRISTO . AVSPICE . REGNO., arms crowned between C and R crowned, a small B over the edge of the crown.

A variety has CAROLVS at full length, without the small B, or C R ; another is dated 1636 over the crown.

Ordinary specimens, 3s. to 5s.

Half Noble (24 to 30 grains), by Briot and Falconer.

Obv., similar to the Noble, but XL (for Forty Pence Scots = $3\frac{1}{2}$d. English) behind the head; *rev.*, SALVS . REIPVB . SVPREMA . LEX, a thistle crowned.

On Briot's pieces there is a small B under the bust.

Falconer's pieces have a small F over the crown on *rev.*

There is a rare variety with a thistle instead of XL behind the bust and, on *rev.*, crowned arms as on the Noble.

Ordinary specimens, 1s. 6d. to 2s. 6d.

A Noble and Half Noble (unpublished), sold together for 10s. 6d.

Six varieties of the Half Noble, four by Briot and two by Falconer, sold for 5s.

Four varieties, one by Briot, and three by Falconer, 12s.

Quarter Noble (9 to 13 grains).—By Briot and Falconer.

Obv., similar to the Half Noble, but XX behind the bust, for value twenty pence Scots = $1\frac{3}{4}$d. English ; *rev.*, IVS . THRONVM FIRMAT. Briot's pieces are distinguished by a small B, and Falconer's by a small F.

Ordinary specimens, 1s. to 2s.

Scots Two Shilling Piece (11 to 16 grains) = 2d. English.

Obv., CAR . D . G . SCOT . AN . FR . & . HIB . R., similar bust ; *rev.*, IVST . THRONVM . FIRMAT., arms of Scotland crowned.

Mixed lots of the preceding coins have sold as follows :

A Noble, two Half Nobles, three Quarter Nobles, and three Two Shilling Pieces, £1 1s.

Two Shillings, a Sixpence, Noble. Half and Quarter Noble, and three Twopennies, £1 10s.

CHARLES I.—CONTINUED.

SILVER.—*Continued.*

Half Crown, Shilling, Noble, Half Noble, Quarter Noble, and Half Groat, 17s.

Two extra fine Shillings, two Nobles, and a Half Noble, 9s.

Briot's Half Crown, Shilling, Half and Quarter Noble, 12s.

COPPER.—Hardhead and Half Hardhead.

Hardhead, Bodle or Turner (about 27 grains).

Same type as the Hardhead of James (Fig. 167), but CAROLVS for IACOBVS., two points behind the lion.

Twelve specimens, varied, sold for 10s. in 1883.

Half Hardhead (about 13 grains).

Same type, but one point behind the lion.

Charles II., 1660—1685.

GOLD.—None.

SILVER.—Four Merk Piece, Two Merk Piece, Merk, Half Merk, Dollar, Half Dollar, Quarter Dollar, Eighth of a Dollar, and Sixteenth of a Dollar.

Four Merk Piece (about 412 grains), by Simon.—Dated 1664, 1665, 1670, 1673, 1674, and 1675.

Obv., CAROLVS . II . DEI . GRA, King's bust laureate in armour to the right, a thistle over (sometimes under) the bust, on some coins a small F under the bust ; *rev.*, MAG . BRI . FRA . ET . HIB . REX., the arms of Scotland, &c., on four shields in form of a cross, CC cyphered and crowned in each angle, $\frac{LIII}{4}$ in the centre for value.

The value of the Merk being 13s. 4d. Scots, the Four Merk Piece was equivalent to £2 13s. 4d. *Scots*, represented by LIII . 4. = 53s. 4d.

Specimens have sold for 11s., £1 11s., £1 16s., and £1 18s.

Two Merk Piece (about 206 grains).—Dated 1664, 1670, 1673, 1674, and 1675.

Type similar to the above, but $\frac{XXVI}{8}$ for value = 26s. 8d. *Scots*.

A very fine specimen, £2. Others, 7s. and £1.

The Four Merk and Two Merk Pieces, together, £2 10s.

Merk (about 103 grains).—Dated 1664 to 1675 inclusive.

Similar to the preceding, but with $\frac{XIII}{4}$ for value.

From 1s. 6d. to 3s. 6d.

Half Merk (about 51 grains).—Dated 1664, 1665, 1668, 1669, 1670-3, and 1675.

Similar to the preceding, but $\frac{VI}{8}$ for value.

From 1s. to 2s.

Sets of the four pieces, 13s., 15s., and £1 2s.

Dollar (about 416 grains).—Dated 1676, 1679, 1680 to 1682.

Obv., same legend as on the preceding coins, but the King's bust, laureate and clothed, is turned to the left ; *rev.*, SCO . ANG . FR . ET . HIB . REX., the arms of Scotland, England, France, and Ireland, in form of a cross, a leaved thistle in each quarter, and two C's interlinked in centre.

CHARLES II.—CONTINUED.

SILVER.—*Continued.*

The Dollar passed for Fifty-six Shillings Scots, and the smaller pieces in proportion.

Very fine examples, £2 5s., £3 18s., and £30. Others, 8s., 10s., 12s. 6d., and 14s.

Half Dollar (about 208 grains).—Dated 1675, 1676, and 1681. Similar to preceding.

Ordinary specimens, from 6s. to 10s. Others, well preserved, 13s. and 15s.

A fine specimen, £1 5s. One in perfect proof condition, £15.

A Dollar and Half Dollar, together, in perfect preservation, sold in 1875 for £8 8s., but realised £45 (Dollar £30, Half Dollar £15) in 1882, as noted above.

Quarter Dollar (about 104 grains).—Dated from 1675 to 1682 inclusive. Similar type.

Ordinary specimens, 2s. 6d. to 4s. 6d.

Eighth of a Dollar (about 52 grains).—Dated 1676, 1677, 1679, 1680 to 1682. Similar type.

Ordinary specimens, 1s. 6d. to 3s. 6d.

Sixteenth of a Dollar (about 26 grains).—Dated 1677 to 1681.

Obv., same type; but *rev.* has a St. Andrew's cross with a crown in centre, and in the angles a thistle, rose, fleur-de-lis, and harp.

Ordinary specimens, 1s. 6d. to 3s. 6d.

The Dollar, Quarter, Eighth, and Sixteenth, together, £1 10s.

Sets of the five pieces, £1 5s. and £2 5s.

COPPER.—Turner, Half Turner, Bawbee, and Bodle.

The Turner and Bodle were current for Twopence Scots, the Half Turner for One Penny Scots, and the Bawbee for Sixpence Scots.

Turner (36 to 46 grains).

Obv., CAR . D . G . SCOT . ANG . FRA . ET . HIB . R., in centre C R crowned; *rev.*, a leaved thistle, and motto NEMO . ME . IMPVNE . LACESSET. (See Fig. 169.)

Some specimens have II over C. R., and others have the numerals after C. R.

Half Turner (18 to 22 grains).

Obv., CAR . D . G . SCO . ANG . FR . ET . HIB . R., the numerals II between C and R crowned; *rev.*, similar to the Turner.

Bawbee (120 to 130 grains).—Dated 1677, 1678, and 1679.

Obv., CAR . II . D . G . SCO . AN . FR . ET . HIB . R., King's bust laureate to left; *rev.*, NEMO . ME . IMPVNE . LACESSET, and date, surrounding a leaved thistle crowned. (See Fig. 170.)

Bodle (about 44 grains).—Dated 1677 and 1678.

Obv., CAR . II . D . G . SCO . ANG . FRA . ET . HIB . REX, a sword and sceptre in saltire under a crown; *rev.*, NEMO, &c., a leaved thistle with date over. (See Fig. 168.)

Three Bawbees and a Bodle, 8s.

Three Bawbees and three Bodles, 5s.

H

CHARLES II.—CONTINUED.

COPPER.—*Continued*.

A Bodle of 1678, 12s.   Another, the finest known, £1 12s.

Four Turners, two Half Turners, three Bawbees, and a Bodle, from the Wingate collection, sold for 15s.

James VII. (II. of England), 1685—1688.

GOLD.—None.

SILVER.—Forty Shilling Piece and Ten Shilling Piece.

A Sixty Shilling Piece was struck but never put into circulation.

Forty Shilling Piece (286 grains).—Dated 1687 and 1688.

Obv., IACOBVS . II . DEI . GRATIA, the King's bust laureate to the right, 40 under; *rev.*, MAG . BRIT . FRA . ET . HIB . REX and date, the arms of Scotland, &c., crowned : on the edge NEMO . ME . IMPVNE . LACESSET . ANNO . REGNI . QVARTO (*or* QVINTO).   (See Fig. 119.)

Ordinary specimens, 7s. 6d. to 10s.   One, very fine, £1 10s.

Ten Shilling Piece (71½ grains).—Dated 1687 and 1688.

Obv., similar to the Forty Shilling Piece, but 10, for value, under the bust ; *rev.*, MAG . BR, &c., but the arms arranged in form of a cross.   (See Fig. 121.)

Ordinary specimens, 2s. 6d. to 4s. 6d.

Forty and Ten Shilling Pieces, together, 17s., 18s., and £1 4s.

The *Sixty Shilling Piece*, dated 1688, similar to the Forty Shilling Piece, has sold for 16s., £1 4s., £1 16s., £1 18s., £2 2s., £2 14s., £2 16s., £2 18s., £3 5s., £4 2s., and £6 10s.

The Sixty, Forty, and Ten Shilling Pieces, together, £1 10s.

COPPER.—None.

William and Mary, 1688—1694.

GOLD.—None.

SILVER.—Sixty Shilling Piece, Forty Shilling Piece, Twenty Shilling Piece, Ten Shilling Piece, and Five Shilling Piece.

Sixty Shilling Piece (430 grains).—Dated 1691 and 1692.

Obv., GVLIELMVS . ET . MARIA . DEI . GRA., busts of the King and Queen to the left, 60 under; *rev.*, arms of Scotland, &c., crowned, and the date; on the edge PROTEGIT . ET . ORNAT . ANNO . REGNI . TERTIO (*or* QVARTO).   (See Fig. 120.)

Ordinary specimens, 8s. 6d. to 12s. 6d.   Fine examples, £1 10s., £3, and £3 12s.

Forty Shilling Piece (288 grains).—Dated 1690 to 1694, inclusive.   Type similar, but 40 under the busts.

Ordinary specimens, 7s. 6d. to 10s.   Fine examples, 16s., 18s., £1 and £2.

Twenty Shilling Piece (144 grains).—Dated 1691, 1693, and 1694.   Type similar, but 20 under the bust.

A fine example dated 1693, sold for £4 in 1883.

Ten Shilling Piece (72 grains).—Dated 1690 to 1692 and 1694.   Type similar, but 10 under the bust.

Ordinary specimens, 2s. 6d. to 4s. 6d.

WILLIAM AND MARY.—CONTINUED.

SILVER.—*Continued.*

The Sixty, Forty, and Ten Shilling Pieces, together, £1 15s.

Five Shilling Piece (36 grains).—Dated 1691 and 1694.

Obv., Similar to the preceding, but 5 under the busts; *rev.*, MAG . BR . &c., and the date, W M in cypher crowned. (For *rev.*, see Fig. 122).

Sets of the five pieces, £1 3s. and £1 7s.

COPPER.—Bawbee and Bodle.

Bawbee (about 130 grains).—Dated 1691, 1692, 1693, and 1694.

Obv., GVL . ET . MAR . D . G . MAG . BR . FR . ET . HIB . REX . ET . REGINA, the King's and Queen's busts to the left; *rev.*, as the Bawbee of Charles II. (See *rev.* of Fig. 170.)

Bodle (about 44 grains).—Dated 1691 to 1694.

Ordinary specimens, 9d. to 1s.

Obv., D . G . MAG . BR . FR . ET . HIB . REX . ET . REGINA, W M in cypher, crowned (very similar to the *rev.* of the Five Shilling Piece represented by Fig. 122); *rev.*, as the Bodle of Charles II. (see *rev.* of Fig. 168).

Three Bawbees and four Bodles sold for 7s.

A Bawbee, very fine, and four Bodles, sold for 16s.

William III., 1694—1702.

GOLD.—Pistole and Half Pistole.

Pistole (106 grains).—Dated 1701.

Obv., GVLIELMVS . DEI . GRATIA., the King's bust laureate to the left, under it the Sun rising out of the waves; *rev.*, MAG . BRIT . FRA . ET . HIB . REX . 1701, royal arms crowned between W and R, both crowned.

Specimens have sold for £1 1s., £2 10s., £3, £3 6s., £4 4s., and one, in 1875, for £5 7s. 6d., which was re-sold for £4 15s. in 1883.

Half Pistole (53 grains).—Dated 1701.

Similar to the Pistole, but no waves under the Sun.

Specimens have sold for 11s., £1 12s., £1 13s., £2 12s., £2 16s., £3 4s., £3 12s., £4 4s., £4 11s., and £4 15s.

The Pistole and Half Pistole together, £1 19s., £2 4s, £7 15s., and £8 15s.

SILVER.—Forty Shilling Piece, Twenty Shilling Piece, Ten Shilling Piece, and Five Shilling Piece.

Weights same as those of William and Mary.

Forty Shilling Piece.—Dated 1695, 1696, 1697, 1698, and 1699.

Obv., GVLIELMVS . DEI . GRATIA, the King's bust laureate to the left, 40 under the bust; *rev.*, MAG . BRIT . FRA . ET . HIB . REX, arms, &c.; on the edge PROTEGIT, &c.

Ordinary specimens, 7s. 6d. to 10s. Fine examples, 16s. and £1 1s.; one, extra fine, £3 10s.

Twenty Shilling Piece.—Dated 1695 to 1699, inclusive.

Similar to the preceding, but 20 under the bust, and no inscription on the edge.

H 2

WILLIAM III.—CONTINUED.

SILVER.—*Continued.*

From 5s. to 8s. 6d. Two, very fine, £1 1s.

Ten Shilling Piece.—Dated 1695 to 1699, inclusive.
Similar to the preceding, but 10 under the bust.
From 2s. 6d. to 4s. 6d.
Sets of the three pieces, 10s. and 14s.

The above three pieces, with Anne's Ten and Five Shilling Pieces, together, 17s.

Five Shilling Piece.—Dated 1695, 1696, 1697, 1699, 1700, 1701, and 1702.

Obv., GVL . D . G . MAG . BR . FR . & . HIB . REX, bust to left with 5 under it; *rev.*, NEMO . ME . IMPVNE . LACESSET and date, a three-leaved thistle crowned. (See Fig. 123.)

From 1s. 6d. to 2s. 6d. Four fine examples, of different dates, 10s.

A set of the Forty, Twenty, Ten, and Five Shilling pieces, sold for 10s. in 1883.

COPPER.—Bawbee and Bodle.

Bawbee (120 to 130 grains).—Dated 1695, 1696, and 1697.

Obv., GVL . D . G . MAG . BR . FR . ET . HIB . REX, King's bust laureate to the left; *rev.*, similar to the Bawbee of Charles II. (See Fig. 170.)

Bodle (about 47 grains).—Dated 1695, 1696, and 1697.

Obv., same legend as on the preceding, a sword and sceptre in saltire with crown over; *rev.*, similar to the Bodle of Charles II., but the thistle is crowned. (See Fig. 168.)

A Bawbee and three Bodles, together, 12s.

Two fine Bawbees, and two Bodles (one with GVLIELMVS in full), 9s.

A Bawbee and three Bodles of William and Mary, with a Bawbee and three Bodles of William, sold together for 6s. in 1883.

Anne, 1702—1714.

GOLD.—None.

SILVER.—Before the Union, Ten Shilling Piece and Five Shilling Piece Scots.

After the Union the following coins were struck at the Edinburgh mint : Crown, Half Crown, Shilling, and Sixpence.

Scots Ten Shilling Piece (70 grains).—Equal to tenpence English, dated 1705 and 1706.

Obv., ANNA . DEI . GRATIA, the Queen's bust to the left, a thistle on her bosom, 10 under it; *rev.*, MAG . BRIT . FRA . ET . HIB . REG., arms of Scotland, &c., crowned, and date.

From 2s. 6d. to 4s. 6d.

A Ten Shilling and Five Shilling Piece, both reading ANNA DEI . GRATIA, sold for 8s. in 1883.

A piece of Ten Shillings, with three of Five Shillings, extra fine, sold for £1 8s.

ANNE.—CONTINUED.

SILVER.—*Continued.*

Scots Five Shilling Piece (35 grains).—Equal to fivepence English. Dated 1705, 1706, and 1707.

Obv., AN . D . G . MAG . BR . FR . & HIB . R, bust as on the preceding, but 5 under it; *rev.*, similar to the Five Shilling Piece of William. (See Fig. 123.)

Same pieces, dated 1705, have ANNA . DEI . GRATIA on *obv.* From 1s. 6d. to 2s. 6d.

The coins minted at Edinburgh after the Union were of the same design, standard, and value as the coins struck at the Royal Mint in London. They are distinguished by E or E* placed under the bust.

The varieties of these pieces are :

Crowns.—1707 E and 1708 E.

Half Crowns.—1707 E, 1708 E, and 1709 E.

Shillings.—1707 E, 1707 E*, 1708 E, 1708 E*, and 1709 E*.

Sixpences.—1707 E, 1708 E, 1708 E*, and 1709 E*.

The Sixpence, 1709 E*, is given on the authority of the sale catalogue of the collection of the Rev. Henry Christmas, 1864, Lot 833.

They have realised the following prices :

Crown, 6s. 6d., 8s , 9s., 10s. 6d., 17s. 6d., 18s., and £1 5s.

Half Crown, 4s., 5s. 6d., 6s., and 14s.

Shilling, 4s. ; an exceptional specimen, £2 3s.

Sixpence, 2s. 6d. Three, varied, all well preserved, sold for 5s. 6d. in 1883.

Crown, Half Crown, Shilling, and Sixpence, 1707 E, extra fine, £3 15s.

Crown and Half Crown, 1708 E ; Shilling, 1708 E* ; and Sixpence, 1708 E* and 1709 E*, 13s.

Crown and Half Crown, 1708 E ; Shilling, 1708 E* and 1709 E* ; and Sixpence, 1708 E*, £3.

Crown and Half Crown, 1708 E ; Shillings, 1707 E, 1708 E, and 1708 E* ; and Sixpence, 1708 E*, 13s.

Crown and Half Crown, 1707 E, £1 1s.

Half Crown, 1708 E, and Shillings, 1708 E and 1709 E*, £1.

Shilling, 1707 E. and Sixpence, 1708 E*, £1 5s.

Shilling, 1709 E*, and Sixpence, 1708 E*, sold together for 5s. in 1883.

COPPER.—None.

ADDENDA.

The following prices of Scottish coins have been noted since the preceding pages were printed :

David I.

Penny.—Berwick, £5 ; Roxburgh, £6, in 1883.

Alexander III.

Pennies.—Third coinage, sold in 1883 :
Aberdeen, £2. £2 10s.. and £5 10s. ; Berwick, £1 2s.
Dunbar, 8s. 6d. and 14s. ; Forres, £5 10s.; Perth, 11s., and
£1 2s.; St. Andrews, £5 5s.
Halfpenny.—One in 1882, £2 12s. ; one in 1883, £1 10s. ;
another, *fine*, realized only 2s. 6d.
Farthing.—One, four mullets of six points, £10 10s., in 1883.

John Baliol.

Penny.—In 1882, 6s., £2 8s., and £2 12s.
Halfpenny.—In 1882, £2 ; in 1883, 12s., and £2 10s.

Robert Bruce.

Penny.—In 1882, 11s. ; in 1883, 13s., 14s., 15s., 18s., £1 3s.,
and £1 17s.

David II.

Groat.—Aberdeen, 19s. and £3 14s. ; Edinburgh, 17s., £1 2s.,
and two unpublished, £2 10s., and 9s., each.
Half Groat.—Aberdeen, in 1882, £2 15s. 6d. ; in 1883, 6s.,
and £3 4s. Edinburgh, in 1883, three 7s., three 10s., one 14s.,
and one, £1 1s.

Robert II.

St. Andrew.—£6, and *Lion*, £6 5s. in 1882.
Halfpenny.—Edinburgh, £3, and £1, in 1883.

Robert III.

St. Andrew.—£3 15s., £4 9s., £6, and £7 10s.
Penny.—Edinburgh, £6 2s. 6d.

James I.

Half St. Andrew.—£32 11s., in 1883.
Lion.—In 1882, £3 14s., £4 15s, and £6 10s.; in 1883,
£6 5s., and £7 10s.
Half Lion.—£5 5s. and £8 10s.
Groat.—Edinburgh, £2 12s. ; Linlithgow, £1; and Stirling,
£13.

James II.

Lion.—£6 5s. in 1882.
Groat.—Second coinage, Edinburgh, £4; and Stirling, £11,
in 1883.

James III.

Rider.—£10 10s. ; *Unicorn*, EXVRGAT, £10 10s.
Half Unicorn.—£1 13s.
Groat.—Edinburgh, £2 12s. ; Berwick, £5 7s. 6d.
Black Farthing (coinage of 1466).—£2 5s., and £2 15s.

James IV.

Two-thirds St. Andrew.—With IIII., £33 12s.
Two-thirds Rider.—£8.

JAMES IV.—CONTINUED.

    Unicorn.—With X, £5 10s.
    Groat.—Fifth issue, with IIII., 6s., and £1 16s.

James V.

    Ecu.—£26. *Bonnet Piece,* 1540, £9 19s., £6, £4 6s., and £4 10s. in 1883.
    One-third Bonnet Piece.—£12.
    Groat.—First coinage, fine, £1 12s.
    One-third Groat.—£3 8s., £1 2s., and 7s. 6d.

Mary.

    Half Lion.—1543, £28, and £17 17s. in 1883.
    Lion.—1553, £3 5s.
    Half Ryal.—1555, £14 10s.
    Testoon (undated COR HVMILE).—£9 19s. 6d.
    Testoon.—1555, £3 6s. ; *Half Testoon,* 1555, £1 18s.
    Testoon (with portrait).—1561, £12 10s., £8 15s., and £1 12s.
    Ryal (Mary and Henry).—1565, £3 2s. ; and *One-third Ryal,* 1565, £2 15s.
    Two-thirds Ryal.—1566, £3 10s. ; 1567, £2 12s.
    Ryal (Mary *sola*).—£1 11s.
    Two-thirds Ryal.—£2 14s.
    Penny (with bust).—A fine specimen, 5s.

James VI.

    £20 Piece.—1576, £31, in 1883.
    Rider.—1593, £8 10s. ; 1594, £5 10s.; 1595, £1 14s.
    Sword and Sceptre.—1601, £1 7s. ; 1602, £1 4s. and 15s.; 1603, £6 and £3.
    Half Sword and Sceptre.—1601, £1 5s. and 10s. ; 1602, 13s.
    Quarter Unit, or Crown.—Second coinage, £1 8s.
    Eighth of Unit, or Half Crown.—Second coinage, 11s.
    Forty Shilling Piece.—1582, £29 8s.
    Half Hardhead (*Lion* on rev.).—£3 15s.

Charles I.

    Briot's Half Unit.—A specimen, in beautiful medallic relief, realized £7, in December, 1883.

IRISH COINS.

PRIOR to the introduction of a regular coinage, Rings of gold, silver and brass, formed the earliest currency in Ireland. The late Sir William Betham established the fact that these Rings, as well as Fibulæ of gold, at one time supposed to have been used merely as personal ornaments, not only passed as money in Ireland, but were graduated according to troy weight in multiples of the half-pennyweight or twelve grains.

No Irish coins have been discovered which can be assigned to a period earlier than the arrival of the Danes in Ireland. Without attempting to give a complete list of the coins attributed to the Danish Princes who ruled over the provinces of Dublin, Limerick and Waterford, from about the year 853 to 1177, when Prince John, son of Henry II., was appointed Lord of Ireland, a sufficient idea of the Hiberno-Danish coins may be formed from the following descriptions and accompanying illustrations.

Simon's "Essay on Irish Coins," and Lindsay's "View of the Coinage of Ireland," may be consulted for further details.

An account of more recent discoveries will be found in the papers (referred to hereafter) by Dr. Aquilla Smith, of Dublin, the greatest authority on the subject.

THE HIBERNO-DANISH KINGS.
Kings of Dublin.

Ifars I., 870—872.

SILVER.—Penny.

Penny (9½ to 10½ grains).

Obv., full face bearded, the legend is scarcely intelligible, the letters NND are supposed to stand for Normanorum Dyflin or Dominus, the other letters being intended for IMA CVNVNC; rev., a long double cross, having a cross in one angle, a figure supposed to be a hand* in the opposite angle, and a pellet in each of the two remaining angles. (See Fig. 124.)

Lindsay valued this coin at 3s.

---

* In a paper entitled "The Human Hand on Hiberno-Danish Coins," contributed to the *Numismatic Chronicle* (vol. iii., 3rd series, 1883), Dr. Aquilla Smith gives it as his opinion that the symbol, usually termed a *hand*, which appears on the reverse of a large number of Hiberno-Danish coins (see Figs. 124 and 127), is really a *branch*, having three, four, or sometimes six *leaves* projecting from one side, and that the hand as a symbol is rare on these coins. On a very few coins the bones of three human arms, forearms, and hands, are represented in the form of a triskelion, while the bones of a hand are shown on a small number only.

Anlaf IV., 962—981.

SILVER.—Penny.

Penny (28 grains).

Obv., profile to left, inscription OELDFO, &c., or in modern characters OLAF . REX . DIFLI ; rev., long double cross. (See Fig. 125.)

This coin was valued by Lindsay at £1 10s.

The coins represented by Figs. 124 and 125 are commented upon in a paper, " When was Money first Coined in Ireland ? " by Aquilla Smith, Esq., M.D., M.R.I.A., contained in the Numismatic Chronicle, vol. ii., 3rd series, 1882. For reasons given at length in this paper, Dr. Smith is convinced that the coins attributed to Ifars I. belong to a period much later than the undoubted Dublin coins of Sihtric III., and that the coin (Fig. 125) attributed to Anlaf IV., was struck by Olaf I. of Sweden, 1015—1026. Dr. Smith considers that the chronological series of these coins begins with Sihtric III. of Dublin, the only Hiberno-Danish King whose coins are known with certainty. Sihtric III. was contemporary with Ethelred II., King of England.

Sihtric III., 989—1029.

SILVER.—Penny. Three types.

First (21 to 23 grains).—The King's head, with helmet, to left ; rev., long double cross, with moneyer's name and place of mintage. Some very rude specimens weigh only from 10 to 18 grains.

Second (18 to 27 grains).—Bare head, with sceptre to left ; rev., short double cross, C R V X in the angles. (See Fig. 126.)

Third.—Head to left, wearing a cap with two streamers or ribbons at back ; rev., a small cross, surrounded by the legend.

First type, from 3s. to 7s. 6d. Seven, all fine, sold for 14s.

Second type, from 6s. to 8s. Specially fine examples have realised £1 and £1 10s.

Third type, extra rare, £1.

Anlaf V., 1029—1034.

SILVER.—Penny.

Obv., a cross surrounded by a rude attempt at the words ONLAF and DIFNLIN (= Dublin). (See Fig. 128.)

Valued by Lindsay at 15s.

Anlaf VI., 1041—1050.

SILVER.—Penny (16 to 18 grains).

No head on obv. (See Figs. 129 and 130.)

Valued by Lindsay at 10s.

Ifars III., 1050—1054.

SILVER.—Penny (11 to 15 grains).—Several types.

Penny (13 grains).—Obv., bare head to left ; rev., long double cross, a hand in two quarters, a cross and a pellet in two opposite quarters. (See Fig. 127.)

Common type valued by Lindsay at 4s.

IFARS III.—CONTINUED.

SILVER.—*Continued*

> *Penny* (11 grains).—*Obv.*, head with radiated crown to left, and inscription intended for R . IFARZ . N . DIFMX . DI., that is King Ifars of the Northmen of Dublin ; *rev*, similar to a type of Edward the Confessor, legend + FREDNE . ON . EOFR, *i.e.*, of York. (See Fig. 131.)

> Of the greatest rarity. Valued by Lindsay at £1.

> *Penny.*—*Obv.*, head with helmet to left, legend IF. CVNVNC. (See Fig. 132.)

> Extra rare, value 15s.

> *Penny*, without head.—Value 10s.

Askill McTorquil, 1159—1171.

SILVER.—*Penny* (12 grains).

> *Obv.*, rude head to left, legend ANCIL . COV reversed and retrograde, apparently intended for AZKIL COVNVNC. (See Fig. 133.)

> Lindsay says that this coin, which is very neatly executed, is remarkable for bearing, on the King's neck and also on the *reverse*, figures of the articles formerly supposed to be Fibulæ, but which were varieties of the Ring Money previously referred to.

> Valued by Lindsay at 15s.

Kings of Waterford.

SILVER PENNIES, of similar type to the coins already described, were struck between 853 and 1036 by the Danish Kings of Waterford.

Regnald II., 1023—1036.

SILVER.—*Penny.*

> A coin assigned by Lindsay to this Prince is represented by Fig. 134.

> Mixed lots of these Hiberno-Danish coins have realised the following prices :

> Nine sold for 6s. in 1864; seven sold for 5s. in 1854; and twelve sold for 12s. in 1881.

> Six of Sihtric, varied, 13s. ; and seven, similar, 14s.

> Two Crux Pennies of Sihtric III., five Dublin Pennies of Henry III., and a Waterford Penny of Edward I., sold for 18s.

Ethelred and Canute, 978—1035.

SILVER PENNIES, bearing the names of Ethelred and Canute and place of mintage Dublin, are generally classed as Irish coins. These pieces are inferior in workmanship, and often in metal, to the English coins, and were, it is supposed, struck by Irish Kings in imitation of English money.

> The Ethelred coins are worth from 5s. to 10s.

> Lindsay valued coins bearing the name of CNVT, struck at Dublin, at £3. One sold in 1824 for £3 8s.

BRACTEATE COINS.

These coins, illustrations of which are given in Figs. 135, 136, 137 and 138, are very thin, weighing, when perfect, not more than from seven to ten grains. They have a device struck on one side only, and no legend occurs on any of them. Lindsay considered them to have been copied from English coins, beginning with those of William the Conqueror and ending with those of John or Henry III., the probable period of their mintage being the early part of the thirteenth century. In Lindsay's opinion, they are genuine and unquestionable specimens of the coins of native Irish Princes.

Few Bracteate coins had been found in Ireland until November, 1837, when a very large hoard was dug up near Fermoy.

Fig. 135 (7 grains) has a long single cross with a small square in the centre and a large fleur-de-lis in each angle, and is apparently copied from the *rev.* of a Penny of Harold I.

Fig. 136 (4 grains) is the only coin found at Fermoy which has a rude imitation of letters round the margin. The general design appears to be taken from the *rev.* of a Pax Penny of William I.

Fig. 137 (7 grains) has long single cross with quatrefoil and trefoil alternately in angles, and may have been copied from a Penny of Henry I.

Fig. 138 (4¾ grains) shows a somewhat intricate design, seemingly taken from two coins of Henry I.

Value, 1s. each.

KINGS OF ENGLAND.

John, as Lord of Ireland, 1177—1199.

SILVER.—Halfpenny and Farthing.

Halfpenny (11½ grains).—Struck at Dublin and Waterford. *Obv.*, + IOHANNES . DOM . *or* DOMI, *or* DOMIN . (in one instance DOMIN . IBER), surrounding a full-faced head in a circle (see Fig. 140); *rev.*, a short double cross in a circle, with an annulet in each angle, encircled by the name of the moneyer and mint, as ADAM ON . DWE ., NORMAN . ON . DWELI (= Dublin), MARC . ON . WATER ., WHILELMVS . ON . WA . (= Waterford).

One variety has on *obv.*, IOHANNES . DO . ON . WA ., *retrograde.*

Fine specimens, Dublin, 5s. ; Waterford, 10s.

Farthing (4¼ to 5½ grains).—Struck at Dublin and Waterford. *Obv.*, a lozenge, or large mascle, with ornamented points, in a circle of pellets, without any legend ; *rev.*, a long single cross extending nearly to the edge, having in each angle a letter, the four letters forming part of the moneyer's name, thus TOMA., ALEX., NICO., &c.

From 5s. to 10s.

JOHN.—CONTINUED.

SILVER.—*Continued.*

*Patrick Farthing** (4½ to 6 grains).—Struck at Carrickfergus and Downpatrick by John De Curcy.†

The type of the *obv.* is almost identical on all the specimens known, but there are three distinct types of *rev.*

Obv., a short single cross within an inner circle, surrounded by + PATRICII (= Crux Patricii).

Rev., first type, a short double cross, encircled by the legend + GOANDQVRCI (= GOAN or JOANnes De CVRCI).

Rev., second type, a short double cross or a cross potent voided, in an inner circle, surrounded by + CRAGF or CRAGFEVF (= Carrickfergus).

Rev., third type, a short single cross with a crescent in each angle, surrounded by + D' or DE . DVNO (= Downpatrick). This type of *rev.* is very similar to that of the first issue of William the Lion (see page 59).

Coins of the first type were probably struck between 1185 and 1189.

Value from 2s. 6d. to 5s.

John, as King, 1199—1216.

SILVER.—Penny, Halfpenny and Farthing.

Penny (22½ grains).—Struck at Dublin, Limerick and Waterford.

Obv., IOHANNES . REX, in a triangle the King's bust full-faced, with crown fleury, sceptre in right hand, and a rose of five leaves at the King's left side ; *rev.*, in a triangle a crescent having over it a blazing star, a small star in each angle of the triangle, legend the name of the moneyer and mint, as WILLEM . ON . DIVE (= Divelin or Dublin) or ON . LIME (= Limerick) or ON . WAT (= Waterford).

Dublin mint, from 3s. 6d. to 5s. 6d.

Limerick mint, from 6s. to 7s.

Waterford mint, from 10s. to £1

Halfpenny (11¼ grains).—Struck at Dublin and Limerick.

Obv., the King's full-faced bust. in a triangle, a star in each angle, legend IOHAN (or IOHANNES) REX ; *rev.*, in a triangle a crescent, with a cross above it, a star in each angle, with the name of moneyer and mint. (See Fig. 139.)

Dublin mint, about 5s. ; Limerick mint, about 10s.

Farthing (5½ grains).

Obv., IOHAN . RE, full-faced bust in a triangle, a small star in each angle ; *rev.*, in a triangle a blazing star, with the name of the moneyer.

From 5s. to 10s.

Lindsay valued this coin at £5, and stated (in 1839) that only three specimens were known, one (the Rev. Mr. Martin's) having sold for £9 9s. At the sale of the Martin cabinet in 1859, the

---

* A full account of these Farthings was first published by Dr. Aquilla Smith in the *Numismatic Chronicle*, 1863.

† John De Curcy, created Earl of Ulster by Henry II. in 1181, was constituted sole Governor of Ireland in 1185. He was removed from that office in 1199, when he retired to his earldom, and finally quitted Ireland in 1204.

JOHN.—CONTINUED.

SILVER.—*Continued.*

Farthing, Halfpenny and Penny, head in a triangle, together with a full-faced Halfpenny and Mascle Farthing, realised £1 2s.

Henry III., 1216—1272.

SILVER.—Penny and Halfpenny.

Penny (22¼ grains).—Struck at Dublin.

Obv., HENRICVS. REX. III. in a triangle, as on the Penny of John, the King's bust full-faced, with crown fleury, sceptre in right hand, a rose of five leaves to his left; *rev.,* a long double cross extending to the edge, with name of moneyer and mint in a circle, as DAVI. ON. DIVELI, *or* RICARD. ON. DIVE.

From 2s. 6d. to 5s.

Halfpenny (11¼ grains).—Struck at Dublin.

Similar to the Penny.

This coin is described and figured by Simon, but Lindsay observed that it must be extremely rare, as he had never seen one, and was not aware of there being one in any collection. Nevertheless, Lindsay valued the coin at £7. No specimen is now known.

Edward I., II., and III., 1272—1377.

From the Royal Proclamations it would appear that a large quantity of money must have been struck in Ireland by Edward I. and III. No mode of distinguishing their coins has been approved of, but Lindsay was inclined to assign coins having the Roman N in the legend to Edward I. or II., and those with the English n to Edward III. The number of dots or pellets under the bust has been rejected as a criterion, as some coins have four dots and others none.

SILVER.—Penny, Halfpenny and Farthing.

Penny (22½ grains).—Struck at Cork, Dublin and Waterford.

Obv., EDW. R. ANGL. DNS. HYB., the King's full-faced bust crowned, in a triangle, the base of which is above the King's head and the apex below the bust (see Fig. 141); *rev.,* long cross with three pellets in each angle, as on the English Penny, with CIVITAS and the name of the place of mintage, as COR-CACIE, DVBLINIE. *or* WATERFOR, sometimes VATERFOR.

Cork mint, 5s. to 7s. 6d.

Dublin mint, 2s. 6d. to 5s.

Waterford mint, 3s. to 6s.

Penny (22½ grains).—Struck at Dublin and Waterford.

Obv., + EDW. R. ANGL. DNS. HYB., no triangle, bust in a *circle,* as on the English Penny; *rev.,* as before.

Dublin mint, 12s. One sold for £2 5s. in 1881.

Waterford mint, 18s.

Halfpenny (11¼ grains).—Struck at Cork, Dublin and Waterford.

Similar to the Triangle Penny.

Dublin and Waterford mints, 3s. to 5s.

EDWARD I., II., AND III.—CONTINUED.

SILVER—*continued.*

Lindsay valued the Cork Halfpenny at £3. and stated that only three were known.

Farthing (5¼ grains).—Struck at Dublin and Waterford. Similar to the Halfpenny. but, on *obv.*, E . R . ANGLIE . Dublin mint, 5s. to 6s.

Waterford mint, 7s. 6d. to 10s. A fine specimen of the Waterford mint sold for £1 6s. in 1873.

A set, Penny, Halfpenny and Farthing, in brilliant preservation, sold for 6s. in 1864.

Richard II., 1377—1399.

No Irish coins of this King have been discovered.

Henry IV., 1399—1413.

There is no record that any Irish coins were struck during this reign.

Henry V., 1413—1422.

Simon and other distinguished numismatists have assigned Irish coins to this King, but Lindsay takes a different view, because, among other reasons, no records have been discovered which refer to an Irish coinage from the reign of Edward III. until the 38th year of Henry VI., 1459-60. The coins assigned to Henry V. will be described under Henry VII.

Henry VI., 1422—1461.

SILVER.—Groat and Penny.

There are two varieties of the Penny, the first being similar to the English type.

Penny, first issue (12¼ grains).—Struck at Dublin about 1425. *Obv.*, + HENRICVS . DNS . HIBNIE . with an annulet at the end, front-faced bust, crowned, in a circle, a star of six points at the left side of the King's neck; *rev.*, long cross with three pellets in each quarter, CIVITAS . DVBLINIE. There is an annulet after CIVI.

Note.—The star at side of the neck and annulet in legend indicate that this coin might have been struck by Henry V.

A specimen, now in the British Museum, sold for £1 17s. in 1859 ; another specimen is known in a private collection.

Groat (about 45 grains).—Struck at Dublin, about 1460. *Obv.*, an open crown, in a double tressure of twelve arches, no legend, (for type see Fig. 142) ; *rev.*, long cross with three pellets in each angle, an annulet between the pellets in two quarters, surrounded by the legend, in one circle only, CIVITAS . DVBLINIE.

A Groat and Penny, of similar type, sold for 8s. in 1854.

A Groat, extremely fine, realised £1 11s. in 1873.

Penny, second issue (about 9½ grains).—Struck at Dublin, about 1460.

Similar to the Groat.

Valued by Lindsay at £1 10s.

HENRY VI.—CONTINUED.

COPPER.—Patrick or Half Farthing, struck in 1460.

The standard weight was 7½ grains, but specimens actually weigh 6, 7, 9 and 11 grains each.

Patrick (7½ grains).

Obv., a small crown in a circle, surrounded by PATRIK, followed by an annulet and a small branch, which complete the circle ; *rev.*, a broad plain cross, with P in one angle.

A variety is known without the P on *rev.*

Value, 5s.

Edward IV.,* 1461—1483.

SILVER.—Double Groat, Groat, Half Groat, Penny, Halfpenny and Farthing.

Seven coinages.

First coinage.—Groats, Half Groats, and Peonies, of the same stamp and standard as the coinage of the 38th year of Henry VI., were authorised to be struck in Dublin, Trim and Galway, and Halfpence and Farthings in Dublin. Ten Groats were to be coined from a Tower ounce of 450 grains troy, which would give 45 grains to the Groat. Of this coinage the Groat and Penny of the Dublin mint only are now known. The earliest coin known from the mint of Trim was struck in 1467, and it does not appear that silver coins were ever made in Galway. It is probable that the Half Groat was never struck, as Half Groats did not occur in either of the subsequent coinages, or previous to the fourth issue in 1467. The Halfpenny and Farthing are still to be discovered.

Groat (38 to 44½ grains).—Struck at Dublin.

Obv., a large crown in a double tressure of eight, nine, or ten arches, sometimes having suns or roses in the outer angles, no legend ; *rev.*, long cross with pellets, those in alternate angles being joined by annulets, legend CIVITAS DVBLINIE. (See Fig. 142).

These Groats may be distinguished from the similar type of Henry VI. by having fewer than twelve arches in the tressure which incloses the crown, and having generally roses or suns round the tressure.

Valued by Lindsay at £1 10s.

Penny (9 to 12 grains).—Struck at Dublin.

Similar to the Groat, but without roses on *obv.*

A variety (10½ grains) has on *obv.*, the crown in a beaded *circle*; and on *rev.*, CIVITAS . DVBLIN, no annulets between the pellets.

Valued by Lindsay at £1 10s. One sold for £2 3s.

Another variety is without either a tressure or circle of pellets on *obv.*

Second coinage, of the 3rd year, 1463-4.

The Groat should weigh 45 grains.

---

* See Dr. Aquilla Smith's paper on the Irish Coins of Edward the Fourth, published in the Transactions of the Royal Irish Academy, vol. xix., 1840. Also see Sainthill's "Olla Podrida," vol. ii., 1853.

EDWARD IV.—CONTINUED.

SILVER.—*Continued.*

Groat (about 40 grains).—Struck at Dublin and Waterford.

Obv., crown in a double treasure, surrounded by the legend EDWARDVS . DI . GRA . DNS . HYBERNIE, m.m. a rose ; or cross fleury ; *rev.*, POSVI, &c., in outer circle ; CIVITAS . DVBLINIE (*or* WATERFORD) in inner circle ; the pellets in angles of the cross are sometimes joined by annulets.

One of Dublin mint sold for 6s. in 1854, and for £1 6s. in 1859 ; two sold for £1 2s. in 1881.

One of Waterford mint sold for 8s. in 1854.

Penny (9¼ grains).—Struck at Dublin.

Obv., crown in a dotted circle, surrounded by + EDWARD . DI . G . DNS . HYB. ; *rev.*, long cross and pellets, CIVITAS . DVBLIN.

Lindsay considered this coin unique, and valued it at £5.

Penny.—Struck at Waterford.

A fragment, the only specimen known, has on *obv.* the crown within a double treasure, with trefoils at its points ; *rev.*, long cross and pellets, CIVITAS W. . . .

Halfpence and *Farthings* were also ordered to be made at Waterford, but none have been discovered.

No coins of this issue are known of the mints of Limerick or Trim.

Third coinage, of the 5th year, 1465-6.

Groat (28 grains).—Struck at Dublin.

Obv., a small cross on the centre of an expanded rose of five leaves, within a double treasure, a pellet in each of the outside angles, legend EDWARDVS . DEI . GRA . DNS . HYBERNI, m.m. rose; *rev.*, POSVI, &c. in outer circle, CIVITAS . DVBLINIE, in inner circle ; within the inner circle a sun of sixteen rays, having an annulet *or* a rose in the centre, m.m. rose.

Penny (8¼ grains).—Struck at Dublin.

Type similar to the Groat.

Obv., EDW . D . G . DNS . HYBERN, small cross in centre of a rose of five leaves, within a circle ; *rev.*, CIVITAS . DVBLINIE, surrounding a sun of sixteen rays, with a rose in the centre.

Both extremely rare. Lindsay valued this Groat and Penny at £3 each.

In 1859 a Groat and Penny sold together for 5s., and in 1864 a Penny (described as " extremely rare, but two or three known ") realised 5s.

A Penny of this type, but having, on *rev.*, a sun of eleven rays, sold for £1 5s., in 1854.

Fourth coinage, of the 7th year, 1467-8.—Ordered to be coined at Carlingford, Drogheda, Dublin, Galway, Limerick and Trim.

At this time, consequent upon its great scarcity in Ireland, silver was raised to double the value it had in the last year of Henry VI. A coin called a Double (weighing 45 grains) was ordered to be struck and to pass current in Ireland for eight

EDWARD IV.—CONTINUED.

SILVER.—*Continued.*

pence. Groats, Half Groats, Pence, Halfpence, and Farthings, were also ordered to be coined. Of the Dublin mint are known the Double Groat, Groat, Half Groat, and Penny; of the Drogheda mint, the Double Groat, Groat, and Penny; and of the Trim mint, the Double Groat, Groat, and Half Groat. No coins of this issue struck at Limerick or Waterford have been discovered, and it does not appear that silver coins were ever minted in Carlingford or Galway.

Double Groat (about 45 grains).—Those struck at Dublin, Drogheda, and Trim, only are known.

Obv., EDWARDVS . DEI . GRA . DNS . HYBERN, full-faced bust, crowned, in a tressure, m.m. rose; *rev.*, CIVITAS . DVBLINIE (*or* VILLA . DE . DROGHEDA *or* DE TRIM), surrounding a large sun of twenty-four rays, having a rose in the centre. (For type of *rev.*, see Fig. 143.)

Valued by Lindsay at £1 10s.

In 1854 a Double Groat (described as a Groat) of Drogheda sold for £1 5s.

In 1859 one of Dublin realised £1 18s.; in 1864 one sold for £1; and in 1873 another sold for £4 6s.

These pieces are described as Groats in the sale catalogues, 1854, 1859, and 1873.

Groat (about 22 grains).—Struck at Dublin, Drogheda, and Trim.

Obv., similar to the Double Groat, but legend contracted; *rev.*, similar to the Double Groat, CIVITAS . DVBLIN, *or* VILLA . DE . DROGHEDA, *or* DE TRIM, m.m. rose. (See Fig. 143).

The Dublin Groat (described by Lindsay as a Half Groat) was valued by him at £2.

The Trim Groat is unique.

In 1854 a Dublin Groat sold for £1 3s., and in 1873 for £4 1s.; in 1859 one sold for £1 8s.

These coins were termed Half Groats in the sale catalogues.

In 1859 a Groat and Half Groat (described as a Half Groat and Penny) sold for 15s.

The Groat struck at Trim was valued by Lindsay, who termed it a Half Groat, at £5, and described as unique.

Half Groat.—Struck at Dublin and Trim.

The Half Groat now appears for the first time in the Irish series.

Half Groat (11 Grains).—Struck at Dublin.

Obv., EDWAR . D . G . D . HYBER, bust in a circle; *rev.*, CIVITAS . DVBLIN, same type as the Groat.

The Half Groat of Dublin was valued by Lindsay (who styled it a Penny) at £2 10s.

In 1854 one (described as a Penny) sold for £1 14s.

Half Groat (11¼ grains).—Struck at Trim. Unique.

Obv., EDWARDVS . DI . GRA . DNS . HYBE; *rev.*, VILLA . DE . TRIM.

I

EDWARD IV.—CONTINUED.

SILVER.—*Continued.*

The following is the description of a coin weighing 14½ grains, which may have been a pattern for a Half Groat of this coinage :

Obv., + EDWAR . R . ANGL . D . HYB, bust in a circle ; *rev.*, a large sun of ten rays, surrounded by CIVITAS . DVBLINI.

Penny (5¾ grains).—Struck at Drogheda.

Obv., the King's head in a beaded circle without a tressure, + EDWARD . D . G . DN ; *rev.*, VILLA . DE . DROGH, surrounding a sun of twenty-four rays.

Penny.—Struck at Dublin.

Similar to the preceding Penny, except that the sun on *rev.* has sixteen rays.

Fifth coinage, presumably of the 10th year, 1470.

Prior to the important issue of money of the English type (noticed as the *sixth* coinage) certain coins were struck at Drogheda and Dublin, which are not described in any of the public Acts. They are distinguished from the coins of the English type by having a rose in the centre of the cross on the *rev.*, and no pellets in the angles. Groats, Pennies, and Half-pennies are known.

By an Act of 1470, the coinage of 1467-8 was reduced to half its original value. The Groat issued in 1470 should, therefore, weigh 45 grains, and the smaller pieces in proportion, but the actual weight of the Groat varies from 27 to 32 grains.

Groat (27 to 29 grains).—Struck at Drogheda. Of this type and mint no coins, except Groats, are known.

Obv., crowned bust, within a double tressure, a sun at right side of the crown and a rose at left, a sun at left of the neck and a rose at right, EDWARDVS . DEI . GRA . DNS . HYBER ; *rev.*, a long cross, extending to the edge of the coin, with a rose on its centre ; in outer circle, POSVI, etc. ; in inner circle, VILLA . DROGHEDA.

In another variety the suns and roses at the sides of the crown and neck are transposed.

Valued by Lindsay at 6s. In 1873, one sold for 11s.

Groat (32 grains).—Struck at Dublin.

Almost similar to preceding Groat ; *rev.*, CIVITAS . DVBLINIE.

Valued by Lindsay at 3s. 6d. In 1854, a very fine specimen realised 15s.

Penny (6 to 7 grains).—Struck at Dublin.

Obv., bust in a circle, a sun at right side of crown, a rose at left ; *rev.*, in one circle, CIVITAS . DVBLINIE.

A variety has a sun to left of neck, and a rose to right. Value from 3s. to 5s.

Halfpenny (about 3 grains).—Struck at Dublin.

Obv., full-faced bust, crowned, in a circle ; *rev.*, long cross, with a rose in the centre, CIVITAS . DVBLIN.

One specimen has a rose at each side of the neck ; another has a small cross at each side of the crown.

Valued by Lindsay at £1.

EDWARD IV.—CONTINUED.

SILVER.—*Continued.*

Some Dublin Pennies, probably coined at this time, are like those last described, except that they have roses and suns in the angles of the cross on *rev.*

Penny (6 to 9 grains).

Obv., crowned bust in a circle, surrounded by the king's name, &c., and a rose and sun at sides of crown and neck; *rev.*, CIVITAS . DVBLIN ; in the quarters of the cross there are alternately two roses and a sun and two suns and a rose, instead of pellets as in the sixth coinage.

A variety (9½ grains) has: *obv.*, EDW . . DI . GRA . REX . NGI . T ; *rev.*, CIVITAS . DVBLIN, and three stars in each angle of the cross.

Henry VI. (restored), 1470.

SILVER.—Groat and Penny.

Groat (26 to 31 grains).—Struck at Dublin.

Obv., full-faced bust with a broad and flat crown, within a tressure of nine arches, HENBICVS . DI . GBA . DNS . HYBEBNIE, m.m. plain cross, small saltire, four pellets, &c.; *rev.*, long cross and pellets, POSVI, &c., in outer circle, CIVITAS DVBLINIE in inner circle, m.m. plain cross, trefoil, pierced cross, &c.

These Groats are attributed to Henry VI., as struck in 1470, although no documentary evidence exists to prove that the King exercised his prerogatives in Ireland after his restoration. Throughout the legend on both sides the letter R is shaped like B, a peculiarity which marks the English light Groats of Henry VI., struck in 1470. The above Groats are further distinguished from those of a similar type of Henry VII. by having "Dominus Hibernie" for the King's title instead of "Rex Angl."

Penny (5 grains).—Similar to the fifth coinage of Edward IV.

Obv., full-faced bust crowned in a dotted circle, HENBICVS . DNS . HIB., m.m. pierced cross; *rev.*, CIVIT, &c., a long plain cross with a rose on the centre, and no pellets in the quarters.

Edward IV.—CONTINUED.

SILVER.—*Continued.*

Sixth coinage.—Similar to the English type.* The order, given in the 10th year, 1470, directed that the *reverse* should be like the Calais Groats (see Fig. 144, Calais Half Groat), and that five sorts of silver coins, viz., Groats, Half Groats, Pennies, Halfpennies and Farthings, should be struck at Dublin, Drogheda and Trim.

Waterford was recognised as a royal mint, but coins struck at Cork, Limerick, Youghal, Kinsale and Kilmallock, were

---

* In 1472 the English Groats, Half Groats, and Pennies of Edward III., Richard II., and Henry IV., V., and VI., were ordered to pass in Ireland at fivepence the Groat, and the smaller coins in proportion. In 1475 the value of these Groats was raised to sixpence in Ireland, and the contemporary English Groat was to be current in Ireland for fivepence.

I 2

EDWARD IV.—CONTINUED.

SILVER.—*Continued.*

declared unlawful. No coins are known of the last three places.

The Groats should weigh nearly 44 grains, but are seldom more than 35 grains, and in 1473 the weight was reduced by law to a little over 32 grains.

Groats.—Struck at Cork, Drogheda, Dublin, Limerick, Trim, Waterford and Wexford.

Obv., EDWARDVS . DEI . GRA . DNS . HYBERNIE. (on one specimen EDWARDVS . DEI . GRA . REX . AGL . Z . FRA), full-faced bust, crowned, in a tressure ; *rev.*, POSVI, &c., and in inner circle CIVITAS . DVBLINIE, *or* WATERFORD, *or* CORCAGIE, *or* LIMIRICI, *or* VILLA . DE . DROGHEDA, *or* DE . TRIM, *or* WEIXFOR.

A variety of the Drogheda Groat has the King's name spelt EDVARDVS, and a Limerick Groat has LIMERICI.

There are two varieties of *reverse* :

First, three pellets in each of the quarters of the cross.

Second, three pellets in two of the quarters, and two pellets and a star (*or* a rose) in the other quarters.

Some coins have a rose, sun, annulet, &c., at the sides of the head, and on the bust the letter G (for Germyn Lynch. the Master of the Mint), *or* L (for Limerick), and V or W (for Waterford).

Lindsay valued these Groats as under :

Cork, £1 10s. In 1854 one sold for £10, and another for £3 18s.

Drogheda, 4s. to 6s.

Dublin, 2s. 6d. to 3s. 6d.

Limerick, 10s.

Trim, 4s.

Waterford, 3s.

Wexford, £2.

Half Groat (15 to 19 grains).—Struck at Drogheda, Dublin, Limerick, Trim, and Waterford.

Obv., EDWARD . DI . GRA . DNS . HYBER, full-faced bust, crowned, in a tressure; *rev.*, POSVI, &c., CIVITAS . DVBLIN, *or* LIMIRICI, *or* WATERFO., cross and pellets. The Limerick Half Groat has L on breast, a rose on each side of the bust, and two pellets and a rose in two quarters of *rev.*

Dublin, 15s.

Limerick, £1 10s. In 1854 a specimen, together with five Pennies struck at Dublin, Limerick and Waterford, sold for £1 16s.

Penny (6¼ to 10¼ grains).—Struck at Cork, Drogheda, Dublin, Limerick. Trim, and Waterford.

Obv., EDWAR . DI . GR . DNS . HYBE, *or* IBERNIE (*or* EDWARD . REX . ANG . Z . FR), full-faced bust, crowned, in a circle ; *rev.*, cross and pellets, CIVITAS . DVBLIN, *or* CORCAGIE, *or* LIMIRICI, *or* WATERFORD, *or* WATFOR, *or* VILLA . DE . DROGHEDA, *or* DE . TRIM.

Some specimens have at each side of the bust, a small cross,

EDWARD IV.—CONTINUED.

SILVER.—*Continued.*

an annulet, a pellet, a sun, a rose and star, a rose and sun, or a quatrefoil; and on *rev.*, a rose on centre of the cross, with three pellets in each quarter, and sometimes with a rose in two of the quarters.

Drogheda, 7s.
Dublin, 4s.
Limerick, £1.
Waterford, 10s.

Halfpenny.—Struck at Dublin.

Obv., EDWA, &c., full-faced bust, crowned, in a circle; *rev.*, long cross, a rose on the centre, and pellets in the angles.

Farthing.—None have been discovered.

Seventh coinage, of the year 1478—the Three Crowns* money (see Fig. 145): Groat, Half Groat, Penny, Halfpenny, and Farthing.

Groat (24 to 32 grains).—Four varieties.

First variety.—*Obv.*, REX . ANGL . FRANCIE, arms of England in a shield over across pommete; *rev.*, Three Crowns in .pale, on a cross pommete, encircled by DOMINVS . HYBERNIE.

Some Groats of this sort have on the *obv.*, at each side of the arms of England, a small shield bearing a saltire, the arms of Fitz Gerald, Earl of Kildare, and Lord Justice of Ireland, in 1479.

On some specimens the Kildare arms appear in the form of the figure 8. The legend on *rev.* is DOMINOS . YBEEN, and the Three Crowns are contained within a tressure of eight or nine points.

From 1s. 6d. to 2s. 6d.

Second variety.—Similar to the preceding, but on *obv.*, REX . ANGLIE . FRANCI (*or* FRANCIE), and on *rev.*, ET . REX . HYBERNIE, the crowns within a tressure.

From 5s. to 10s.

Third variety.—Similar to first variety, but DOMINVS . HYBERNIE on *obv.* as well as on *rev.*

From 2s. 6d. to 3s. 6d.

Fourth variety.—Similar to first variety, but EDWARDVS *or* EDWAR . REX . ANGLIE . FRANCI on *obv.*

From 3s. 6d. to 4s. 6d.

Half Groat (11 to 14½ grains).—Four varieties.

The Half Groats have no tressure on *rev.*

First variety.—Similar to the first Groat.

From 2s. to 3s.

Second variety.—*Obv.*, like the second Groat, but CIVITAS DVBLIN on *rev.*

From 3s. to 4s.

Third variety.—Similar to the third Groat.

Only one Half Groat bearing the Fitz Gerald arms is known; it has the word DOMINOS only on each side.

---

* The THREE CROWNS *in pale on a field azure* were the arms of Ireland from the reign of Richard II. to that of Henry VIII.

EDWARD IV.—CONTINUED.

SILVER.—*Continued.*

Fourth variety.—Similar type, but EDWARD . DOM . HYBE . on *obv.*, and CIVITAS . DVBLINIE on *rev.*

From 4s. to 5s.

Penny (about 7 grains).—Same type.

Obv., REX . ANGL . Z . FRANCIE *or* REX . ANGL . FRANC ; *rev.*, DOMINVS . HYBERN, *or* DOMNVS . HYBENIE.

From 5s. to 10s.

Halfpenny (5 grains).

Of similar type to the Penny.

Farthing (about 2 grains).

Of similar type to the Penny.

According to Lindsay, *unique* and worth 10s.

BILLON.—By an Act of the second year of Edward IV. (1461), a coin of copper mixed with silver was ordered to be struck at Dublin, having on *obv.*, a cross with name of the place of mintage, and on *rev.*, a crown, with suns and roses. No specimen of this coinage is known to exist.

COPPER.—Farthing. Three issues.

First issue (10¼ grains).—Struck about 1461.

Obv., a crown, surrounded by roses and suns alternately in place of a legend ; *rev.*, a cross, encircled by the legend CIVITAS DVBLINI, a sun between the words.

Value, 5s.

Second issue (9¼ grains).—Struck about 1463.

Obv., PATRICIVS, full-faced bust of St. Patrick with mitre ; *rev.*, long cross with broad ends, a sun in two quarters and a rose in the other two, surrounded by SALVATOR, suns and roses alternately between the letters in each quarter.

Value, 10s.

Third issue (10 grains).—Struck about 1467.

Obv., EDWARDVS . D., &c., Three Crowns, two above and one below, on a shield, in a dotted circle ; *rev.*, long cross, CIVITAS . DVBLINIE surrounding a sun of sixteen rays, having a small rose on the centre.

Value, 5s.

BRASS.—Half Farthing.—Two issues.

First issue (4¾ grains).—Struck in 1463, and corresponding in type with the Silver Penny of the second coinage.

Obv., a crown in the centre, surrounded by roses and crosses (the latter intended to represent suns) in place of a legend ; *rev.*, a long single cross extending to the edge of the coin, with three pellets in each quarter ; legend obliterated.

Second issue (3¼ grains).—Struck in 1470, and corresponding with the Silver Penny of the sixth coinage.

Obv., full-faced bust, crowned, in a circle ; *rev.*, long cross, with pellets in the angles, and small strokes or lines in place of a legend.

Unique, valued at 5s.

Mixed lots of the coins of Edward IV. have sold as under :

In 1854, at the Cuff sale, five Groats sixth issue, of Dublin,

EDWARD IV.—CONTINUED.

Limerick and Waterford, a Groat of seventh issue, and two Dublin Pennies, sold for 9s.; also seven Groats, varied, of the sixth issue, sold for 10s.; and another lot of seven Groats sold for 8s. A lot of six coins, comprising Groats of Drogheda, Trim and Waterford, and Pennies of Dublin and Waterford, realised 18s.

In 1859, at the Martin sale, a Groat of Drogheda sixth issue, a Groat of seventh issue, with arms of Kildare, and a Dublin Penny of second issue, sold for 16s.; another lot, comprising three Groats and a Half Groat of sixth issue, two Half Groats of seventh issue, and three Dublin Pennies, varied, realised £1 8s.

In 1864, at the Christmas sale, a Groat of second and third issue, and two Half Groats, seventh issue, sold for 17s.; a Groat of second, third and fourth issues, sold for £1 3s.; five Groats of sixth issue, and five Groats of seventh issue, all well preserved, realised £1; two Half Groats of sixth issue, and four Half Groats of seventh issue, sold for 19s.

In 1873, at the Bergne sale, two Groats of Dublin and Waterford, and five Dublin Pennies, varied, sold for 11s.

In 1881, at the Neligan sale, seven Groats, Dublin, Drogheda, Limerick, and Waterford, sold for £1 2s.; and fourteen Groats, varied, sold for £1 5s.

In 1881, at the Reynell sale, a Double Groat of Dublin, and four Groats, one of first coinage and three of sixth coinage, sold for £2 2s.

The following table shows the legal weight of the Groat at different periods during this reign :

1461—65, 45 grains	1470—73, 43$\frac{7}{11}$ grains.*
1465—67, 36 „	1473—79, 32$\frac{1}{2}$ „
1467—70, 22$\frac{1}{2}$ „	1479—83, 31 „

Edward V., April to June, 1483.

SILVER.—Groat.

Groat (Three Crowns type).—Struck at Waterford.

Obv., shield with the arms of England within a tressure of four arches, outside which, in each of the lower angles, is a small cross, legend EDW . . . &c. ; *rev.*, the Three Crowns within a tressure of nine arches, the letter E (in old English character) under the lowest crown, legend CIVITAS . WAT . . .

Mr. Sainthill ("Olla Podrida," vol. ii.) thought it very probable that Groats of this type were coined during the short period that Edward the Fifth was on the throne. The E would be a marked distinction from his father's coinage, without occasioning the loss of any dies that might have been sunk.

---

* It was enacted in 1470 that eleven Groats should make an ounce Troy; each Groat should, therefore, weigh 43$\frac{7}{11}$ grains. Dr. Smith presumes that the Troy ounce was erroneously substituted for that of the Tower, and consequently that the Groat of this year should weigh 40$\frac{10}{11}$ grains.

Richard III., 1483—1485.

SILVER.—Three coinages, similar to the fifth, sixth, and seventh coinages of Edward IV.

First coinage.—Groat and Penny.

Groat (28¼ to 30½ grains).—Struck at Drogheda, from an altered die of Edward IV.

Obv., RICARDVS . DEI . GRA . DNS . HYB., full-faced bust, crowned, in a tressure, a rose and sun alternately at each side of the head, m.m. rose; *rev.*, POSVI, &c., and in inner circle VILLA . DROGHEDA, a large rose on centre of the cross, no pellets in the angles, m.m. rose.

Valued by Lindsay at £5.

In 1854, one sold for £6; and another, not quite so fine, realised £1 8s.

In 1859, one sold for £1 11s.; and in 1873, one sold for £6.

Penny (about 8 grains).—Struck at Drogheda.

Obv., RIC., &c., full-faced bust, crowned, in a circle, rose and sun alternately at each side, m.m. rose; *rev.*, VILLA . DROGHEDA, a large rose on centre of the cross, no pellets in the angles.

Valued by Lindsay at £1 10s.; one sold for £1 1s. in 1864.

Second coinage.—Penny.

Penny (7 grains).—Struck at Waterford.

Obv., RICARD . DNS . HYB, full-faced bust, crowned, in a circle; *rev.*, CIVITAS . WATERFORD, a rose on the centre of the cross and three pellets in each of the angles.

Valued by Lindsay at 15s.

Third coinage.—Groat.   Two varieties.

Groat (25¼ to 30½ grains).—First variety.

Obv., RICAR . REX . ANGL (*or* ANGLE) FRANC, the arms of England on a cross pommete; *rev.*, DOMINVS . HYBERNIE, three crowns in pale on a cross pommete.

Valued by Lindsay at £1 5s., in fine condition.

In 1854, one sold for £1 1s., and another for 19s.

In 1859, a specimen, well preserved, realised 12s.

Groat (22 grains).—Second variety.

Obv., RICARDVS . DEI . GRAIA . REX, the arms of England on a cross trefoil within a tressure of four arches; *rev.*, CIVI . WATTOORFOORD, three broad flat crowns of equal size in pale on a cross trefoil.

A specimen, believed by Dr. A. Smith to be unique, is now in the Royal Irish Academy.

In 1864, a Groat with bust, and one with the three crowns, sold together for £1 2s.

Henry VII.,* 1485—1509.

SILVER.—Groat, Half Groat and Penny.   Four coinages.

First coinage.—*Obv.*, the arms of England; *rev.*, the Three Crowns.   (See Fig. 145.)   Of this coinage there are four varieties.

---

* See Dr. A. Smith's Monograph on the "Irish Coins of Henry VII.," published in the "Transactions of the Royal Irish Academy," vol. xix., 1840.

HENRY VII.—CONTINUED.

SILVER.—*Continued.*

Groat, first variety (24 to 29 grains).

Obv., REX . ANGLIE . FRANCIE (*or* FRANC) ; *rev.*, DOMINVS . HIBERN . *or* HIBERNIE (*or* DOMINOS . YBERNIE), the letter h under the lower crown ; the Three Crowns within a beaded circle, or sometimes within a treasure. One specimen has the arms on *obv.*, in a tressure of four arches within the beaded circle.

Another has the Fitz Gerald arms on each side of the shield on *obv.* The letter h under the crowns distinguishes it from the similar coin of Edward IV.

From 2s. to 3s. 6d.

Groat, second variety (27 grains).

Obv., DOMINVS, *or* DOMINOS, . HYBERNIE ; *rev.*, same legend.

From 5s. to 7s.

Groat, third variety (30 grains), intermediate between the Groats of the second and fourth varieties.

Obv. HENRICVS . DI . GRACIA ; *rev.* DOMINOS YBERNIE, instead of the place of mintage.

Groat, fourth variety (22 to 28½ grains). Struck at Dublin and Waterford.

Obv., HENRIC . DI . GRACIA ; *rev.*, CIVITAS . DVBLINIE, type as first variety.

A Groat of Waterford (30 grains) has *obv.*, HENRICVS . DI . GRACIA REX, arms in a tressure of four arches ; *rev.*, CIVITAS . WATERFOR . *or* WATERFORD, the Three Crowns in a tressure of nine arches, with h under the lower crown.

The legends on other Waterford Groats vary from the preceding.

Dublin Groat, 5s. to 10s.

Waterford Groat, 2s. to 3s.

Half Groat (13 to 15½ grains), first coinage.

First variety.—Similar to first variety Groat.

Second variety.—Similar to fourth variety Groat, but without h under the crowns.

Obv., HENRICVS . DI . ORAI ; *rev.*, CIVITAS . DVBBL .

Another has *obv.*, HENRIC . DOM . OBAR ; *rev.*, CIVITAS . DVBLINIE.

From 5s. to 7s.

Penny (6 to 7 grains).—Two varieties known, similar to the first and fourth varieties of Groats.

First variety (6 grains).

Obv., arms of England in a circle of pellets; REX . ANGLIE ; *rev.*, the Three Crowns in a circle of pellets not quartered by a cross, DOMINVS . YRERNI, h under the crowns.

Second variety (7 grains).

Obv., HENRICVS . REX . AN. ; *rev.*, CIVITAS . DVBLIN.

Valued by Lindsay at 15s., in fine condition.

In 1854, two Groats, a Half Groat and Penny, sold for 9s.

Second coinage.—Groat and Half Groat.

HENRY VII.—CONTINUED.

SILVER.—Continued.

Groat, second coinage (26¼ to 29 grains).—The bust with open crown in a tressure of six, seven, nine, eleven or twelve arches.

Obv., HENRIC (or HENRICVS) DEI . GRACIA . REX . AGLI ; rev., POSVI, &c., and in inner circle, CIVITAS . DVBLINIE, cross and pellets, sometimes **h** in centre of cross.

From 5s. to 10s.

A Groat (32 grains) of the Waterford mint is known.

The legend, which is much defaced, appears to have been

Obv., HENRIC . DEI . GRA . REX . ANGLI . FRANC ; rev., POSVI, &c., and CIVITAS . WATERFORD.

Half Groat, second coinage (16 grains).

Obv., full-faced bust, with open crown in a tressure, HENRIC . DI . GRA . REX . ANLIE ; rev., POSVI, &c., CIVITAS . DVLIN, cross and pellets.

In 1859, two Groats and a Half Groat, with open crown, together with five coins of Henry VIII., sold for £1 13s.

Third coinage.—Groat, Half Groat, and Penny.

Groat, third coinage (26 to 30 grains).—The bust with double-arched crown in a tressure of four, six, seven, eight, nine or ten arches.

Obv., HENRIC . DEI . GRA . REX . ANGL . FR ; rev., POSVI, &c., and CIVITAS . DVBLINIE.

One variety is said to have a boar's head in centre of cross, and another has the letter **h**.

From 3s. to 4s.

Half Groat.—Type of third coinage Groat.

Obv., bust with double-arched crown, in a tressure of nine points ; rev., POSVI, &c., CIVITAS . DVXLIN.

Valued by Lindsay at £1 10s.

Penny, third coinage (5¼ grains).

Obv., **h** under a large double-arched crown, HENR . . ; rev., CIVITAS, &c., cross with three pellets in each angle.

Described by Lindsay as unique and valued at £3.

Fourth coinage.—Groats only.

Groat (24 to 29¼ grains).—The bust with flat crown in a beaded circle.

These Groats were assigned by Simon to Henry V.

Obv., HENRICVS . DI . GRA . REX . AGL, full-faced bust, crowned ; rev., POSVI, &c., in inner circle, CIVITAS . (*sometimes* SIVITAS) DVBLINE, or DVBLIN, or DVBL, cross and pellets.

Some specimens have, on each side of the head, a cinquefoil, or quatrefoil, or a cross and annulet, or a small cross.

From 3s. to 4s.

In 1854, two Groats of this coinage with a Groat of Edward IV., first issue, sold for 10s.

Henry VIII.,* 1509—1547.

SILVER.—Groat, Half Groat, Sixpence, Threepence, Three Halfpence, and Three Farthings. Four types.

---

* See Dr. A. Smith's paper on the "Irish Coins of Henry VIII.," in the *Numismatic Chronicle*, vol. xix., new series, 1879.

HENRY VIII.—CONTINUED.

SILVER.—*Continued.*

First type, prior to 1541.—Groat and Half Groat.

Groat (35 to 38 grains).

Obv., arms of England, crowned, on a cross fourchy, HENRIC . VIII . D . G . R . AGL . Z ; *rev.,* harp, crowned, between H and R, both crowned, FRANCE . DOMINVS . HIBERNIE.

A variety (presumably the first coinage of this King) omits the VIII. after HENRIC, and has GRA . REX.

Similar Groats have, instead of h—R at side of the harp, h—A (for Henry and Anne Boleyn *or* Anne of Cleves), h—I (for Henry and Jane Seymour), and h—K (for Henry and Katherine Howard).

From 1s. 6d. to 2s. 6d.

In 1854, six, varied, sold for 6s. ; five, varied, 8s. ; and seven, varied, 4s. 6d.

Half Groat (19 to 21 grains).—Same type as the Groat, with h—A, h—I, *or* h—K, at side of harp.

A variety has 8 for VIII after HENRIC.

Very rare ; valued by Lindsay, in fine condition, at £1 5s., £1 10s., and £1 respectively.

In 1854, a Groat and Half Groat, with H . A., both in fine preservation, sold for 10s. ; and a Groat and Half Groat with H . K., realised 9s.

In 1864, three Groats, H . R ., H . A ., H . I., and a Half Groat, H . A., all very fine, sold for 13s.

In 1873, three Groats, with H . A ., H . I., and H . K. at side of the harp, and a Half Groat, realised £1 11s.

Second type, 1541.—Groats only (35 to 39½ grains), of base metal, 9oz. 6dwt. fine.

Obv., same type as the preceding, HENRIC . VIII. DI . GRACIA . ANGLIE, arms of England ; *rev.,* FRANCIE . ET . HIBERNIE . REX ., harp crowned between h—R, both crowned.

From 2s. 6d. to 3s. 6d., in fine condition.

Third type, 1544.—Sixpence, Threepence, Three Halfpenny and Three Farthing Pieces. Base metal, 8oz. fine and 4oz. alloy.

Sixpence (35 to 44 grains).

Obv., the King's bust, nearly full-faced, crowned, HENRIC . 8 . D . G . AGL . FRA . Z . HIB . REX. (see Fig. 146) ; *rev.,* CIVITAS . DVBLINIE, the arms of England on a cross fleury, m.m. harp, boar's head, sun, P, &c.

From 2s. 6d. to 3s. 6d.

Threepence (18 to 22 grains).

Type similar to the Sixpence.

From 3s. to 5s.

Three Halfpenny Piece (9 to 11 grains).

Same type ; *obv.,* H . D . G . ROSA . SINE . SPINE.; *rev.,* CIVITAS . DVBLIN. *or* DVBLINIE.

A variety reads SIN . SPI.

HENRY VIII.—CONTINUED.

SILVER.—*Continued.*

One of these coins was valued at £2 by Lindsay, who supposed it to be "perhaps unique."

In 1854, four Sixpences, two Threepenny and one Three-Halfpenny Piece, sold for 8s.; and a similar lot, but with one additional piece, also realised 8s. At the same sale, two Sixpences, a Threepenny and two Three-Halfpenny Pieces, together with three Groats of Henry VII., third coinage, sold for 7s.

In 1859, a Sixpence, Threepence, and Three-Halfpenny Piece, with a Groat and Half Groat (H . A.), and also two Groats and a Half Groat of Henry VII., sold for £1 13s.

In 1864, two Sixpences, very fine, two Threepences, fine, and a Three-Halfpenny Piece, sold for 9s.; and at the same sale a Sixpence, Threepence, and Three-Halfpenny Piece, all fine, realised 8s.

In 1873, two Sixpences, a Threepence, and Three-Halfpenny Piece, all fine, sold for £1 9s.

Three-Farthing Piece (5½ grains).

Similar type. *Obv.*, H . D . G . ROSA . SINE . SP.; *rev.*, CIVITAS . DVBLIN.

Valued by Lindsay, as being unique, at £2.

In 1859, this coin was sold for £2 11s.

In 1864, one (probably the same) sold for £3.

Fourth type, 1546.—Sixpence only. Similar to Groat of second type. Very base metal, 4oz. fine silver to 8oz. alloy.

Sixpence (34 to 40 grains).

Obv., HENRIC . VIII. DI . GRACIA . AGLIE, the arms of England, crowned, on a cross fourchy; *rev.*, FRANCIE . ET . HIBERNIE . REX . 37., harp crowned between h and R, also crowned, m.m. fleur-de-lis on each side.

A variety has *obv.*, HENRIC . 8 . D.G . ANGL . FRANC; *rev.*, W . ET . HIBERNIE . REX . 38. (See Fig. 147.)

The figures 37 and 38 in *rev.* legends of the preceding coins indicate the year of the King's reign in which they were struck.

Another variety has; *obv.*, HENRIC . 8 . DEI . GRACIA . ANGLIE, and, *rev.*, W . FRANCIE . ET . HIBERNIE . REX.

The W at beginning of *rev.* legend should correctly be WS in monogram, the initials of William Sherrington, Master of the Mint at Bristol, where these coins were struck.

From 2s. 6d. to 3s. 6d.

Edward VI., 1547—1553.

Whether or not Irish coins were struck by Edward VI. is a moot point among numismatists. Lindsay thought it certain that money was coined in Ireland during this reign, although none had been discovered. "Have we no Irish coins of Edward VI.?" is the title of a paper* by the Rev. Canon Pownall, who writes

---

* *Numismatic Chronicle*, vol. i., third series, 1881.

EDWARD VI.—CONTINUED.

thus: "We possess Irish coins of Henry VIII., although there was no Irish mint at work in Henry's time. And we are supposed to have no Irish coins of Edward VI., though it can be shown that in his reign the mint in Dublin was at work." The writer's opinion (in which, however, Dr. Aquilla Smith does not concur) is that the Testoons of Edward VI., dated 1551 and 1552, with mint mark a *harp* (and probably also those of same date with mint mark a fleur-de-lis and a rose), were struck at Dublin. These Testoons are very base, although the coinage of fine silver in England began in 1551. Hawkins observed* : "It is not easy to account for this date (MDLII.) on a base shilling, as the money of fine silver was certainly in circulation in the preceding year." But if these base Testoons are detached from the English money of the same date and classed as Irish coins, nothing, in Canon Pownall's opinion, remains to occasion surprise.

Many of these pieces are only latten, and look as if they had not been even washed with silver. Those with mint mark harp are of the basest sort, and were ordered, in the third year of Elizabeth, to pass for twopence farthing only. They vary in weight. One (74¾ grains), with m.m. harp on both sides, reads, Obv., EDWARD . VI . D. G . AGL . FRAN . Z . HB . REX ; rev., TIMOR . DOMINI . FONS . VITE . M . DLII, the letters E and R on either side of the Arms.

They are of the type shown in Fig. 79, except that the letter M on rev. is of the Lombardic not the Roman shape.

Mary,† 1553—1554.

SILVER.—Shilling, Groat, Half Groat and Penny.
Shilling (90 to 96 grains).—Dated 1553 and 1554.
Obv., MARIA . D . G . ANG . FRA . Z . HIB . REGIN, or REGINA, or HIBE REGIN, crowned bust to the left, with necklace, a fleur-de-lis after Maria, and annulets between the words, m.m. annulet; rev., VERITAS . TEMPORIS . FILIA . MDLIII, the harp crowned between M and R, also crowned. A fleur-de-lis after VERITAS, and annulets between the words.
A variety has VERTAS and the date MDLIIII.
Specimens have sold for 6s., £1 5s., £2 10s., and £4 4s.
Tolerably well executed forgeries of the Shilling are met with occasionally; they are readily known by the want of the flange or cross line at the base of the initial letters M . R on rev.
Groat (about 32 grains).
Similar to the Shilling, except that it is not dated. (See Fig. 148.)
Specimens have sold for £3 11s., £14 5s., and £29 10s.
In Fig. 148 the fleur-de-lis after MARIA and the annulets between the words are unfortunately omitted.

---

* "The Silver Coins of England," 2nd ed., p. 289.
† See Dr. A. Smith's paper on the "Irish Coins of Mary," published in the "Proceedings of the Kilkenny Archæological Society," vol. iii., 1856.

MARY.—CONTINUED.

SILVER.—*Continued.*

A forgery of the Groat has a pomegranate after the Queen's name, and the date MDLIII on *rev.*

Half Groat (about 16 grains).

Obv., MARIA . D . G . A . FR . Z . HIB . REGI, similar to the Groat.

Valued by Lindsay at £4.

A forgery of the Half Groat omits the crown over the harp on *rev.*

A Groat and Half Groat of Mary, with a Shilling and five Groats of Philip and Mary, sold for £2 2s. (1881).

Penny (8 grains).

Same type as the Half Groat, but on *obv.*, M . D . G . ROSA . SINE . SPIN.

Described by Lindsay as unique, and valued at £7.

In 1859 one sold for £3 10s.

Philip and Mary, 1554—1558.

SILVER.—Shilling and Groat, of base metal, 3oz. silver to 9oz. alloy.

In 1557 the circulation of the base English Rose-Pennies of Henry VIII. and Edward VI. was prohibited in England and restricted to Ireland.

Shilling (144 grains).—Dated 1555.

Obv., PHILIP . ET . MARIA . D . G . REX . ET . REGINA . ANGL, *or* ANG, busts of the King and Queen face to face, a crown over, the date 1555 below the busts, m.m. rose; *rev.*, POSVIMVS, &c., the harp crowned between P and M both crowned, m.m. rose or portcullis.

From 7s. 6d. to 10s., in good condition.

These Shillings are seldom found in a fine state.

Groat (48 grains).—Dated 1555, 1556, 1557 and 1558.

Similar to the Shilling, but the date is placed over the busts, with the crown between, thus, 15——55.

From 1s. 6d. to 2s. 6d.

Two Shillings and a Groat, in fine condition, sold for 17s. ; a similar lot but not so good, sold for 10s.   (1854).

A Shilling and a Groat, both fine, sold for 12s.   (1864).

A Shilling and two Groats, realised 17s.   (1873).

A Shilling of Mary, a Shilling and Groat of Philip and Mary, with nine coins, varied, of Elizabeth and James I., sold for £1 5s. (1859).

Elizabeth, 1558—1602.

SILVER.—Three coinages.

First Coinage, 1558.—Shilling and Groat of base metal, 3oz. silver to 9oz. alloy.

Second Coinage, 1561.—Shilling and Groat of good silver.

Third Coinage, 1598.—Shilling, Sixpence, and Threepence of base metal, 3oz. silver to 9oz. alloy.

ELIZABETH.—CONTINUED.

SILVER.—*Continued.*

Shilling, first coinage (144 grains).

Obv., ELIZABETH . D . G . ANG . FRA . Z . HIB . REG .
or REGI . or REGINA, crowned bust to the left, m.m. rose ;
rev., POSVI, &c., crowned harp between E and R also crowned,
m.m. rose.

From 3s. to 5s.

Groat, first coinage (48 grains).

Similar to the preceding Shilling.

From 2s. 6d. to 3s. 6d.

Shilling, second coinage (about 72 grains).—Dated 1561.

Obv., ELIZABETH . D . G . A . F . ET . HIBERNIE . REG .
or REGI, crowned bust to the left in a dotted circle, m.m.
harp ; *rev.*. POSVI, &c., a crowned shield, bearing three harps
(two above, one below), the date, 1561, on each side of the
shield, thus, 15——61. (See Fig. 149.)

From 5s. to 7s. 6d.

Groat, second coinage (about 24 grains).—Dated 1561.

Similar to the Shilling.

Valued by Lindsay at 10s.

Shilling, third coinage (72 to 88 grains).

Obv., ELIZABETH . D . G . ANG . FRA . ET . HIBER .
REG . or RE, the arms of England on a shield, in a dotted circle,
m.m. trefoil, star, &c.; *rev.,* POSVI, &c., the harp crowned.

From 2s. 6d. to 5s.

A very fine specimen realised £1 3s. in 1864.

Sixpence, third coinage (38 to 47 grains).

Similar to the preceding Shilling.

From 2s. to 5s.

Threepence (about 20 grains).

Similar to the preceding Shilling.

Valued by Lindsay at 12s.

A specimen, with three other coins, was sold for 6s. in 1854.

COPPER.—Penny and Halfpenny.

Penny (27 to 30 grains).—Dated 1601 and 1602.

Obv., ELIZABETH . D . G . AN . FR . ET . HIBER . RE,
the arms of England between E and R, m.m., star, cross, &c.;
rev., POSVI, &c., crowned harp between 16——01, or
16——02.

From 6d. to 1s. 6d.

Halfpenny (about 15 grains).—Dated 1601 and 1602.

Similar to the Penny.

From 1s. to 2s. 6d.

Mixed lots of Elizabeth's coins have realised the following
prices :

In 1854, a Shilling and Groat, first issue, with a Sixpence
and Threepence, sold for 6s.

A Shilling of third issue, with a Sixpence and Threepence, and
two copper coins 1601 and 1602, sold for 8s.

A Shilling and Groat of second issue, with two Shillings and
a Sixpence of James I., sold for 11s.

ELIZABETH.—CONTINUED.

In 1864, a Shilling, first issue, with a Shilling and Groat, second issue, all in fine condition, sold for 14s.

In 1873, a Shilling and Groat both 1561, and a Shilling without bust, the last two remarkably fine, sold for £4.

In 1881, a Shilling, Sixpence and Threepence, and a copper Penny, sold for 11s.

James I., 1603—1624.

SILVER.—Shilling and Sixpence ; two coinages, of 9oz. silver to 3oz. alloy.

Shilling, first coinage (about 70 grains).—1603.

Obv., IACOBVS . D . G . ANG . SCO . FRA . ET . HIB . REX., crowned bust to the right, m.m., bell or martlet; *rev.*, EXVRGAT . DEVS . DISSIPENTVR . INIMICI, the harp crowned, m.m., as on *obv.*

From 2s. 6d. to 5s.

Sixpence, first coinage (about 35 grains).

Similar to the Shilling, but *rev.* legend is TVEATVR . VNITA . DEVS.

From 1s. 6d. to 3s. 6d.

Shilling, second coinage (about 70 grains).—1604 to 1613.

Obv., IACOBVS . D . G . MAG . BRIT . FRA . ET . HIB . REX., same type as the preceding Shilling ; *rev.*, HENRICVS . ROSAS . REGNA . IACOBVS., same type as the preceding Shilling, m.m. rose, martlet, cinquefoil, or shell.

From 2s. to 3s.

Sixpence, second coinage (about 35 grains).

Similar to the second coinage Shilling, but *rev.* legend TVEATVR . VNITA . DEVS.

From 1s. 6d. to 2s. 6d.

COPPER.—Farthing. There is a Half-farthing of similar type, supposed to have been struck as a pattern.

Farthing (about 12 grains).—Issued in 1613.

Obv., IACO . D . G . MAG . BRI; *or* BRIT., two sceptres, in saltire, through a crown ; *rev.*, FRA . ET . HIB . REX., harp crowned (see Fig. 174), various m.m.

From 6d. to 1s.

Charles I., 1625—1649.

No regal money, except the copper Farthing, was coined in Ireland during this reign.

Siege Pieces were struck in gold, silver and copper.

COPPER.—Farthing.

Farthing (6 to 10 grains).—Struck in 1625.

Obv., CAROLVS . D . G . MAG . BRIT., two sceptres in saltire, through a crown, in an inner circle ; *rev.*, FRAN . ET . HIB . REX, harp crowned in an inner circle, various m.m.

Another variety has, on *obv.*, CARO . D . G . MAG . BRI .

CHARLES I.—CONTINUED.

COPPER.—*Continued.*

or BRIT., without the inner circle; *rev.*, FRA . ET . HIB . REX, no inner circle.

From 6d. to 1s.

The English Rose Farthing (described at page 35) was ordered to be struck in 1635 and to pass current equally in England and Ireland.

Irish Siege Pieces, or Money of Necessity.[*]

GOLD.—Pistole.

Dr. A. Smith, in the paper referred to below, observes that the fact of a coinage of gold having been issued in Ireland has only been established within the last few years, by the discovery of two or three pieces. These coins are stamped on each side, $4 : \text{dw}^{\text{tt.}}$ within a double circle which extends to the margin; $7 . \text{gr} :$ the inner circle is linear, the outer one beaded.

SILVER.—Inchiquin, Ormond, Kilkenny and Cork money.

Inchiquin money, 1642.—Crown, Half Crown, Shilling, Ninepence, Sixpence, Groat, and Threepence, of very irregular shapes.

Crown (464 grains).—Two varieties.

First.—An irregular polygon, having $19 : 8$ $^{\text{dw gr}}$ stamped in a circle, on both sides.

Specimens have realised £2 2s., £3, £3 14s., £5, and £7 12s. 6d.

A Crown (probably unique) on octagonal plate, stamped on both sides with the weight reversed, in an engrained circle, sold for £17 in 1881.

Second.—A nearly circular piece, having V.s. stamped on both sides.

£1, £2 16s., £3 11s., and £4 4s.

Half Crown (232 grains).—Two varieties.

First.—An irregular oblong, having $9 : 16.$ $^{\text{dw}^{\text{t}} \text{ g}}$ stamped, in a circle, on both sides.

£1 11s., £2 3s., £2 10s., £2 15s., £3, £3 5s., £5, and £5 10s.

Second.—An irregular oblong, having $\text{II} \ \text{VI}$ $^{\text{S} \quad \text{D}}$ in a circle, stamped on both sides.

£2, £2 18s., £3 1s., £3 8s., and £5.

A Crown and Half Crown, both first variety, £13; ditto, both second variety, £10 10s.

Shilling (93 grains).—An irregularly shaped piece.

Obv., in a circle, $3 : 21$, $^{\text{dw gr}}$ stamped on both sides.

---

[*] See Dr. A. Smith's "Money of Necessity issued in Ireland in the Reign of Charles the First," published in the Proceedings of the Kilkenny Archæological Society, vol. iii., new series, 1861.

IRISH SIEGE PIECES.—CONTINUED.

SILVER.—*Continued*.

£2 15s., £3 3s., £3 7s., £4 7s., £4 10s., £4 15s., £5 7s. 6d., and £6.

A Half Crown, first variety, and Shilling, sold together for £8 in 1881.

Ninepence (68 grains).—Two varieties.

First.—An irregularly shaped piece.

Obv. and rev., in a circle 2 : 20, stamped on both sides.

One sold for 17s. in 1859.

Second.—*Obv.*, as above; *rev.*, nine annulets within a circle.

One sold for £27 in 1854.

Sixpence (46 grains).—Two varieties.

First.—In a circle, 1 : 22, stamped on both sides.

Specimens have sold for £5, £5 2s. 6d., £9 2s. 6d., and £10 10s.

Second.—*Obv.*, as before; *rev.*, six large annulets.

One sold for £1 1s. in 1859.

A specimen, having obv. plain, and rev. six annulets, sold for £10 10s. in 1854.

Groat (30 grains).—Two varieties.

First.—In a beaded circle, 1 . 6, stamped on both sides.

A specimen sold for £5 2s. 6d. in 1859, and another for £8 12s. 6d. in 1881.

Second.—*Obv.*, like the preceding, but rev., four large annulets.

One sold for £10 15s. in 1854, and for £10 12s. 6d. in 1873.

Threepence (23 grains).—Obv., 23 in a beaded circle; rev., three large annulets.

Described by Lindsay as being perhaps unique, and valued at £2.

The only specimen known is in the British Museum.

Forgeries of the Crown, Half Crown, Shilling, Sixpence, and Fourpence, were manufactured in Dublin. They are very black, and were exposed to the fumes of burning sulphur for the purpose of giving them an antique appearance.

Ormond Money,[*] 1643.—Crown, Half Crown, Shilling, Sixpence, Groat, Threepence, and Twopence.[†]

This money was ordered, by royal proclamation, to be current coin of Ireland. (For type, see Fig. 150.)

Crown (449 to 464 grains). The exact weight should be 456 grains.

Obv., C . R. crowned, within a double circle, the outer one beaded; rev., V, in a double circle.

£1 5s., £2 3s., £3 1s., and £3 11s.

* See Dr. A. Smith's paper on "The Ormonde Money," published in the Proceedings of the Kilkenny Archæological Society, vol. iii., 1856.

† Simon and Lindsay both mention a Penny of this money, but no authentic specimen is known, and the Penny is not mentioned in the King's commission, which directed what denominations should be coined.

IRISH SIEGE PIECES.—CONTINUED.

SILVER.—*Continued.*

Half Crown (225 to 247 grains). The weight should be 228 grains.

Similar to the Crown, but II VI on *rev.*
From 15s. to £1 5s.; one sold for £1 15s. in 1854.

Shilling (82 to 88½ grains). The weight should be 91½ grains.

Similar, but XII on *rev.*
From 7s. 6d. to 15s.

Sixpence (40 to 45 grains). The weight should be 45½ grains.

Similar, but VI on *rev.* (See Fig. 150.)
From 3s. 6d. to 7s. 6d.

Groat (22 to 30½ grains). The weight should be 30½ grains.

Similar, but IIII on *rev.*
From 5s. to 10s.

Threepence (15 to 22½ grains). The weight should be 22½ grains.

Similar, but III on *rev.*
From 5s. to 7s. 6d.

Twopence (12½ to 15 grains). The weight should be 15½ grains.

Similar, but II on *rev.*
From 7s. 6d. to 12s. 6d.

Sets of the Ormond money have realised £2 3s., £2 6s., £2 14s., £3 4s., £4 15s., £5 4s., and £6 11s.

Kilkenny Money.—Crown and Half Crown, coined in imitation of the Ormond Money, and the Blacksmith's Half Crown.

Crown (353 grains).—Known as the Rebel Crown.

Obv., large cross in a plain circle, outside which is a beaded circle, and between the circles a small star opposite one arm of the cross; *rev.*, V within two circles, as on *obv.*

Specimens have realised £3 10s., £4 1s., £4 15s., £5 7s. 6d., £7 10s., £8 5s., and £10 10s.

Half Crown (176 grains).—The Rebel Half Crown.

Obv., large cross in a double circle; *rev.*, II. VI, in a double circle.

Specimens have sold for 12s., £5 15s., £6 2s. 6d., £6 5s., £10 10s., and £11 15s.

Blacksmith's Half Crown (211 to 231 grains).—Struck at Kilkenny, in November, 1642, by order of the Confederate Catholics, in imitation of the Tower Half Crown. Hawkins terms it the Blacksmith's Half Crown, on account of its extreme rudeness. The m.m. on *obv.* is a cross, and on *rev.* a harp.

Cork Money.—Shilling and Sixpence.

Shilling (69 to 75 grains).—An irregular octagon.

Obv., in a circle, CORK with 1647 under it, in the centre of the coin is a dot or point; *rev.*, in a circle XII.

£2 2s. and £3.

K 2

IRISH SIEGE PIECES.—CONTINUED.

SILVER.—*Continued.*

Sixpence (34 to 37 grains).

Obv., similar to the Shilling ; *rev.*, in a beaded circle, VI.
£1 12s., £1 15s., and £2 10s.

A Shilling and Sixpence, together, sold for £2 1s. in 1859.

A Shilling and two Sixpences sold for £7 5s. in 1881.

COPPER *and* BRASS.—Struck at Bandon, Cork, Dublin, Kilkenny,
Kinsale, and Youghal.

Bandon.—Copper (31 grains) of an irregular octagon
shape.

Obv., the letters B . B . (= Bandon Bridge, the ancient name
of the town of Bandon) within a circle of small lozenges ; *rev.*,
three castles, one above and two below, within a circle as on
obv.

Cork.—Pieces struck in brass were, it is supposed, coined
about the same time as the Cork Shilling and Sixpence.

First variety.—Circular piece (57½ grains).

Obv., the word CORKE under a crown ; *rev.*, without legend or
device.

Valued by Lindsay at 3s.

Second variety.—Square piece (40 grains).

Obv., the word CORK in a beaded circle; *rev.*, a rudely designed
castle in a circle of small lozenges.

Valued by Lindsay at 5s.

Dublin Money will be found described at the end of this
reign.

Kilkenny.—Copper Halfpence and Farthings were coined by
order of the Confederate Catholics (October, 1642), who adopted
the type and legends of the Copper Farthings of Charles I.,
issued in 1625. (See page 128.)

These pieces are very rudely and imperfectly struck.

Halfpenny (51 to 125 grains).—The standard weight was
90 grains.

Obv., CAROLVS (or CARO) . D . G . MAG . BRI., two
sceptres in saltire through a crown, surrounded by two beaded
circles; *rev.*, FRAN . ET . HIBER . REX., harp crowned
between C and R within a beaded circle.

Farthing.—The standard weight was 45 grains.

Type of the Halfpenny, legend CARO *or* CAR . D . G .
MAG . BRI, and FRA . ET . HIB . REX.

Value from 2s. 6d. to 3s. 6d.

Kinsale.—A square copper piece (44 to 55 grains).

Obv., the letters K . S. within a circle of pellets ; *rev.*,
a chequered shield, the arms of Kinsale, surrounded by
pellets.

Youghal.—There are several varieties of these pieces, two
of which are as follows :

First.—Square piece (56 grains).

Obv., Y . T ., with 1646 below, within a double circle ; *rev.*, a
ship with one mast within a double circle.

Valued by Lindsay at 3s.

IRISH SIEGE PIECES.—CONTINUED.

COPPER *and* BRASS.—*Continued.*

Second.—Square piece (14 grains).

Obv., the letters Y. T., with a bird above and 1646 below, all within a circle ; *rev.*, a ship within a circle.

Valued by Lindsay at 5s.

Dublin Money.—St. Patrick's Halfpenny and Farthing.*

Halfpenny (130 to 148 grains).

Obv., FLOREAT . REX, King David kneeling, playing on a harp, a crown over ; *rev.*, ECCE . GREX., St. Patrick standing with a crozier in his left hand, and trefoil in his right, which he holds extended over people standing before him, at his left side a shield bearing the arms of Dublin, three castles.

The crown over the harp is of a different metal to that of the coin, being brass upon copper or copper upon brass. (For *obv.*, see *obv.* of Fig. 172.)

From 2s. to 3s.

According to Simon ("Essay on Irish Coins"); specimens of the preceding Halfpenny were struck in silver, which, he supposed, the Kilkenny Assembly intended should pass for Shillings.

A proof in silver (unique) is now in the Royal Irish Academy.

Farthing (77 to 102 grains).

Obv., similar to the Halfpenny ; *rev.*, QVIESCAT . PLEBS., St. Patrick standing with crozier in his left hand, and his right extended over reptiles, a church behind. (See Fig. 172.)

From 6d. to 1s.

Commonwealth, 1649—1660.

COPPER.—Farthing (67 grains).

Obv., A . CORKE . FARTHING, shield, bearing St. George's cross, between two branches ; *rev.*, same legend, surrounding a harp.

Valued by Lindsay at 3s. 6d.

Lindsay described a similar piece, weighing only 13 grains, which he valued at 5s.

Charles II., 1660—1685.

SILVER.—Crown and Half Crown. Struck in Ireland previous to his Restoration.

Crown (427 grains).

Obv., CAR . II . D . G . MAG . BRIT., roses between the words, an imperial crown within a plain circle ; *rev.*, FRA . ET .

HYB . REX . F . D., &c., roses between the words, V̊ in a plain circle ; m.m. on both sides, a fleur-de-lis.

Specimens have sold for £1 11s., £3 4s., £3 7s., £3 15s., £4, £5 2s. 6d., £6 15s., £8 10s., and £17.

---

* Dr. Aquilla Smith, in his paper "On the Copper Coin commonly called St. Patrick's" (Kilkenny Archæological Society's Transactions, vol. iii., 1850), gives it as his opinion that the St. Patrick's were issued in Dublin some time between the Restoration and the year 1680, when regal copper Halfpence were coined for Ireland.

CHARLES II.—CONTINUED.

SILVER.—*Continued.*
Half Crown (219 grains).
Obv., similar to the Crown, but a fleur-de-lis or a quatrefoil
between the words; *rev.*, same as the Crown, but II . VI within
the circle.   Simon's figure of this piece has nothing between the
words.
Specimens have realised £3 3s., £3 15s., £4, £5 5s., £5 10s.,
and £13.
COPPER.—Halfpenny and Farthing.
Halfpenny (105 to 119 grains).—Dated 1680 to 1684.
Obv., CAROLVS . II . DEI . GRATIA., the King's bust
laureate to the right; *rev.*, MAG . BR . FRA . ET . HIB .
REX., a harp crowned between the date, as 16—80.
From 1s. to 2s.
Farthing (22 to 28 grains).—Struck in 1660.
Obv., CAROLVS . II . D . G . M . B., two sceptres in
saltire through a crown; *rev.*, FRA . ET . HIB . REX., a
harp crowned, m.m. fleur-de-lis.
From 1s. to 2s.

James II.,* 1685—1688.

SILVER.—None.
COPPER.—Halfpenny (101 to 130 grains).   Dated 1685 to 1688.
Obv., IACOBVS . II . DEI . GRATIA, bust laureate to the
left; *rev.*, MAG . BR . FRA . ET . HIB . REX., harp crowned
between the date, as 16—85.
From 1s. to 2s.
GUN MONEY.†—Crown, Half Crown, Shilling, and Sixpence, 1689
and 1690.
Crown (159 to 245 grains).—Dated 1690.
Obv., IAC . II . DEI . GRA . MAG . BRI . FRA . ET . HIB .
REX., the King in armour, on horseback, riding to the left,
head bare but laureated, sword drawn; *rev.*, CHRISTO .
VICTORE . TRIVMPHO, a large crown in the centre, the arms
of England, Scotland, France, and Ireland, each in a crowned
shield, arranged crosswise, the English arms between ANO and
DOM, and the French arms dividing the date 16—90.   (See
Fig. 202.)
The Crowns exhibit no variation of type or legend, but differ
greatly in weight.
From 1s. to 2s. 6d.
Half Crown.—Two issues, dated 1689 and 1690, the first
being the heavier.
Obv., IACOBVS . II . DEI . GRATIA, laureate bust to the
left; *rev.*, MAG . BR . FRA . ET . HIB . REX., two sceptres

---

* See Dr. A. Smith's paper on the Money of Necessity issued in Ireland in the reign of
James the Second.—*Numismatic Chronicle*, vol. x., 1870.
† Made from old brass guns, broken bells, old copper, brass and pewter; worth from 3d.
to 4d. the lb., but ordered to pass current for from £5 to £10 sterling the pound weight.

JAMES II.—CONTINUED.

GUN MONEY.—*Continued.*

in saltire, through a crown, between I and R, XXX above the crown, the date being above the XXX, below the crown the name of the month in which the piece was issued. (See Fig. 199.)

The following dates occur:

Large Half Crown (115 to 259 grains): 1689, July, August, ditto (date under crown), September, October, 8ber, November, December, January, February, and March; 1690, March, April, and May. None of June, 1689.

Small Half Crown (104 to 196 grains): 1690, April, May, June, July, August, September, and October.

From 1s. to 1s. 6d.

Shilling.—Two issues, the first being the heavier, dated 1689 and 1690.

Rev., similar to the Half Crown (Fig. 199), but XII above the crown instead of XXX. The *obv.* is similar to the *obv.* of Fig. 201.

Large Shilling (72 to 122 grains).—Dated for every month of 1689, except April and May; also dated 8ber, 9r, and 10r: a variety of 9r has a castle below the bust. Dated 1690, March and April.

Small Shilling (66 to 105 grains).—Dated 1690, April, May, June, July, August, and September.

From 6d. to 1s.

Sixpence (44 to 65 grains).—Dated 1689 and 1690.

Similar to the Shilling, but VI above the crown in place of XII.

Dated 1689, June, July, August, September, 7ber, October, November, December, January, February, and March; also 1690, March, April, May, and June.

From 1s. to 2s.

In 1864, a fine collection of Gun Money, comprising fifteen Crowns, twenty-six Half Crowns, fifty-eight Shillings, and eighteen Sixpences, all, with few exceptions, very fine, sold for £5 5s.

Proofs of the Gun Money were struck in gold and silver, and examples are in the British Museum and in private collections.

The following prices have been realised:

Proofs in Gold:

Crown, £15 10s.

Half Crown, £3 15s.

Shilling, £1 10s. and £6 10s.

Sixpence, 18s.

Proofs in Silver:

Crown, £3 3s., £4 6s., £5 10s., and £9 2s. 6d.

Half Crown, £3 10s.

Crown and Half Crown together, 11s. in 1859.

Shilling and Sixpence together, £1 11s. and £2 8s.

Sixpence, 6s.

JAMES II.—CONTINUED.

GUN MONEY.—*Proofs in Silver, continued.*

Crown, Half Crown, and Shilling, £9 15s. (1880).

Crown, Half Crown, and three Shillings, £5 15s. (1881).

Half Crown, Two Shillings, and a Sixpence, £2 4s. (1854).

Half Crown, Shilling, and Sixpence, £1 13s. (1864).

Shilling, three Sixpences, and a copper Sixpence, £3 10s. (1881).

WHITE METAL.*—*Groat,* 1689.

Groat (51 grains).—Size of the Gun Money Sixpence.

Obv., IACOBVS . II . DEI . GRATIA, laureate bust to the left; *rev.,* MAG . BR . FRA . ET. HIB . REX, 1689, harp crowned between II—IL

Valued by Lindsay at 15s.

PEWTER.—Crown (two varieties), Penny (two varieties), and Halfpenny (three varieties).

Crown (346 grains), first variety.—Dated 1689.

Obv., the King in armour on horseback to the left, head bare, laureated, in his right hand a drawn sword erect, legend IACOBVS . II . DEI . GRATIA, in large letters, a small circular piece of Prince's metal is inserted in the fore and hind quarters of the horse; *rev.,* MAG . BR . FRA . ET . HIB . REX, 1689, in the centre a piece of Prince's metal, on which is stamped a large crown.

This coin is in the British Museum, and seems to be a pattern for a Crown piece.

Crown (281 grains), second variety.—Dated 1690.

Similar to the Gun Money Crown (Fig. 202), but on the edge the legend MELIORIS . TESSERA . FATI . ANNO . REGNI . SEXTO.

Specimens have sold for £1 16s., £1 19s., £3 1s., £3 13s. 6d., £4 15s., £5 15s. 6d., £6 16s. 6d., and £13 15s.

Penny (107 to 130 grains), first variety (size of the large Gun Money Shilling).—Dated 1689 and 1690.

Obv., similar to the Gun Money Shilling; *rev.,* MAG . BR . FRA . ET . HIB . REX, 1689., harp crowned, a piece of Prince's metal in the centre. (Similar to Fig. 201.)

From 5s. to 10s.

Penny (95 grains), second variety.—Dated 1690.

Obv., like *obv.* of Fig. 160, but 1^D behind the head; *rev.,* MAG . BR . FRA . ET . HIB . REX., harp crowned between 16—90., piece of Prince's metal in the centre.

From 5s. to 10s. One sold for £2 1s. in 1859.

Halfpenny (72 grains), first variety.—Dated 1689 and 1690.

Similar to the Penny, first variety, except that the King's hair is short.

From 3s. to 7s.

Halfpenny (71¼ grains), second variety.—Dated 1690.

Obv., IACOBVS . II . DEI . GRATIA., small bust to left,

---

* See Dr. A. Smith's paper on the "Irish Pewter Coins of James II.," in the Proceedings of the Kilkenny Archæological Society, vol. iii., 18.6.

JAMES II.—CONTINUED.

PEWTER.—*Continued.*

with short hair, a small ornament under the bust; *rev.*, legend as on first variety Penny, but the date is divided by the Crown, 16—90.

From 3s. to 7s.

Halfpenny, third variety.—Probably struck at Limerick.

Obv., IACOBVS . II . DEI . GRATIA., the King on horseback, riding to the left, wearing a hat, and with drawn sword, two specks of brass upon the horse; *rev.*, MAG . BR . FRA . ET . HIB . REX . 1689, two sceptres in saltire through a crown of brass, a lion over the crown, a harp under, the word HALF to the left of the crown, and PENNY to the right. (See Fig. 200.)

Valued by Lindsay at £1, but no specimen is now known in any public or private collection.

BRASS.—Halfpenny, two varieties.

Halfpenny, first variety.—Dated 1690 (see Fig. 201).

From 2s. to 3s.

Halfpenny, second variety (about 87 grains).—Dated 1691. Struck at Limerick, and called a HIBERNIA.

Obv., similar to *obv.* of Fig. 201, but the bust clothed; *rev.*, HIBERNIA . 1691, the figure of Hibernia seated, the right hand upraised holding a cross, the left arm leaning upon a harp.

Some of the former Gun Money Shillings were re-stamped with the above designs.

From 6d. to 1s.

William and Mary, 1689—1694.

COPPER.—Halfpenny, dated 1690 to 1694.

Halfpenny (106 to 116 grains).

Obv., GVLIELMVS . ET . MARIA . DEI . GRATIA., busts of the King and Queen to the right; *rev.*, MAG . BR . FR . ET . HIB . REX . ET . REGINA., harp crowned, date divided by the crown, thus 16—90.

From 6d. to 1s. 6d.

William III., 1694—1702.

COPPER.—Halfpenny (106 to 116 grains), dated 1695 and 1696.

Obv., GVLIELMVS . III . DEI . GRA., bust laureate to the right; *rev.*, MAG . BR . FRA . ET . HIB . REX., harp, crowned, dividing the date, thus 16—95. On some pieces the bust is bare; on others it is in armour.

From 1s. to 2s.

Anne, 1702—1714.

No Irish money was struck in this reign.

George I., 1714—1727.

COPPER.—Halfpenny, two varieties, and Farthing.

Halfpenny, first variety (108 grains).—Dated 1722.

Obv., GEORGIUS . DEI . GRATIA . REX., laureated bust
to the right; *rev.,* as Fig. 176.

From 1s. to 2s.

Halfpenny, second variety (96 to 120 grains).—Dated 1722,
1723, and 1724.

Obv., as first variety ; *rev.,* as Fig. 177.

From 6d. to 1s. 6d.

Farthing (about 59 grains).—Dated 1723 and 1724.

Similar to the preceding Halfpenny.

From 1s. to 1s. 6d.

A pattern Halfpenny is represented by Fig. 175.—Dated 1722
and 1723.

George II., 1727—1760.

COPPER.—Halfpenny and Farthing, two varieties, with young and
with old head.

Halfpenny (about 134 grains).— Dated, with young head,
1736, 1737, 1738, 1741 1742, 1743, 1744, 1746, 1747, 1748,
1749, 1750, 1751, 1752, 1753, and 1755 ; and, with old head,
1760.

Obv., GEORGIUS . II . REX., laureate bust to the left;
rev., HIBERNIA and date, a harp crowned.   (See Fig. 173.)

The omission of DEI GRATIA from these coins caused much
comment at the time.

From 6d. to 1s. 6d.

Farthing (64 to 71 grains).—Dated, with young head, 1737,
1738, and 1744, and, with old head, 1760.

Similar to the Halfpenny.

From 6d. to 1s. 6d.

NOTE.—In all the above coins the name is spelt GEORGIUS,
from 1736 to 1746 inclusive, after that date GEORGIVS.

VOCE POPULI* Halfpenny and Farthing, dated 1760.

Halfpenny (about 109 grains).—Dated 1760.

Obv., laureate bust (supposed to be that of the young Pre-
tender) to right, surrounded by VOCE . POPULI ; *rev.,* female
seated, looking to the left, a harp at her left side, legend
HIBERNIA, the date 1760 in exergue.

One variety has the letter P (supposed to stand for *Princeps*)
in front of the face, another has P under the bust, and a third
variety has P on the *rev.*

From 6d. to 1s.

Farthing (about 55 grains).—Dated 1760.

Similar to the Halfpenny.

From 1s. to 1s. 6d.

---

* Some account of the Voce Populi money is contained in Dr. Aquilla Smith's paper, "On
Copper Tokens issued in Ireland from 1728 to 1761," published in the Kilkenny Archæological Society's Transactions, third series, vol. i., p. 417.

George III., 1760—1820.

SILVER.—Bank of Ireland Tokens for Six Shillings, Thirty Pence, Ten Pence, and Five Pence, Irish.

Six Shilling Token (415 grains).—Dated 1804.

Obv., GEORGIUS . III . DEI . GRATIA . REX., laureated bust in armour to right; *rev.*, BANK OF IRELAND TOKEN. SIX SHILLINGS.—1804., Hibernia seated, looking to the left, with a palm-branch in her right hand, and the left leaning on a harp. (See Fig. 151.)

From 6s. to 10s.

Thirty Pence Token (192 grains).—Dated 1808.

Obv., legend and bust as on the first variety Ten Pence, with date 1808; *rev.*, type as the Six Shilling piece, with legend BANK TOKEN encircling Hibernia, XXX PENCE IRISH in exergue.

From 3s. 6d. to 4s. 6d.

Ten Pence Token.—Two varieties.

First variety (64 grains).—Dated 1805, and 1806.

Obv., GEORGIVS . III . DEI . GRATIA, laureated bust in armour to right; *rev.*, across the field in six lines BANK TOKEN TEN PENCE IRISH. 1805., edge milled.

From 1s. 6d. to 2s.

Second variety (55 grains).—Dated 1813.

Obv., GEORGIUS . III . DEI . GRATIA . REX., bust to right; *rev.*, in a wreath of shamrock, BANK TOKEN 10 PENCE IRISH 1813, in five lines, across the field, edge plain.

From 1s. 6d. to 2s.

Five Pence Token (32 grains).—Dated 1805 and 1806.

Obv., similar to the Tenpence of same date; *rev.*, BANK TOKEN FIVE PENCE IRISH 1805., in six lines across the field, edge milled.

From 1s. 6d. to 2s. 6d.

COPPER.—Penny, Halfpenny, and Farthing.

Penny (266 grains).

Obv., GEORGIUS . III . D . G . REX., bust to right; *rev.*, HIBERNIA, harp crowned, 1805.

From 1s. to 2s.

Halfpenny.—Two varieties.

First variety (81 to 156 grains).—Dated 1766, 1769, 1775, 1776, 1781, 1782, and 1783.

Obv., GEORGIVS . III . REX, bust to right; *rev.*, HIBERNIA and date, harp crowned.

From 1775 inclusive the name is spelt GEORGIUS.

From 9d. to 1s. 6d.

Second variety (134 grains).—Dated 1805.

Similar to the Penny.

From 6d. to 1s.

Farthing (67 grains).—Dated 1805 and 1806.

Similar to the Halfpenny.

From 6d. to 1s.

Pattern Pence and Halfpence were also struck, differing from the above.

George IV., 1820—1830.

SILVER.—None.

COPPER.—Penny and Halfpenny, dated 1822 and 1823.   A Farthing, dated 1822, was struck as a pattern.

Penny (261 to 266 grains).

Obv., GEORGIUS . IV . D . G . REX., laureated bust to left; *rev.*, HIBERNIA, 1822 *or* 1823, harp crowned.

From 2s. to 2s. 6d.

Halfpenny (128 to 130 grains).

Similar to the Penny.

From 2s. to 3s.

This coinage is the last of the Irish series, the currency of Ireland having been subsequently assimilated to that of Great Britain.

COINS OF THE ISLE OF MAN.

In 1406, King Henry IV. bestowed upon Sir John de Standley, or Stanley, the dominion of the Isle of Man, to be held of the Crown of England, on the presentation of a cast of falcons to the King at his coronation. After James, the seventh earl (celebrated in history as "the great Earl" of Derby), had been executed for bringing aid to King Charles II. before the battle of Worcester, the Island was granted to General Lord Fairfax, who held it until the Restoration, when, in 1660, it was restored to Charles, the eighth earl, son of Earl James. James, the tenth earl, dying without issue in 1736, the lordship of Man devolved upon James, second Duke of Athol, a descendant of the Lady Amelia Stanley, youngest daughter of the seventh Earl of Derby.

With a view to put an end to the contraband trade of the Island, its sovereignty and revenues were surrendered to the Crown in 1765 by the Duke of Athol, in consideration of the sum of £70,000.

The earliest coin issued in the Island was the token described below. A description of tokens does not come within the scope of this book, but this piece is mentioned because, by an Act of the House of Keys, it was ordered to be current as a legal tender in the Island.

Copper money only was coined for the Isle of Man, but proofs of some of the pieces, and a few patterns, were struck in silver.

John Murrey, 1668.

COPPER.—*Penny.*

> *Obv.*, IOHN MVRREY ∴ 1668 as a legend round the words HIS . PENNY . I M., in three lines across the field; *rev.*, the Triune, or three legs (the feet pointing to the left), encircled by the legend QVOCVNQVE . GESSERES : STABIT.

> This piece is very small, the diameter being the same as that of a current Farthing of the present year.

The Earl of Derby, 1705—1733.

SILVER.—*Pattern Piece* (220 grains).—1705, struck in silver, 1⅜in. in diameter.

> *Obv.*, the Stanley or Derby crest (eagle and child) under which is the Cap of Maintenance, and above the crest is the motto SANS . CHANGER; *rev.*, the Triune (feet pointing to the right), surrounded by QUOCUNQUE . GESSERIS . STABIT. The edge is engrailed. (For type, see Fig. 183.)

THE EARL OF DERBY.—CONTINUED.

COPPER.—*Penny* and *Halfpenny*, 1709.

Penny.—Obv., the Stanley or Derby crest (eagle and child), under which is the Cap of Maintenance, and above the crest the motto SANS . CHANGER ; *rev.*, the Triune (feet pointing to the left), surrounded by QVOCVNQVE . GESSERIS . STABIT.

From 2s. to 5s.

Halfpenny (80 grains).

Of similar type to the Penny.

From 3s. to 8s.

These coins are of very rude execution, and were *cast*, not struck. On some pieces the date seems to be 1700, but this is owing to the incompleteness of the cast diminishing the 9 to a cipher.

Penny and *Halfpenny*, 1723.

Obv., the Stanley crest and motto; *rev.*, the Triune (the feet pointing to the right), and motto QVOCVNQUE GESSERIS STABIT.

Value 10s. to 15s.

These were struck as patterns. The Halfpenny also occurs in silver. They were never legalised as coins, consequently never circulated as such.

Penny, 1724.—A pattern, supposed to be unique.

Almost similar to the Penny of 1723.

Penny, 1732.—A pattern.

Obv., the Stanley crest in high relief, the date divided, 17 being at the head of the child and 32 at the feet, a small branch, with six or eight leaves, at the head of the cradle ; *rev.*, QUOCUNQUE IECERIS STABIT, between the limbs the initials I and D (for Jacobus Darbiensis, James, the tenth Earl) and the figure 1 denoting one Penny. The feet of the Triune point to the left.

Penny and *Halfpenny*, 1733.

Obv., the Stanley crest and motto, the date (not divided) below the Cap of Maintenance ; *rev.*, the Triune, the feet pointing to the right, QUOCUNQUE . IECERIS . STABIT., the initials I and D and figure for value (1 for One Penny and ½ for a Halfpenny) between the limbs. (See Fig. 183.)

The Penny (142 grains) is the size of the English Halfpenny, and the Halfpenny (85 grains) is the size of the English Farthing.

From 2s. to 5s.

Proofs of these pieces were also struck in silver.

The Duke of Athol, 1758.

COPPER.—Penny and Halfpenny.

Penny (172 grains).

Obv., the monogram A D (Athol Dux) surmounted by a ducal coronet, the date 1758 below the monogram, no legend ; *rev.*, the Triune, feet pointing to the right, without initials or numeral, legend QUOCUNQUE . JECERIS . STABIT. Edge plain. A proof in silver has the edge milled. (See Fig. 184.)

THE DUKE OF ATHOL.—CONTINUED.

COPPER.—*Continued.*
Halfpenny (117 grains).
Similar to the Penny.
Value, 2s. 6d. to 5s.
Forgeries of this Penny and Halfpenny are not uncommon.

George III., 1786—1813.

COPPER.—Penny and Halfpenny.   Three issues : 1786, 1798, and 1813.
Penny (246 grains), 1786.
Obv., the King's head, laureate, to right, GEORGIVS III.
DEI GRATIA., 1786 below the bust; *rev.*, the Triune, feet
pointing to left, QVOCVNQVE IECERIS STABIT. Edge
milled with diagonal lines.
Halfpenny (125 grains), 1786.
Similar to the Penny.
Value 2s. 6d. to 5s.
Penny (330 grains), 1798.
Obv., almost similar to the English Penny of 1797, the King's
head, laureate, to right, legend and date incuse, GEORGIVS III .
D: G . REX, 1798; *rev.*, the Triune, legend incuse, QVO-
CVNQVE IECERIS STABIT.
Halfpenny (167 grains), 1798.
Similar to the Penny, except that the name is spelt GEORGIUS.
Value 2s. to 3s. 6d.
Penny (312 grains), 1813.
Similar, except the date, to the Penny of 1798.
Halfpenny (155 grains), 1813.
Similar to the Penny, the name spelt GEORGIVS as on the
Penny.
Value 2s. to 3s. 6d.

George IV.

No regal money was issued specially for the Isle of Man.

William IV.

No regal money was issued for the Isle of Man.

Victoria, 1839.

COPPER.—Penny, Halfpenny, and Farthing.
Penny (291 grains).
Obv., the Queen's bust to left, legend VICTORIA DEI
GRATIA, date 1839 below the bust; *rev.*, the Triune, feet
pointing to left, QVOCVNQVE IECERIS STABIT.
Halfpenny (145 grains).
Similar to the Penny.
Farthing (72 grains).
Similar to the Penny.
The first and only issue of a Farthing in the Isle of Man.
Set of the three pieces, 2s. 6d. to 5s.

VICTORIA.—CONTINUED.

COPPER.—*Continued.*

In 1840 all coins but those of English type and coinage were suppressed by Act of Parliament.

Mixed lots of these coins have sold as under :

In 1854, Pence and Halfpence dated 1723, 1733, 1758, and 1786 (nine coins, all very fine), sold for 13s. ; and eight others, all fine proofs, dated 1786, 1798, 1813, and 1839, realised 13s.

In 1864, a set of sixteen copper coins, from 1709 to 1839, including a proof Halfpenny of 1786, all fine, sold for £1 2s.

COINS OF BRITISH COLONIES AND DEPENDENCIES.

As supplementary to the preceding pages, a short account of some of the above-named coins may be useful to collectors. Only a limited number of coins are mentioned, as a complete descriptive list would fill a large volume.

AFRICA.

Sierra Leone Company.

SILVER.—Dollar, and pieces of Fifty, Twenty, and Ten Cents. Dated 1791.

Dollar.—*Obv.*, SIERRA LEONE COMPANY, a lion, in the exergue AFRICA (as *obv.* of Fig. 178) ; *rev.*, as *rev.* of Fig. 178, but the word DOLLAR instead of PENNY. The other pieces are similar, with the requisite verbal alterations on *rev.*

COPPER.—Penny and Cent. Dated 1791.

Penny.—*Obv.* and *rev.* as Fig. 178.

Cent.—Smaller than the Penny, but of similar type, the word CENT being substituted for PENNY.

A fine proof set of the above six coins, £1 1s.

AMERICA.

Carolina.

COPPER.—*Halfpenny.*

Obv., an elephant, no legend ; *rev.*, in six lines, GOD PRE-SERVE CAROLINA : AND THE : LORDS : PROPRIETORS 1694. (See Fig. 179.)

One sold for £4 8s. in 1859, and one for £4 7s. in 1864.

Maryland.

Money struck by Cecil, Lord Baltimore, as Proprietor of Maryland, to whom the Province was granted by a Charter dated 20th June, 1632.

SILVER.—Shilling, Sixpence, and Groat.

Shilling (76 grains).—*Obv.* + CÆCILIVS : DNS : TERRÆ-MARIÆ &CT., profile bust to left, with head bare ; *rev.* + CRESCITE : ET : MVLTIPLICAMINI, arms of Lord Baltimore under a crown, with X to left and II. to right, for XII, the value. (See Fig. 153.)

A specimen sold for £4 1s. in 1859.

Sixpence (40 grains).—Similar to the Shilling, excepting V-I. on *rev.* for value.

One sold for £4 4s. in 1859.

L

MARYLAND.—CONTINUED.

SILVER.—*Continued.*

Groat (26 grains).—Similar, but I-V. for value on *rev.*
One sold for £4 18s. in 1859.
Sets of the three coins sold for £11 5s. in 1854, £5 5s. in 1864.
and £12 in 1882.
The Shilling and Sixpence together sold for £3 13s. and £4 6s.
The Shilling and Fourpence together realised £4 6s. in 1876.

COPPER.—*Penny,* believed to be unique.

Obv., almost similar to the Silver Coins; *rev.* + DENARIVM :
TERRÆ-MARIÆ : &c., two flags issuing out of a ducal coronet
the crest of Lord Baltimore (see Fig. 180).
Sold in London in 1859 for £75, and in New York in 1882
for 370 dollars. This coin is in the collection of Mr. L. G.
Parmelee of Boston.

Massachusetts.

SILVER.—Shilling, Sixpence, Threepence, and Twopence, struck at
Boston.

Shilling (72 grains).—1652.

Obv., MASATHVSETS IN, The American pine or oak; *rev.,*
NEW ENGLAND AN DOM , in the centre 1652, with XII
below it.
From 15s. to £1. Specimens have sold for 8s., 15s., 21s.,
23s., and 25s.

Sixpence (36 grains).—1652.

Obv., almost similar to the Shilling, but a different tree;
rev., NEW ENGLAND ANO, with 1652 and VI in the centre.
(See Fig. 152.)
From 10s. to £1.

Threepence (18 grains).—1652.

Obv., MASATHVSETS, a pine tree; *rev.,* NEW ENGLAND,
in centre 1652, III.
From 10s. to £1.

Twopence (12 grains).
Similar to above, but II on *rev.*
From 10s. to £1.
Sets of the four pieces have sold for £2, £2 6s., and £2 16s.
A Shilling, Sixpence, and Threepence sold together for £1 10s.,
and Two Shillings (varied), Sixpence, and Threepence, £4.

New England.

SILVER.—Shilling and Sixpence, struck about 1650.

Shilling (72 grains).—A circular piece, quite plain, except
that close to the edge are the letters NE on the *obv.,* and XII,
for value, on the *rev.*
Specimens have sold for £2 4s., £2 6s., and £3 3s.

Sixpence (36 grains).
Similar to the Shilling, but with VI for value on the *rev.*
Specimens have sold for £4 and £6 6s.

NEW ENGLAND.—CONTINUED.

COPPER.—*Halfpenny.*
> *Obv.*, like *obv.* of Fig. 179 ; *rev.*, in five lines, GOD : PRESERVE NEW ENGLAND. 1694.
> One sold for £15 15s. in 1859.

Rosa Americana.

GEORGE I.

BATH METAL.—Twopence, Penny, and Halfpenny (or more correctly, Penny, Halfpenny, and Farthing). Struck in 1722 and 1723, of a mixed metal resembling brass, known as Bath metal.
> First type.—The Rose, not crowned.
> *Twopence* (otherwise Penny).
> *Obv.*, laureate bust of King George I. to right. GEORGIVS. D : G : MAG : BRI : FRA : ET : HIB : REX; *rev.*, a large Rose, uncrowned, with ROSA AMERICANA. above it, and UTILE DULCI, on a label below. (See Fig. 203.) A rare variety has UTILE DULCI, without a label.
> *Penny* (otherwise Halfpenny).
> *Obv.*, as the preceding coin ; *rev.*, as Fig. 203, but with date, 1722, after ROSA AMERICANA, and UTILE DULCI, not on a label.
> A very fine specimen, £1 5s.
> *Halfpenny* (otherwise Farthing).
> Same type and date as the preceding coin.
> A fine set of the three coins sold for £3 11s. in 1864.
> Second type.—The Rose, crowned as on Fig. 205, and dated 1723.
> The three pieces have *obv.*, the King's bust laureated to right, GEORGIUS . DEI : GRATIA . REX .; *rev.*, as Fig. 205.
> A fine set of the three coins sold for £3 3s. in 1864.

GEORGE II.
> A large piece, supposed to be a unique pattern, has *obv.*, GEORGIVS . II . D . G . REX., laureated bust to left, and *rev.* as Fig. 204.

Barbadoes.

COPPER.—Penny and Halfpenny.
> *Penny.*—Two varieties.
> First variety (½oz.), 1788.—*Obv.*, as *obv.* of Fig. 179 ; *rev.*, BARBADOES PENNY . 1788. A pineapple in the centre.
> It is stated that 5376 were struck.
> Second variety, 1792. (See Fig. 181.)
> *Halfpenny.*—Similar.
> Weight.—Thirty-nine pennies to 16oz. of copper, 39,000 were coined ; seventy-eight halfpennies to 16oz. of copper, 46,800 were coined.

Bermuda.

COPPER.—*Halfpenny*, 1793.
> *Obv.*, GEORGIVS . III . D . G . REX: the King's laureated bust to right; *rev.*, a man-of-war in full sail to the left, above the ship BERMVDA, dated in exergue 1793. (See Fig. 182.)

L 2

THE EAST INDIES.

Elizabeth, 1600.

The earliest coins struck by an English Sovereign for currency in India were authorised by Queen Elizabeth, in January, 1600. The Queen, when she incorporated the East India Company, would not permit it to transport Spanish coin to India, and determined to strike money for circulation in Asia, bearing her name and Royal Arms, in order that the Asiatics might respect her name and know her to be as great a Sovereign as the King of Spain.

The weight of this coinage was regulated by the weight of the Spanish piece of eight reals, and its half, quarter, and eighth. The pieces are now known as the Portcullis Money.

SILVER.—Crown, Half Crown, Shilling, and Sixpence.

Portcullis Crown (425 grains).

Obv., O : ELIZABETH . D : G : ANG : FRA : ET . HIBER : REGINA : the Royal Arms crowned, between E and R, also crowned ; *rev.,* O : POSVI, &c., a large portcullis, crowned. The O at beginning of legend on both sides is the Mint mark, and indicates 1600, the date of the coin. (For type, see Fig. 154.)

Specimens have sold for £1 17s., £4 7s., £4 11s., £4 14s., £5 5s., £6 17s. 6d., £9 2s. 6d., £9 7s. 6d., £10, and £12.

Portcullis Half Crown (210gr.).

Similar to the crown. (See Fig. 154.)

Specimens have realised £1 8s., £4 5s., £4 10s., £6 17s. 6d., and £9.

Portcullis Shilling (109gr.).

Similar to the crown.

Specimens have sold for £1 12s., £1 14s., £3 19s., and £9 5s.

Portcullis Sixpence (53gr.).

Similar to the crown.

Specimens have realised £2 3s., £3 5s., £3 17s. 6d., £4 6s., and £4 12s.

A set of the four coins sold for £12 2s. 6d. in 1864.

Charles II.

SILVER.—Rupee, Half Rupee, Fanam, and Half Fanam.

Rupee.—Bombay, 1678.

Obv., THE RVPEE OF BOMBAIM, in three lines across the field, encircled by the legend BY AVTHORITY OF CHARLES THE SECOND 1678 (see Fig. 155) ; *rev.,* Royal arms, crowned, surrounded by the legend KING OF GREAT BRITAIN FRANCE AND IRELAND.

Specimens have sold for £2 15s., £4, and £5 2s. 6d.

Rupee.—Bombay, without date.

Obv., PAX DEO in two lines, encircled by the legend MONETA : BOMBAIENSIS ; *rev.,* the Arms of the East India Company on a shield, surrounded by four branches. (See Fig. 156.)

Specimens have sold for £2 14s. and £3.

CHARLES II.—CONTINUED.

SILVER.—*Continued.*

Half Rupee.—Similar to above.

The above Rupee and Half Rupee sold together for £3 6s. in 1876.

Rupee.—Bombay.

Obv., HON : SOC : ANG : IND : ORI surrounding a shield containing the arms of the East India Company; *rev.*, MON : BOMBAY ANGLIC REGIMS A° 7°, in five lines across the field, encircled by the legend A : DEO : PAX : & INCREMENTVM : (See Fig. 157.)

Specimens have realised £2 16s. and £6 10s.

Fanam.—Bombay.

Obv., two linked C's with three pellets; *rev.*, an Indian figure. (See Fig. 158.)

Half Fanam.—Similar to above, but smaller.

A Half Rupee, Fanam, and Half Fanam, sold together for £3 in 1876.

COPPER.—*Pice.*

Obv., HON : SOC : ANG : IND : ORI, surrounding the inscription (in five lines) MOET BOMBAY ANGLIC REGIM A° 9°; *rev.*, the arms, as in *obv.* of Fig. 157, encircled with the motto A : DEO : PAX : INCREMENTVM.

James II.

SILVER.—*Rupee.* Bombay, 1687.

Type similar to Fig. 156, but with date, 1687, on *obv.*

A specimen sold for £5 5s. in 1859.

George II.

COPPER.—*Pice.* Bombay.

Obv., a large crown, with G. R. above and BOMB. below; *rev.*, AVSPICIO REGIS ET SENATVS ANGLIÆ. 1728.

George III.

SILVER.—Half Pagoda and Half Dollar.

Half Pagoda.—Madras, 1808.

Obv., HALF PAGODA, &c. In the centre a Pagoda (see Fig. 159); *rev.*, inscription as on *obv.* in Tamil and Telugu characters.

Half Dollar, or *Two-Sookoo Piece,* for Fort Marlborough.

Obv., 2 FORT MARLBRO 1784, in four lines across the field; *rev.*, an inscription in Persian characters.

A specimen sold for £1 2s. in 1859.

COPPER.—*Two Kapangs.* Sumatra.

Obv., UNITED EAST INDIA COMPANY . 1787 . , in centre the arms of the Company ; *rev.*, in Persian characters, Do (*i.e.*, Two) Kapang, with Mohammedan date below. (See Fig. 185.)

Note.—400 Kapangs=1 Dollar.

GEORGE III.—CONTINUED.

  COPPER.—*Continued.*

Pieces of XX, X, V, and I Cash.

Twenty Cash, for Penang or Prince of Wales' Island.

Obv., Arms of the East India Company, with date 1810 ; *rev.,* Pulo Penang. (See Fig. 186.)

Twenty Cash, for Madras, 1803.

Obv., Arms of East India Company, 1803 ; *rev.* (see Fig. 187).

Pieces of Ten and *Five Cash* are similar to the preceding coin, but proportionately smaller, and with value X or V, instead of XX.

One Cash, for Madras, 1803.

Obv., the Company's crest, under it 1803 ; *rev.,* I cash. (See Fig. 188.)

Ceylon.

  SILVER.—*Rupee* (?)

Obv., An elephant, beneath 1809 ; *rev.,* CEYLON GOVERN-MENT, in the centre $\frac{96}{\text{ST}}$.

  COPPER.—Piece of 48 to a Rupee ; also Double Stiver, Stiver, and Half Stiver.

Piece of 48 *to One Rupee.*—1802.

Obv., an elephant, beneath 1802 ; *rev.,* CEYLON GOVERN-MENT, in the centre 48.

Stiver.—1815.

Obv., GEORGIUS III D : G : BRITANNIARUM REX, laureate bust to right ; *rev.,* as Fig. 189.

The Double Stiver and Half Stiver are of similar type and proportionate size. The three pieces correspond with the English Penny, Halfpenny, and Farthing.

APPENDIX.

ENGLISH JUBILEE COINAGE, 1887.

Victoria.

GOLD.—*Five Pound Piece.*—*Obv.*, bust to left, wearing arched crown; head draped: VICTORIA D : G : BRITT : REG : F : D: on truncation, J. E. B. (John Edgar Boehm); *rev.*, St. George and the Dragon, underneath B. P. (Benedetto Pistrucci). Date, below, 1887; edge milled. £5 5s.

Two Pound Piece.—Same types as Five Pound Piece. Date, 1887. £2 5s.

Sovereign.—Same types as Five Pound Piece. Date, 1887.

Half Sovereign.—*Obv.*, bust to left, as on Five Pound Piece: VICTORIA DEI GRATIA; *rev.*, garnished, square shield, crown above arched, BRITANNIARUM REGINA FID : DEF: 1887. 12s.

SILVER.—*Crown.*—Similar types as Five Pound Piece. Date, 1887.

Double Florin, or *Four Shilling Piece.*—*Obv.*, bust to left, &c., as on Half Sovereign; *rev.*, four crowned shields, arranged crosswise, with Star of the Garter in centre, and cantoned with four sceptres, two surmounted by orb, the others with thistle and harp : BRITT : REG : FID : DEF : Date, 1887.

Half Crown.—*Obv.*, bust to left, &c., as on Half Sovereign; *rev.*, square shield, with arched crown above, and surrounded by badge and collar of the Garter: BRITANNIARUM REGINA FID : DEF: Date, below, 1887.

Florin.—Same types as Double Florin. Date, 1887.

Shilling.—*Obv.*, bust to left, as on Five Pound Piece: VICTORIA DEI GRATIA BRITT : REGINA F : D: *rev.*, square shield, with arched crown above, and surrounded by badge of the Garter. Date, below, 1887.

Sixpence.—Two varieties.

First type.—*Obv.*, bust to left, as on Five Pound Piece: VICTORIA DEI GRATIA BRITT : REGINA F : D: *rev.*, square shield, with arched crown above, and surrounded by badge of the Garter. Date, below, 1887. 3s.

Second type.—*Obv.*, bust to left, &c., as on first type; *rev.*, within two branches of laurel and oak, arched crown above, SIXPENCE. Date, below, 1887.

Threepence.—*Obv.*, bust to left, &c., as on Sixpence; *rev.*, within two oak branches, mark of value—3—surrounded by arched crown and dividing date, 1887.

Individual specimens of silver coinage, 5 per cent. above current value. Sets, 18s. 6d.

In his Eighteenth Annual Report, the Deputy Master of the Mint says:—
"The only special feature of the coinage of the year 1887 was the issue
of gold and silver pieces of new designs, which were first put into
circulation on the 21st of June last, the day appointed for the celebration
of the Jubilee of the Queen. The gold coinage executed was not large,
and consisted entirely of coins of the new designs; nor was the amount
of bronze coined above the average. The silver coinage, on the other
hand, was far larger than usual, the demand having been stimulated by
the general wish to possess coins of the new issue. The total number of
good pieces struck was 43,369,043, as against 46,628,573 in 1886, and
their value, real or nominal, £3,014,810 10s. 5d. The total number of
good pieces of the Imperial coinage struck was 33,983,389, and their
value £2,896,065 13s."

. Mr. Fremantle observes:—"The issue of the new coins was received
with some adverse criticism, but it may be observed that there has been
a considerable demand for them on the part of the public, apart from the
ordinary necessities of the circulation. Gold coins of all the authorised
denominations, including the five-pound and two-pound pieces, were
struck during the year, and the value of the five-pound pieces coined
considerably exceeded £250,000. This is the more remarkable as during
the whole of the present reign there had been no demand for either the
five-pound or two-pound piece; nor, indeed, had any dies been prepared
for the latter coin. But very few pieces of either denomination being
met with in circulation, it is evident that nearly the whole number
issued must be hoarded as specimens. The number of sovereigns coined
slightly exceeded one million. As has been the case in most preceding
years, the Bank of England were the only importers of gold bullion for
coinage, and, of the total amount delivered at the Mint for that purpose,
£2,300,000 (or over eighty-one per cent.) consisted of light gold coin
withdrawn from circulation and sent in for re-coinage. The silver
coinage of the year included a new coin, the double-florin. With the
exception of the florin, first issued in 1849, the double-florin is the only
coin of a new denomination which has been added to the Imperial coinage
during the present reign. The total amount of silver coinage struck
during the year was £851,153, and the amount issued £909,768, as
against £430,798 in 1886. This is the largest issue of silver coin in any
year since 1877, except 1883, when, owing to the suspension of all coinage
during the greater part of the preceding year, the amount issued was over
£1,220,000. The total amount of threepences issued during the year
was £38,200. The demand for these coins in 1887 was considerably
under that of recent years. Half-crowns of the nominal value of
£208,225 were issued during the year, as against £130,695 in 1886, and
the total amount of these pieces added to the circulation since their
coinage was resumed in 1874 has been £2,451,710."

Mr. Fremantle adds:—"As the sixpence issued with the series of coins
of the new designs in June last was thought to bear too close a
resemblance to the half-sovereign, and apprehensions were expressed
that the new coin might be gilded and fraudulently passed as a half-
sovereign, it was decided to revert to the reverse of the sixpence in use
since the beginning of the present reign, namely, a wreath formed of olive
and oak branches, with the words 'six pence' in the centre and the date

beneath. Her Majesty having been pleased to approve of the proposed change, a Royal Proclamation was issued on the 29th of November, giving currency to a coin with the design as altered."

The following shows the denominations and amounts of silver coins of the new designs delivered to the Bank of England from the time of their first issue on the 21st of June, to the 31st of December, 1887:—Crowns, £55,300; double-florins, £67,500; half-crowns, £115,400; florins, £97,000; shillings, £116,200; sixpences, £35,600; threepences, £10,100—total, £497,100. So large an amount of silver coin as £574,600 had not been delivered to the Bank for some years, an extraordinary demand having been caused by the issue of the new coins, of which nearly half a million were delivered to the Bank before the close of the year. The worn silver coin withdrawn from circulation by the Bank of England during the year was considerably above the average, having amounted to £280,000.

An appended Memorandum by Mr. Hill, Superintendent of the Operative Department, says:—" A novel feature in the work performed in this department during the past year was the casting of bars for coins of the new designs, namely, gold five-pound and two-pound pieces, and silver crowns and double florins, the amount of metal melted for those bars alone having been—for the gold pieces, 424,803 ounces; and for the silver, 1,511,851 ounces. The amount of gold melted for sovereigns and half-sovereigns, both of the design used from 1837 to 1887, and also of the new design, was 1,314,811 ounces. No less than 7,671,726 ounces, or 235 tons of silver, were converted into bars for the Imperial coinage and for war medals. In addition to the above, 1,152,551 ounces of silver bullion were melted into bars for the various Colonial coinages, and 26,165 ounces of fine silver for the Jubilee Medals. The total weight of silver melted during the year was 8,850,442 ounces, equivalent to 271 tons, or 116 tons over the weight melted in the preceding year. The total number of pieces struck in the Coining Press Room was 50,848,438, a decrease of nearly three millions and a half as compared with the number struck in 1886. The denominations were of 34 different kinds, and included the new five-pound piece, two-pound piece, crown, and double-florin."

In 1888 all the silver coins were issued of the new type; but no gold.

The Maundy money used in 1887 was of the old types, but that issued in 1888 has the new bust of the Queen, as in the Five Pound Piece, but the legend is VICTORIA D : G : BRITANNIAR : REGINA F : D : on all pieces excepting the Threepence, which is the same as the current coin.

The types of the copper coinage of 1887 and 1888 have not changed at all.

LIST OF IMPORTANT SALES OF COINS FROM 1854,

WITH THE TOTAL AMOUNTS REALISED.

Cuff, J. D.	18 days	...	1854	... £7054 0 0
Dymock, Rev. T. F.	4 days	...	1858	... 1928 19 6
Martin, Rev. J. W.	5 days	...	1859	... 2624 7 0
Christmas, Rev. H.	6 days	...	1864	... 1261 15 6
Murchison, Capt.	5 days	...	1864	... 3523 8 0
,, ,, ...	3 days	...	1866	... 1419 16 0
Lindsay, J.	4 days	.	1867	... 1260 3 0
Whitbourn, R.	3 days	...	1869	... 1074 11 6
Bergne, J. B.	11 days	...	1873	... 6102 13 0
Wingate, J. (Scottish Coins)	3 days	...	1875	... 3263 14 0
Johnston, W. H.	5 days	...	1876	... 2498 8 0
Hawkins, E.	1 day	...	1877	... 348 11 0
Moore, General Yorke	3 days	...	1879	... 2087 6 6
Wakeford, G.	2 days	...	1879	... 624 7 0
Sparkes, Geo.	2 days	...	1880	... 3375 18 6
Price, Lake	2 days	...	1880	... 1930 9 0
Nobleman, A (Lord Hastings)	5 days	...	1880	... 3958 19 0
Young, J. Halliburton ...	5 days	...	1881	... 3041 4 0
Brice, W. (Duplicates) ...	1 day	...	1881	... 580 11 0
Rolfe, Rev. S. C. E.	1 day	...	1882	... 648 2 6
*Simpson, Geo. B.	3 days	...	1882	.. 1487 5 0
Wylie, Rev. G.	3 days	...	1882	... 1137 15 0
Montagu, H. (Duplicates) ...	2 days	...	1883	... 1471 18 6
*Mackenzie, Sheriff	2 days	...	1883	
*Hendry, D.	2 days	...	1883	... 1054 5 0
Roach, F.	3 days	...	1884	... 1242 15 6
Henderson, L.	1 day	..	1884	... 264 13 5
Bagot, Lord	3 days	...	1884	... 1642 17 6
Whittal Collection (Part I.) ...	8 days	...	1884	... 3951 0 6
Ford, J. K.	7 days	...	1884	... 4085 1 6
Kirk, A. W.	1 day	...	1884	... 733 16 6
Shepherd, Rev. E. J.	4 days	...	1885	... 5301 3 6
Webb, H.	2 days	...	1885	... 323 9 6
Maynard, Rev. J.	1 day	...	1885	... 1142 7 0
Fothergill, Rev. E.	3 days	...	1885	... 928 12 6
Nation, W. H.	4 days	...	1885	... 1282 14 0

* These Sales were held in Edinburgh.

Whittal Collection (Part II.)	1 day	...	1885	...	£554	2 6
Foljambe, F. J. S.	1 day	...	1885	...	476	9 0
Middleton, J. H.	1 day	...	1885	...	430	7 6
Montague, H. (Duplicates) ...	3 days	...	1886	...	1165	9 0
Webster, W.	4 days	...	1886	...	944	15 6
Domvile, Lady	4 days	...	1886	...	1682	12 0
Ingram, J.	2 days	...	1886	...	1390	9 0
Sanders, J.	3 days	...	1886	...	1047	16 6
Murrell, R. J.	1 day	...	1886	...	1413	15 6
*Shorthouse, E.	4 days	...	1886	...	1571	18 6
Wyndham, C. W.	2 days	...	1886	...	1037	4 6
Williams, J.	4 days	...	1886	...	2123	8 6
White, G. W.	5 days	...	1887	...	1029	4 6
Pownall, Archdeacon	1 day	...	1887	...	517	4 6
Fewkes, J. W.	6 days	...	1887	...	1678	9 0
Mayer, J.	3 days	...	1887	...	1394	1 6
Archdeacon, an (Harrison) ...	5 days	...	1887	...	2313	15 6
Kirby, T. B.	4 days	...	1888	...	1426	17 0

* This Sale was held in Birmingham. All the other Sales were held in London, by Messrs. Sotheby, Wilkinson, & Hodge.

The Sale of Coins collected by Col. THORBURN took place on the 6th, 7th, and 8th July, 1887, at Messrs. SOTHEBY, WILKINSON, & HODGE's sale-room, 13, Wellington Street, Strand, London. The number of Coins was over 4000—there were 457 lots—and the sum total (gross amount) realised by the sale was £1494 11s. 6d. The Coins were mostly in splendid preservation, and included Anglo-Saxon, Anglo-Gallic, Scottish and English gold, silver, and copper, some being of extreme rarity, and many in Mint state. Some of the highest prices are as follows:—A Silver Penny of Alfred, £6 5s.; Sovereign, Henry VIII., 37th year, £12; Sovereign, Edward VI., 3rd year, £18; Sovereign, Queen Mary, 1553, £10 10s.; Portcullis Money Crown, Half-crown, Shilling, and Sixpence, Elizabeth, milled, £25; Pound piece, Oxford Mint, Charles I., £15; Half Broad, Cromwell, Gold, 1656, £32 5s.; Pattern Crown, William IV., Silver, £23; Proof Set, Victoria, Silver, £30; Proof Sets of Copper Coins, Victoria, £14.

INDEX.

INDEX TO THE ILLUSTRATIONS,

WITH A REFERENCE TO THE PAGES WHERE THE FIGURES ARE DESCRIBED.

EMBOSSED PLATES.

*Those marked * are Facsimiles prepared from Coins lent by* MESSRS. W. S. LINCOLN & SONS, *London ; the others are from Coins lent by* MESSRS. SPINK & SONS, *London.*

TONED PLATES.

---

* The R in *rec.* is turned in the wrong direction.

M

* The figure of the *rev.* is incorrect. The date should be 1716, and there should be a rose and a plume alternately in the angles of the cross formed by the shields.

PLATE I.

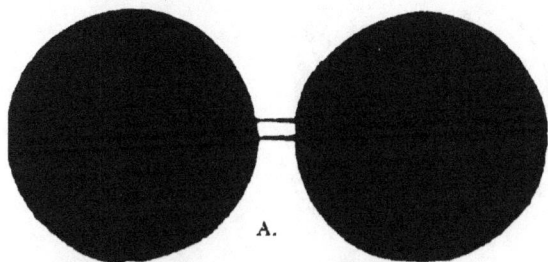

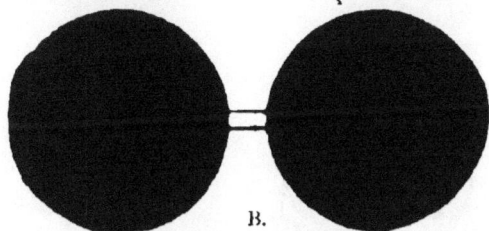

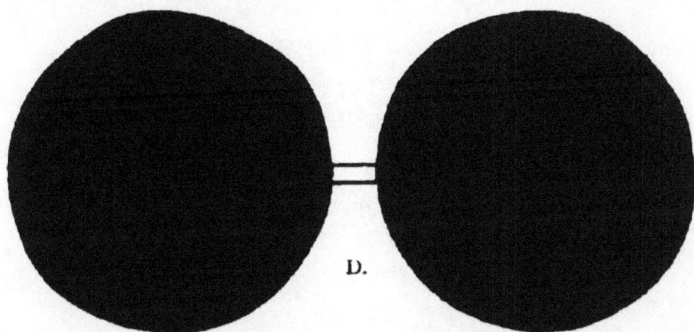

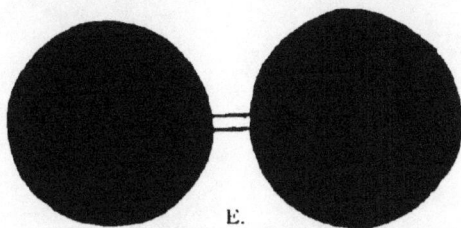

A. Edward III., Noble.
B. Henry VII., Angel.
C. Elizabeth, Hammered Half-Sovereign.
D. James I., Double Real.
E. James I., Half-Laurel.

₀ *Facsimiles prepared from Coins lent by Messrs. W. S. LINCOLN & SON, of London.*

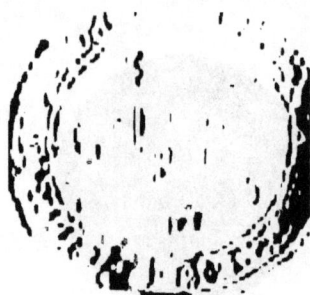

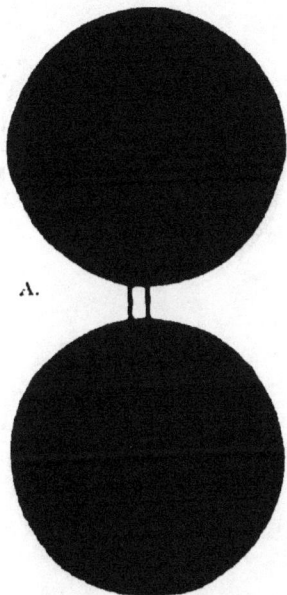

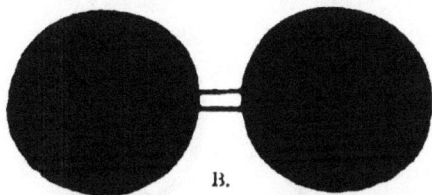

B.

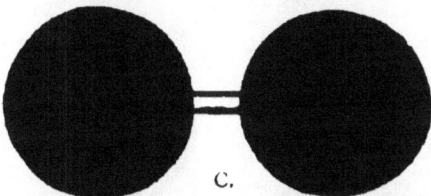

C.

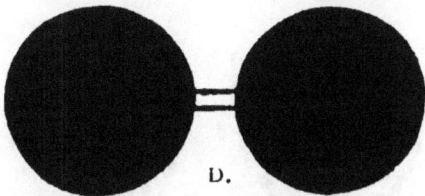

D.

A.

E.

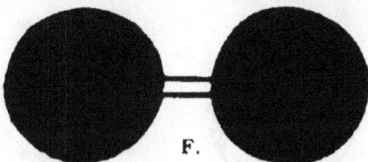

F.

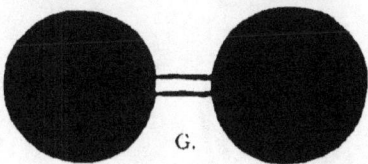

G.

A. Charles II., Five Guinea Piece.
B. Charles II., Guinea.
C. William III., Guinea.
D. George II., Guinea, "Old Head."

E. George III., Guinea, 1785.
F. George III., Spade Half-Guinea.
G. George III., Half-Guinea, 1803.

₀ *Facsimiles prepared from Coins lent by Messrs. W. S. LINCOLN & SON, of London.*

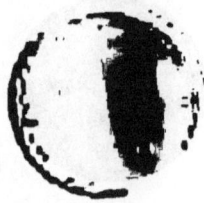

PLATE III.

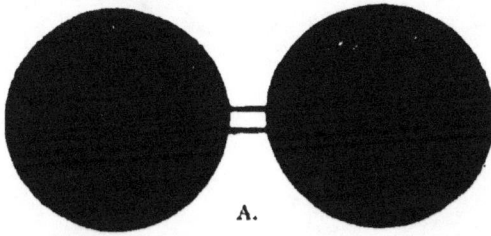

A.

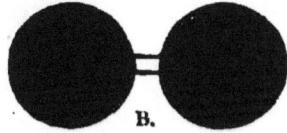

B.

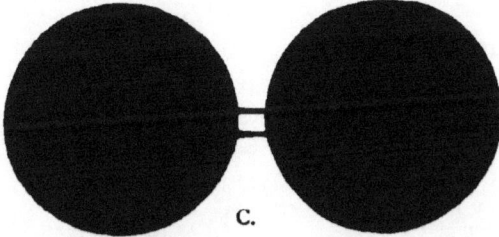

C.

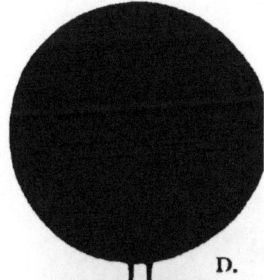

D.

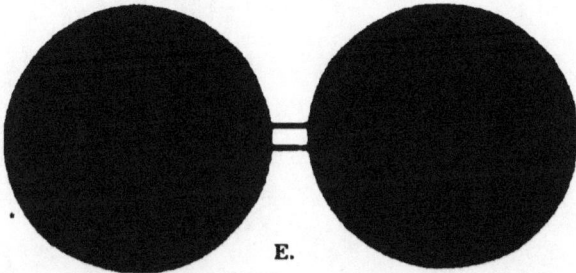

E.

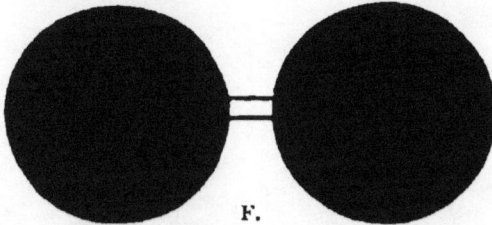

F.

G.

A. Elizabeth, Angel.
B. Elizabeth, Quarter-Angel.
C. Elizabeth, Milled Half-Sovereign.
D. Charles I., Unit.

E. Commonwealth, Twenty-Shilling Piece.
F. Cromwell, Broad.
G. Commonwealth, Five-Shilling Piece.

•°• *Facsimiles prepared from Coins lent by Messrs.* SPINK & SON, *of London.*

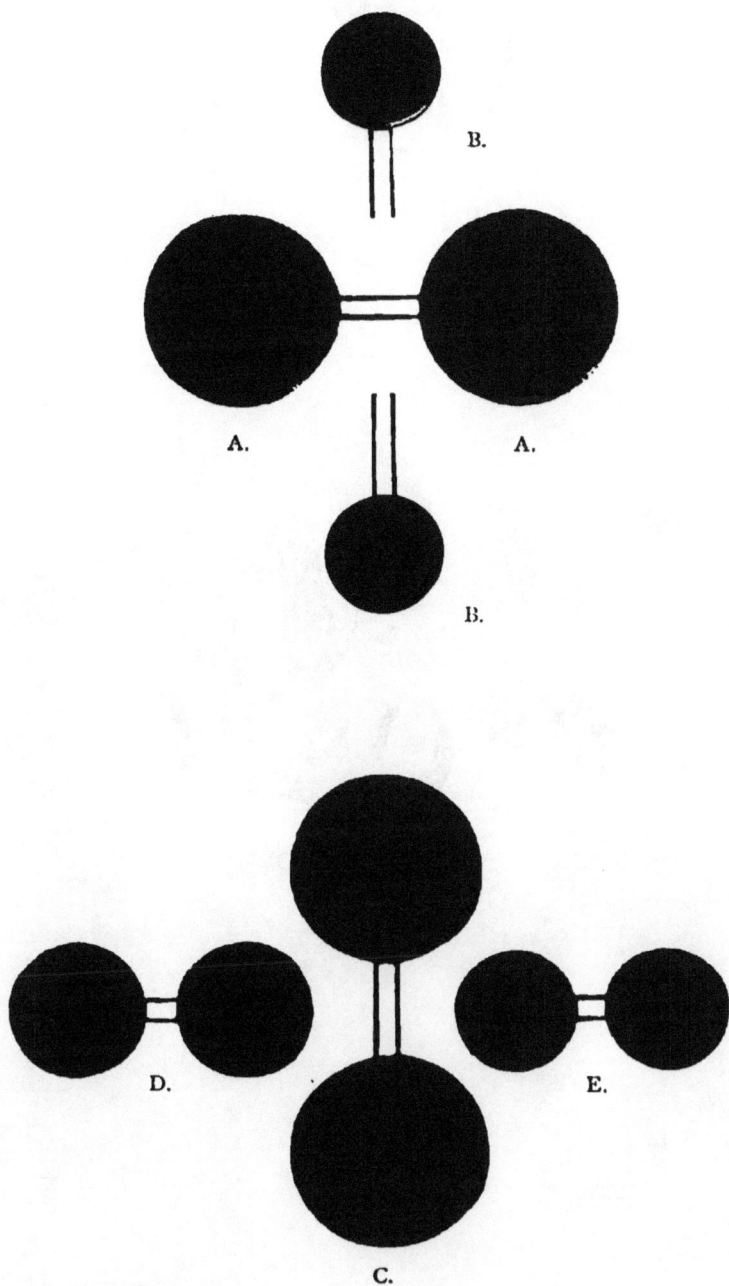

PLATE IV.

B.

A.   A.

B.

D.   E.

C.

A. George I., Guinea.
B. George I., Quarter-Guinea.
C. George III., Guinea, *last issue.*

D. George III., Seven-Shilling Piece.
E. George III., Quarter-Guinea.

°₀° *Facsimiles prepared from Coins lent by Messrs.* SPINK & SON, *of London.*

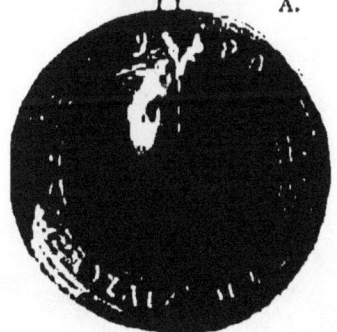

A.

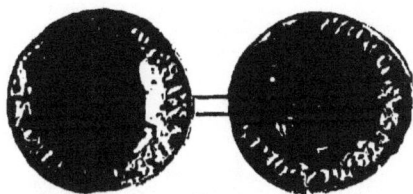

B.

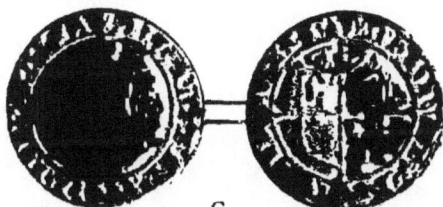

C.

E.

D.

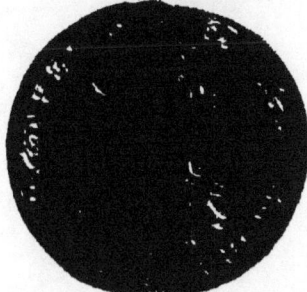

F.

A. Edward VI., Crown.
B. Mary, Groat.
C. Elizabeth, Hammered Sixpence.

D. Charles I., York Shilling.
E. Charles I., Aberystwith Groat.
F. Charles II., Crown, *Rose under Bust.*

•˳• *Facsimiles prepared from Coins lent by Messrs.* W. S. LINCOLN & SON, *of London.*

PLATE VI.

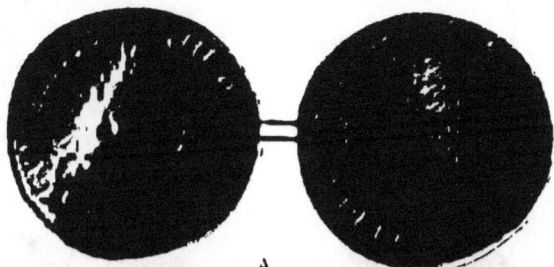

C.

A.

B.

E.

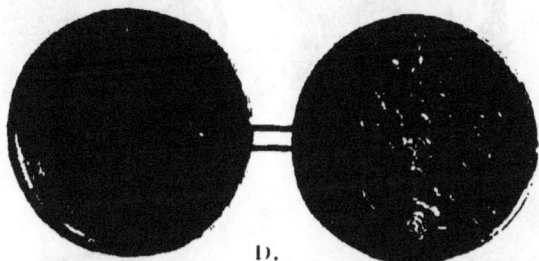

D.

F.

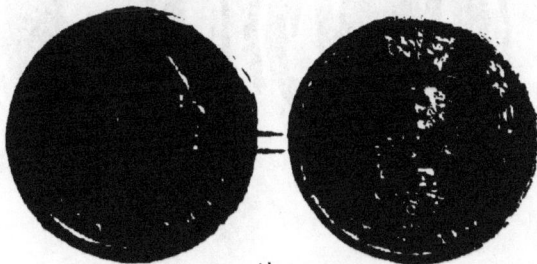

G.

A. William III., Half-Crown.
B. George III., Crown.
C. George III., Sixpence, 1787.
D. George IV., Half-Crown, 1821.

E. George IV., Lion Shilling, 1826.
F. George III., Bank Eighteenpence Token.
G. William IV., Half-Crown.

₀ *Facsimiles prepared from coins lent by Messrs. W. S. LINCOLN & SON, of London.*

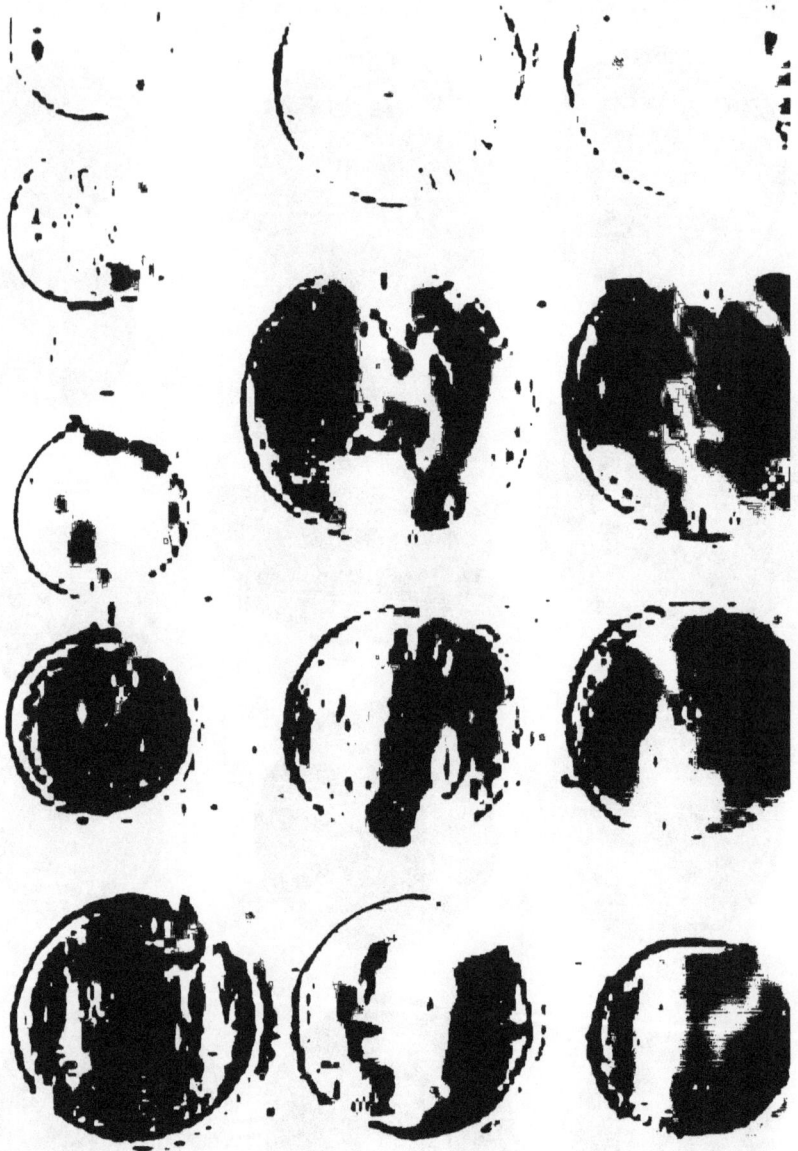

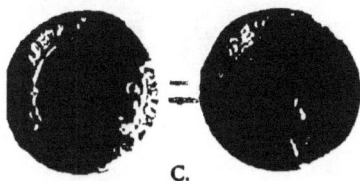

C.

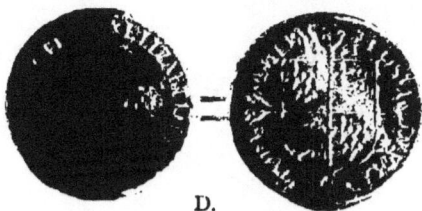

D.

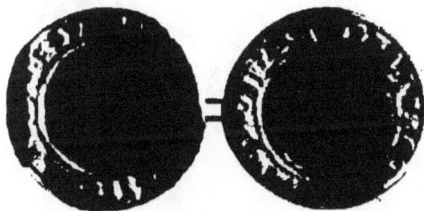

E.

G.

F.

A. Henry VIII., Half-Groat, *first issue.*
B. Henry VIII., Groat, *third issue.*
C. Edward VI., Threepence.
D. Elizabeth, Milled Sixpence.

E. James I., Sixpence.
F. Charles I., Oxford Sixpence.
G. Charles I., Bristol Half-Crown.

⁎ *Facsimiles prepared from Coins lent by Messrs.* SPINK & SON, *of London.*

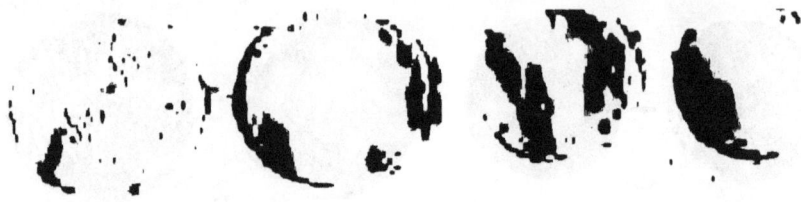

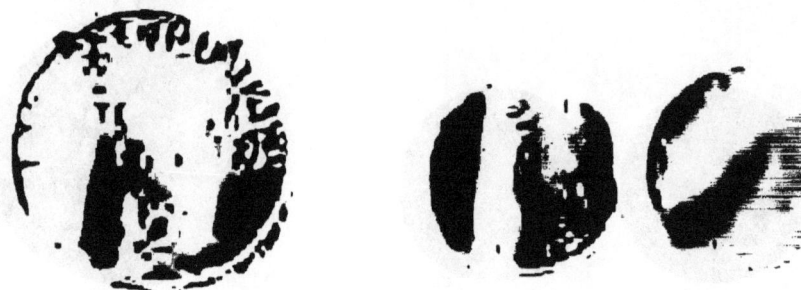

PLATE VIII.

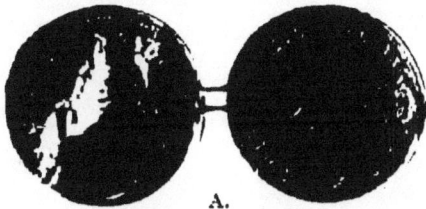

A.

C.

B.

D.

F.

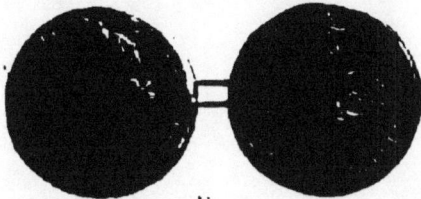

E.

A. James II., Shilling.
B. William and Mary, Shilling.
C. Anne, Half-Crown.

D. George II., Shilling, "Young Head."
E. George II., Shilling, "Old Head."
F. George III., "Northumberland" Shilling.

∗ *Facsimiles prepared from Coins lent by Messrs. SPINK & SON, of London.*

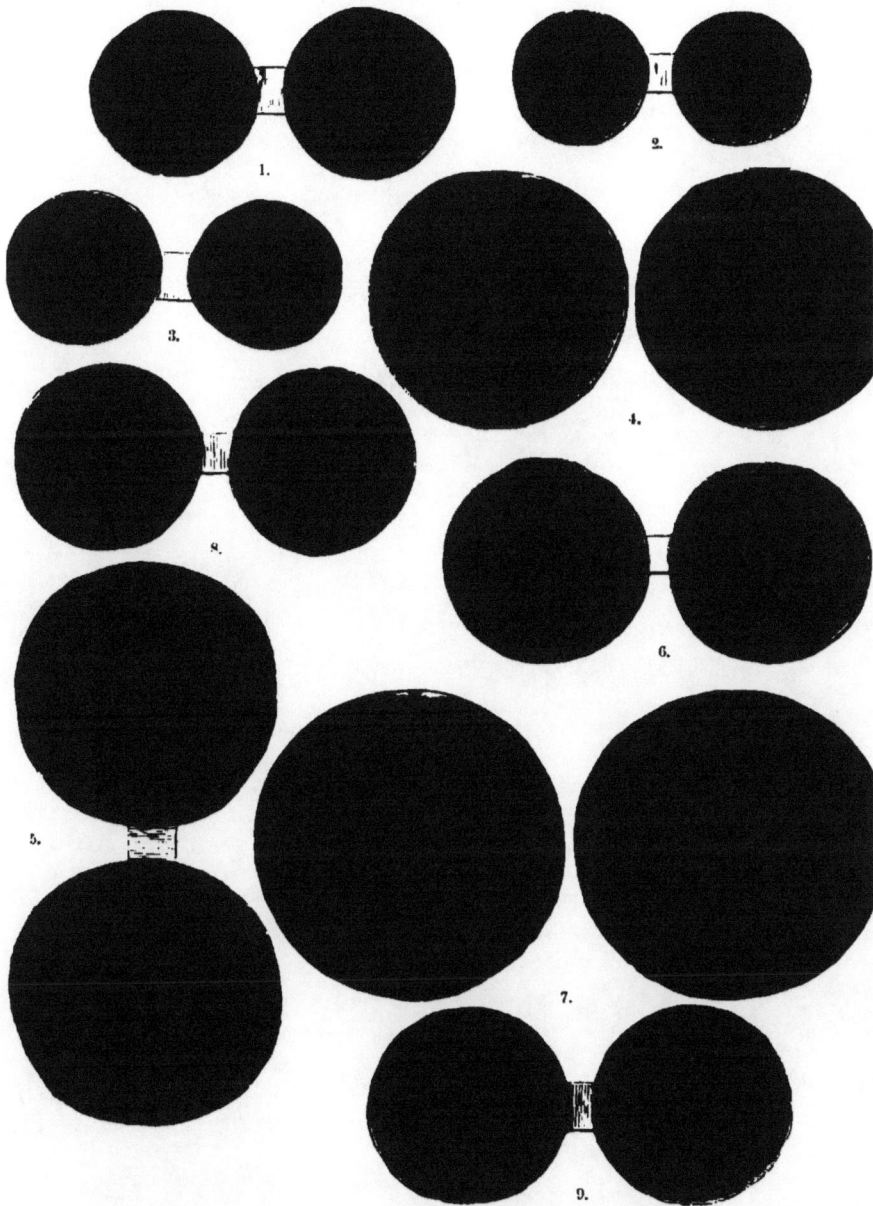

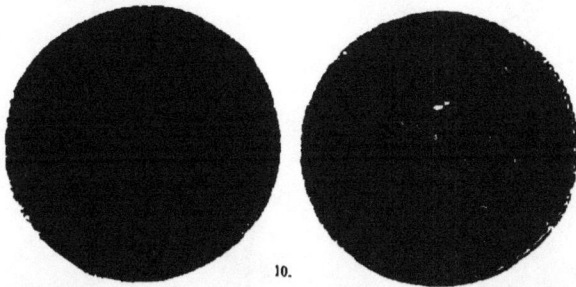

10.

11.   12.

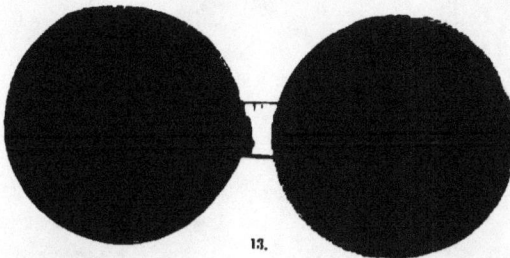

13.

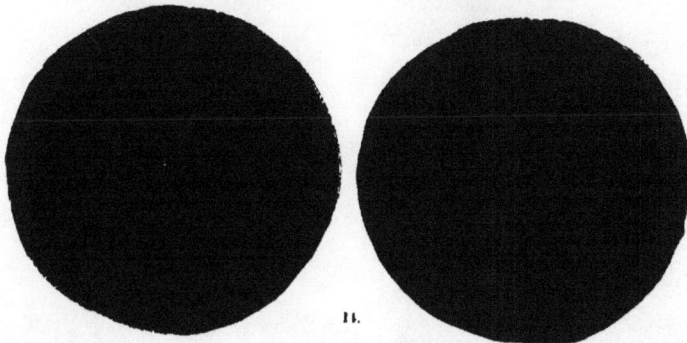

14.

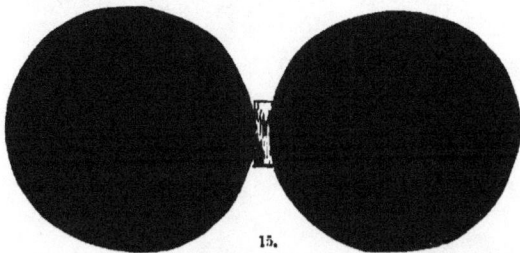

15.

16.   17.

18.   19.

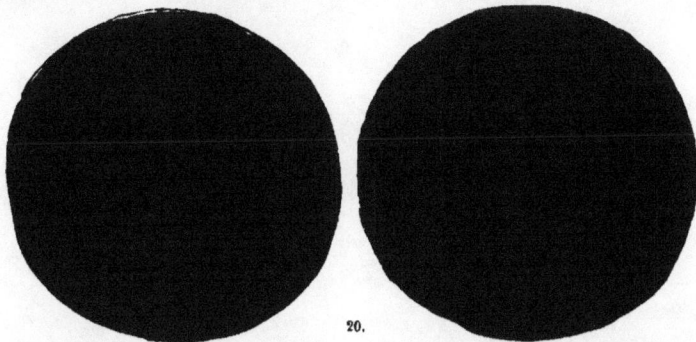

20.

PLATE XII.

21.

22.

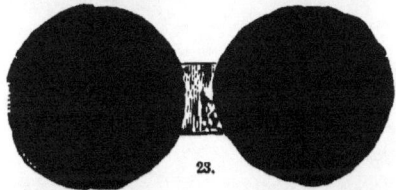
23.

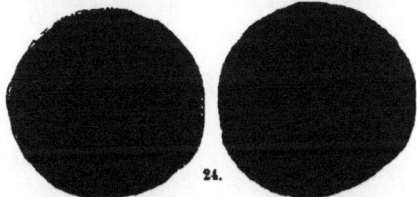
24.

25.

26.

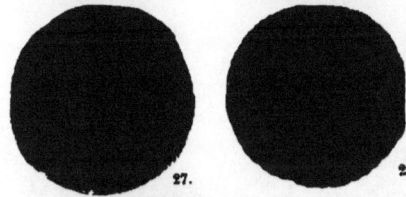
27.

28.

29

30.

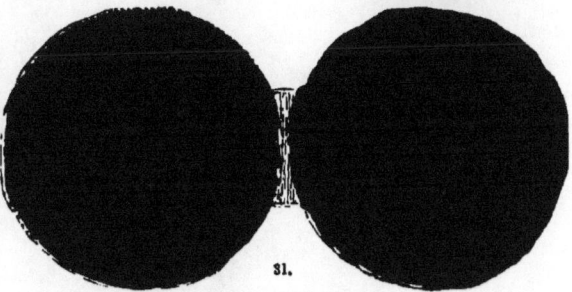
31.

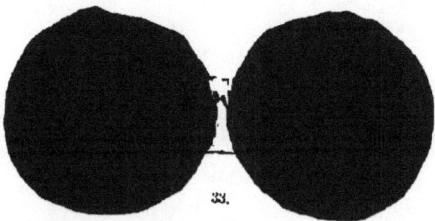

34.

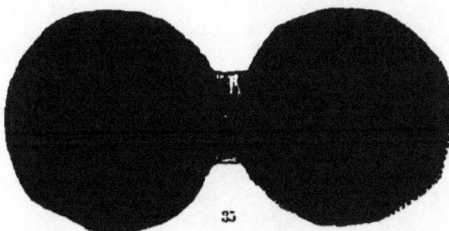

35.

36.

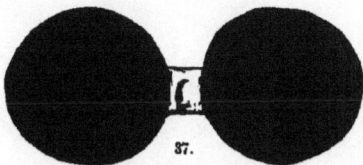

37.

PLATE XIV.

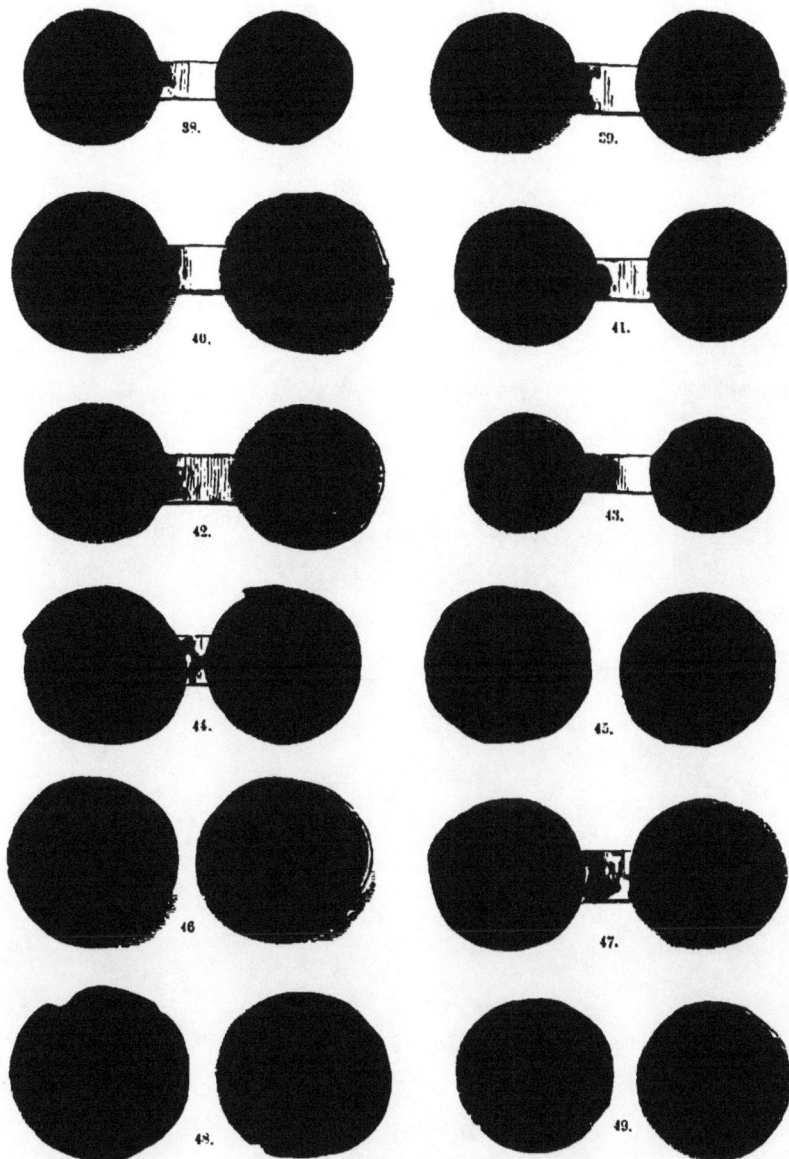

LATE XV.

50.

51.

52.

53.

54.

55.

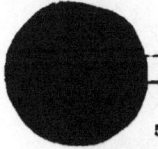
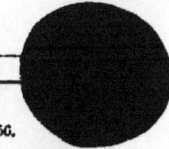

56.

57.

59.

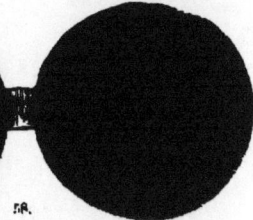

58.

60.

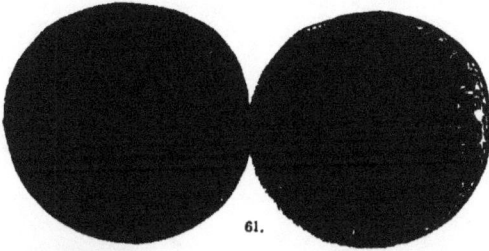

61.

62.

63.

66.

67.

65.

PLATE XVII.

68.

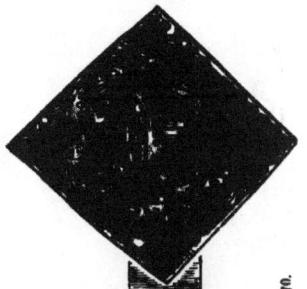

70.

69.

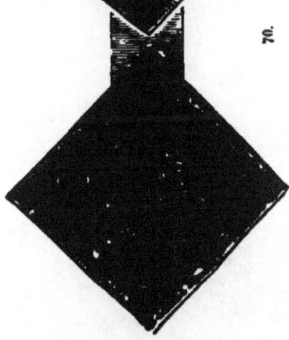

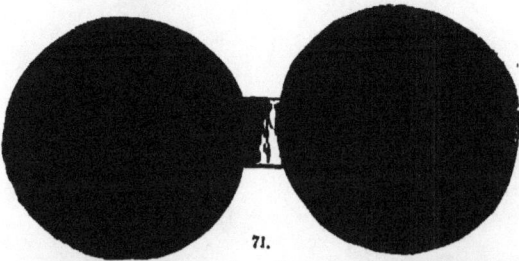

71.

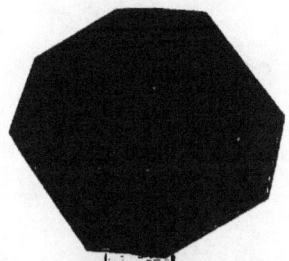

73.

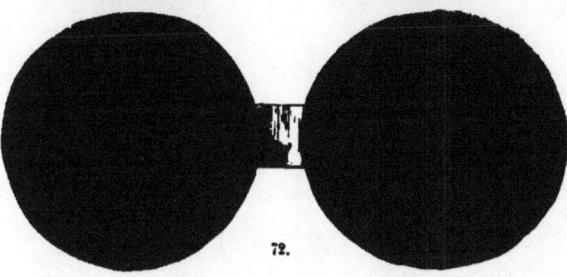

72.

75.

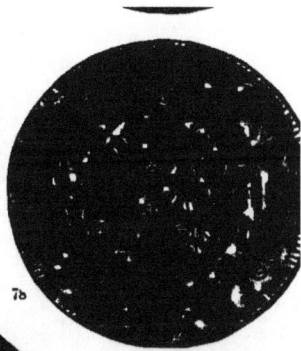

78

76.

79

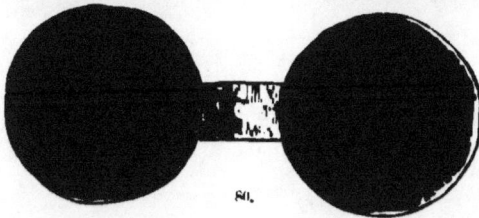

80.

PLATE XIX.

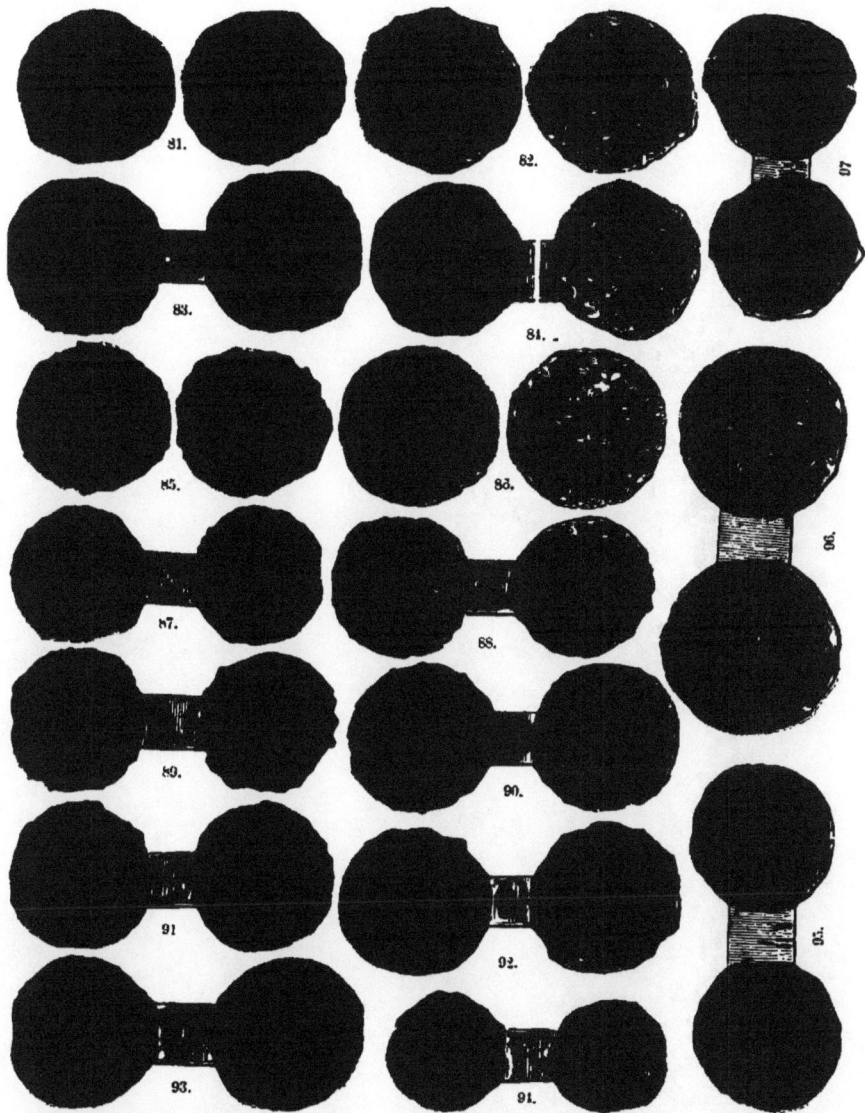

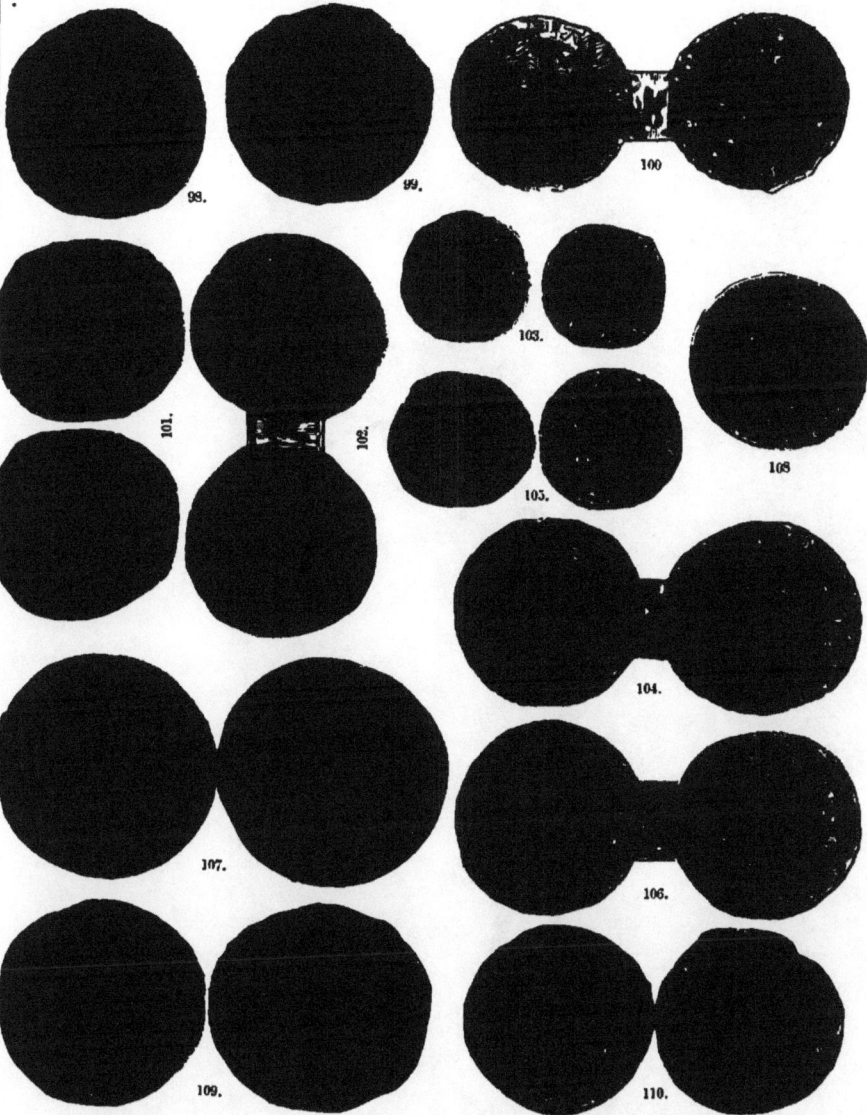

98. 99. 100.

101. 102. 103. 108.

105.

104.

107. 106.

109. 110.

PLATE XXI.

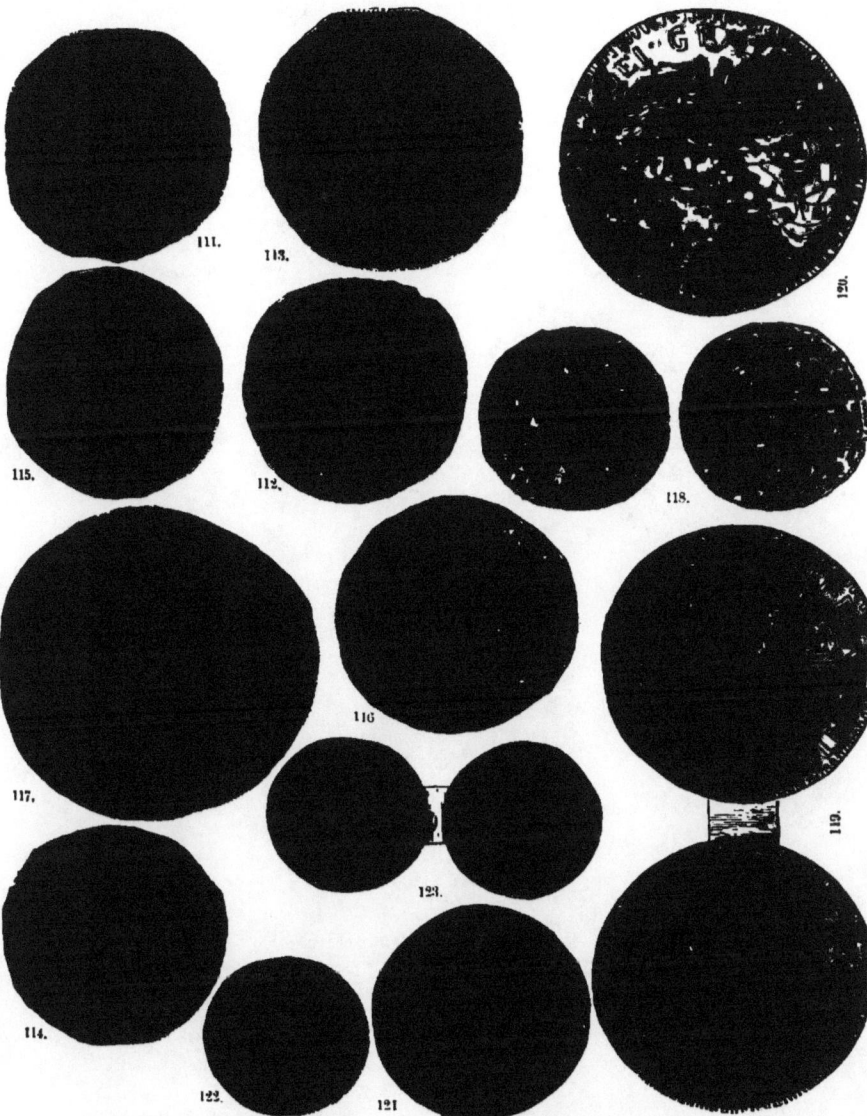

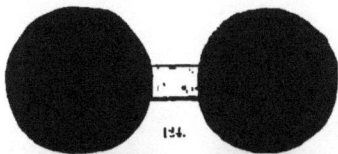

124.

125.

126.

127.

128.

129.

130.

131.

132.

133.

134.

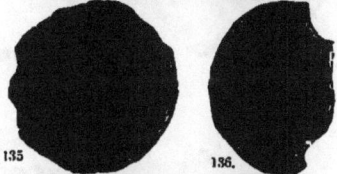

135   136.

137.   138.

139.

PLATE XXIII.

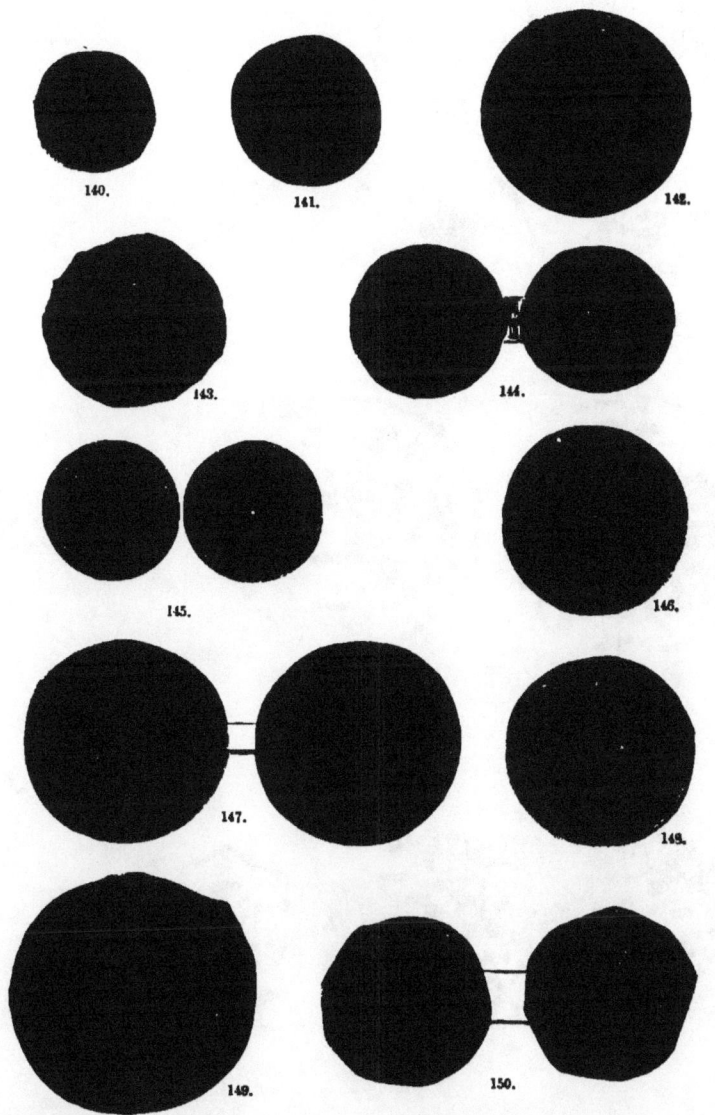

140.

141.

142.

143.

144.

145.

146.

147.

149.

149.

150.

151.

152.

153.

151.

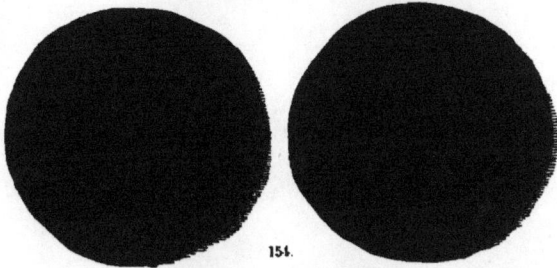

159.

154.

159.

155.

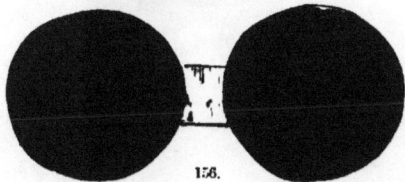

156.

157.

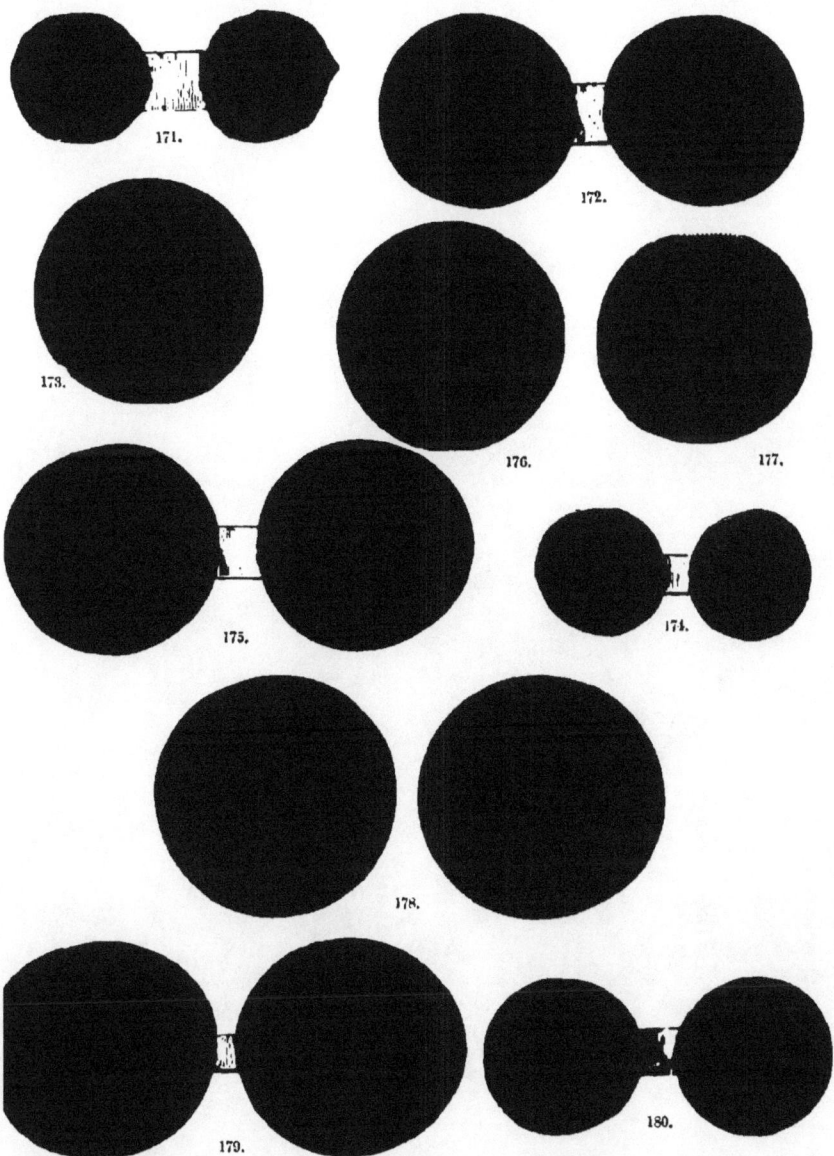

171.

172.

173.

176.

177.

175.

174.

178.

179.

180.

181.

182.

183.

184.

185.

186.

187.

188.

189.

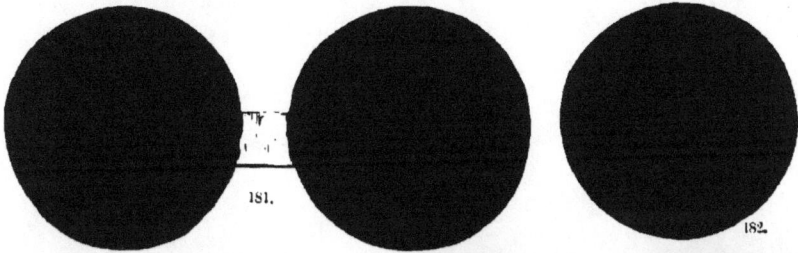

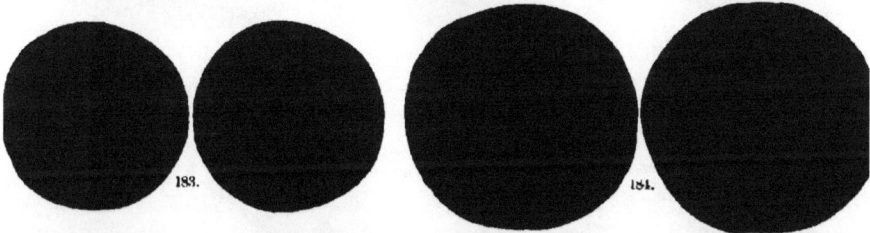

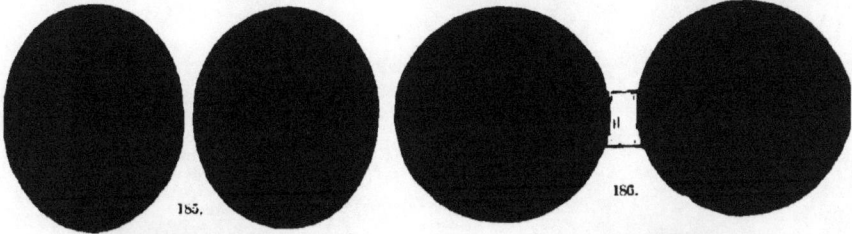

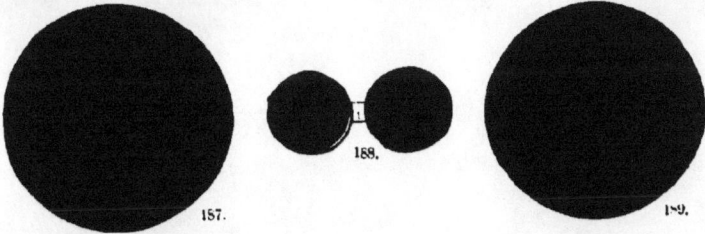

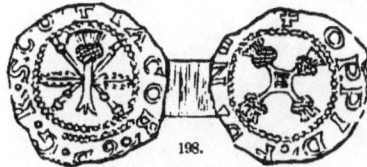

W. S. LINCOLN & SON,

Old-Established Numismatists,

69, NEW OXFORD STREET, LONDON,

HAVE ON VIEW AND SALE A GREAT COLLECTION OF

COINS ✳ AND ✳ MEDALS,

COMPRISING:

GREEK GOLD, SILVER, AND COPPER COINS.
ROMAN GOLD, SILVER, AND BRASS.
ANCIENT BRITISH AND ANGLO-SAXON COINS.
ENGLISH SILVER, FROM WILLIAM I. TO PRESENT REIGN.
ENGLISH GOLD COINS OF NEARLY EVERY REIGN, FROM
    EDWARD III.

The following are a few of the English Silver Coins on View and Sale:

William I. Pennies, 5s., 7s. 6d., 10s.
Henry II. ,,   1s., 2s., 2s. 6d.
Henry III. ,,   1s. 6d., 2s. 6d., 3s. 6d.
Edward I. ,,   1s., 1s. 6d., 2s. 6d.
Edward II. ,,   1s., 1s. 6d., 2s. 6d.
Edward III. Groats, 2s., 3s., 4s.
Henry V. ,,   2s., 2s. 6d., 3s. 6d.
Henry VI. ,,   1s. 6d., 2s. 6d., 3s. 6d.
Edward IV. ,,   1s. 6d., 2s., 3s.
Henry VII. ,,   2s., 3s., 3s. 6d.
Henry VIII. ,,   1s. 6d., 2s., 3s.
Edward VI. Shillings, 2s., 3s. 6d., 5s.
Elizabeth ,,   2s., 3s. 6d., 4s. 6d.
James I. ,,   2s., 3s., 4s.
Charles I. Half-Crowns, 3s. 6d., 5s., 6s.
 ,,   Shillings, 1s. 6d., 2s. 6d., 3s. 6d.

Commonwealth Half-Groats, 1s., 1s. 6d.,
    2s. 6d.
Charles II. Crowns, 6s. 6d., 8s. 6d.,
    12s. 6d.
Charles II. set of four Maundy, 2s. 6d.,
    3s. 6d., 5s.
James II. Crowns, 7s. 6d., 8s. 6d., 12s. 6d.
William and Mary Half-Crowns, 4s., 5s.,
    7s. 6d.
William III. Half-Crowns, 3s. 6d., 4s. 6d.,
    6s.
William III. Crowns, 7s., 8s. 6d., 10s.
Anne Shillings, 1s. 6d., 2s., 3s.
  ,,   Sixpences, 1s., 1s. 6d., 2s. 6d.
George I. Shillings, 1s. 6d., 2s., 3s.
George II. ,,   1s. 6d., 2s., 2s. 6d.
George III. Crowns, 8s. 6d., 10s., 15s.

*Can also supply some of the same Coins at Lower, Intermediate, and
Higher Prices, and many other Denominations of Same and Other Reigns;*

ALSO

**Tokens of the Seventeenth, Eighteenth, and Nineteenth
    Centuries;**
American, Colonial, and Foreign Silver and Copper Coins;
Silver and Bronze Medals of Eminent Men;
War Medals, Decorations, and Commemorative Medals.

All the above-named Coins and Medals are arranged in Cabinets, and separately
priced in plain figures. Intending purchasers are invited to call and make their
own selections, or *bonâ fide* orders with prepayment will be promptly attended to.

NO CONNECTION WITH ANY OTHER HOUSE.

A GUIDE TO

English Pattern Coins,

In Gold, Silver, Copper, & Pewter,

From Edward 1 to Victoria,

WITH THEIR VALUE.

....

BY THE

Rev. G. F. Crowther, M.A.,

Member of the Numismatic Society of London.

ILLUSTRATED.

In Silver Cloth, with Gilt Facsimiles of Coins.

PRICE 5s.

LONDON:

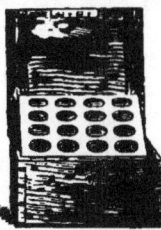

CATALOGUE of
New & Practical
BOOKS

Published by

L. UPCOTT GILL, 170, Strand, London.

INDEX.

Index continued on page 3.

No. 2.—1888.

The Bazaar,
Exchange and Mart,
and
Journal of the Household.

Published Every Monday, Wednesday, and Friday.

Established 20 Years.

PRICE 2d.

Registered as a Newspaper.

CONTENTS. — The plan of the journal is that it shall be a thoroughly practical and useful newspaper in every household, and with this end in view a great variety of information is given, classified in Departments according to the subject.

Although the paper is published three times a week, the literary matter is so arranged that any one may be taken weekly without loss of interest, the three issues being virtually three distinct and separate weekly journals, which can be taken together or each by itself as is most convenient to the reader.

ILLUSTRATIONS. — Numerous Diagrams and more finished Illustrations, specially drawn and engraved for THE BAZAAR, are given.

DRAWING ROOM.—In this Department Art, Music, Science, Amateur Theatricals, and such like, are included. Notices of the Art Galleries, Concerts, New Music, and the doings in the Scientific World, are given, as well as Practical Articles on New Art Work for Amateurs, Playing the Violin, Valuation of Paintings and Engravings, and Correspondence, Questions and Answers on similar matters.

HALL.—A large number of subjects are treated here, such as particulars of Holiday and Health Resorts, Photography, Cycling, the Keeping of Aviary Birds, Management of Aquaria and Small Pets, Popular Natural History, Emigration, Games, Fishing, Ventriloquism, the Microscope, Cats, and Questions, Answers, and Correspondence on the same subjects.

BOUDOIR.—Fashions, Fancy Work of every kind, Dressmaking, Millinery, Knitted Garments, New Materials, Etiquette, and other subjects which Ladies discuss in the Boudoir, form the feature of this Department.

WORKSHOP. — Every branch of Mechanics for Amateurs is here treated in turn : Carpentry, Joinery, Metal Working, Turning, Lacquering, Picture Cleaning, Carriage-building, Making Scientific Apparatus, Furniture Making, Cabinet Work, Painting, Graining, Recipes for various processes, and Questions and Answers for obtaining special information. The Articles are plain, practical, and to the point.

HOUSEKEEPER'S ROOM. —Papers on various points in connection with the Decoration and Arrangement of Houses, Domestic Management, Little Dinners and Luncheons, Oriental Cookery for English Tastes, the Cooking of Special Dishes, Home Dyeing and Cleaning, and other matters of a similar kind, are found in this Department. These papers are reliable and exact, and useful in every household.

GARDEN.—The Cultivation of Hardy Garden Plants, Greenhouse Plants, Ferns, Hardy Orchids, Cacti, Flowering Shrubs, Roses, Fruit and Vegetables, is described in a plain and practical manner, and suited to the requirements of the ordinary amateur. Present work in the Garden for future effect, and practical and seasonable Notes on Bee-keeping, are also given.

LIBRARY.—Here are given Reviews of Books, Articles on the Leading Magazines, Discussions on Literary Topics, Papers on Collectors' Books, and other matters appertaining to the Library.

CURTILAGE. — Dogs, Poultry, Horses, Goat-keeping, Pigeons, Rabbits, Farming for Amateurs, and such like, are treated in this Department. Here, as in all the other Departments, Questions and Answers from Correspondence form a useful feature. Prize Lists of Shows are also given.

EXCHANGE AND MART. — Selling, Buying, and Exchanging amongst *Private* Persons is carried on through this Department, and to so great an extent is it used for this purpose, that the whole of a large Supplement is devoted to it. This Supplement is divided into 22 Departments, and these again are fully sub-divided for perfect ease of reference. A small charge of 1d. for 3 words is made for entering a notice.

TO CORRESPONDENTS. — Under this heading Replies are given, by a large Staff of Experts, to Questions on Law, Literature, Finance and Investments, Art, Bric-à-Brac, Cycling, Travel, Poultry, Pigeons, Pheasants, Dogs, Horses, Farming, Violin, Organ, Piano, o Cage Birds, Fashions, Fancy Work, Cooking, Practical Science, Sport, Housekeeping, Foreign Stamps, and all other subjects except Theology and Politics.

SUBSCRIPTIONS. — These can commence at any time, and be for any length of period, from 1 month to 1 year, but must be prepaid. The terms are as follows :—

ONE ISSUE WEEKLY.

1 month.	3 months.	6 months.	12 months.
-/11	2/8	5/4	10/8

TWO ISSUES WEEKLY:

1 month.	3 months.	6 months.	12 months.
1/9	5/4	10/8	21/4

THREE ISSUES WEEKLY.

1 month.	3 months.	6 months.	12 months.
2/8	8/0	16/0	32/0

Stamps received for small sums. P.O.'s and Cheques to be payable to L. UPCOTT GILL.

SINGLE COPIES. — These may be obtained at all Railway Bookstalls and Newsagents', or will be sent from the Office on receipt of 2½d. in stamps.

OFFICES.—The *Postal* address is 170, Strand, London, W.C. For *Telegrams,* "Bazaar, London."

✦ CATALOGUE ✦

— OF —

PRACTICAL HANDBOOKS

PUBLISHED BY

L. UPCOTT GILL, 170, STRAND, LONDON, W.C.

AMUSEMENTS, ARTISTIC: Being Instructions in Colouring Photographs, Imitation Stained Glass, Decalcomanie, Queen Shell Work, Painting on China, Japanese Lacquer Work, Stencilling, Painting Magic Lantern Slides, Menu and Guest Cards, Spatter Work, Picture and Scrap Screens, Frosted Silver Work, Picture Cleaning and Restoring, Illuminating, and Symbolical Colouring. Illustrated. *In cloth gilt, price 2s. 6d.* "Practical, satisfactory in its treatment, and very interesting."—*The Queen.*

ANGLER, BOOK OF THE ALL-ROUND. A Comprehensive Treatise on Angling in both Fresh and Salt Water. In Four Divisions: 1, Coarse Fish; 2, Pike; 3, Game Fish; 4, Sea Fish. Each Division is complete in itself. By JOHN BICKERDYKE. With over 150 Engravings. *In cloth, price 5s.; also in Monthly parts, price 7d.* LARGE PAPER EDITION (200 copies only, signed and numbered), *bound in Roxburghe, price 21s. to Subscribers.* "Just the sort of treatise that the angling novice requires—a code of simple, practical directions in the high art of catching fish."—*People.*

ANGLING FOR COARSE FISH. Illustrated. A very Complete and Practical Work on Bottom Fishing, according to the methods in use on the Thames, Trent, Norfolk Broads, and elsewhere. (*Being Division I. of above work.*) *Price* 1s.

ANGLING FOR PIKE. A Practical and Comprehensive Work on the most Approved Methods of Fishing for Pike or Jack; including an Account of Some New Tackles for Spinning, Live-baiting, and Trolling. Profusely Illustrated. (*Being Division II. of above work.*) *Price* 1s.

⁂ All Books Post Free.

ANGLING FOR GAME FISH. A Practical Guide to both Wet and Dry Fly-fishing for Salmon, Trout, and Grayling. Well Illustrated. (*Being Division III. of above work.*) *Price* 1s.

ANGLING IN SALT WATER. A Practical Work on Sea Fishing with Rod and Line, from the Shore, Piers, Jetties, Rocks, and from Boats ; together with Some Account of Hand-Lining. Over 50 Engravings. (*Being Division IV. of above work.*) *Price* 1s. "It gives us great pleasure to call attention to this most interesting, practical, and valuable work."—*Fishing Gazette.*

ARBORICULTURE FOR AMATEURS: Being Instructions for the Planting and Cultivation of Trees for Ornament or Use, and Selections and Descriptions of those suited to Special Requirements as to Soil, Situation, &c. By WILLIAM H. ABLETT, Author of "English Trees and Tree Planting," &c. *In cloth gilt, price* 2s. 6d. "Full of practical remarks, tending to make it a reliable and useful guide to amateur gardeners."—*The Farmer.*

ARCHITECTURE, PRACTICAL. As applied to Farm Buildings of every description (Cow, Cattle, and Calf Houses, Stables, Piggeries, Sheep Shelter Sheds, Root and other Stores, Poultry Houses), Dairies, and Country Houses and Cottages. Profusely Illustrated with Diagrams and Plans. By ROBERT SCOTT BURN. *In cloth gilt, price* 5s. "A valuable handbook for ready reference."—*Journal of Forestry.*

BAZAARS AND FANCY FAIRS: A Guide to their Organisation and Management, with Details of Various Devices for Extracting Money from the Visitors. *In paper, price* 1s. "Most amusing. . . . A better book cannot be purchased."—*Ladies' Journal.*

BEE-KEEPING, BOOK OF. A very Practical and Complete Manual on the Proper Management of Bees, especially written for Beginners and Amateurs who have but a few Hives. Fully Illustrated. By W. B. WEBSTER, First-class Expert, B.B.K.A. *Price* 1s.; *in cloth,* 1s. 6d. "The information afforded is of a very practical character, and is precisely that which is required by a beginner."—*The Field.*

BEES AND BEE-KEEPING: Scientific and Practical. By F. R. CHESHIRE, F.L.S., F.R.M.S., Lecturer on Apiculture at South Kensington. Vol. I., SCIENTIFIC. A complete Treatise on the Anatomy and Physiology of the Hive Bee. *In cloth gilt, price* 7s. 6d. VOL. II., PRACTICAL MANAGEMENT OF BEES. *In cloth gilt, price* 8s. 6d. "This is a very interesting book. . . . The illustrations are admirable."—*The Saturday Review.*

BICYCLES AND TRICYCLES OF THE YEAR. Descriptions of the New Inventions and Improvements for the Present Season. Designed to assist intending purchasers in the choice of a machine. Illustrated. By HARRY HEWITT GRIFFIN. (Published Annually.) *In paper, price* 1s. "It is as comprehensive as could be desired. . . . We can readily testify to the strict impartiality of the author."—*The Field.*

BIRDS I HAVE KEPT IN YEARS GONE BY. With
Original Anecdotes, and Full Directions for Keeping them Successfully. By W. T. GREENE, M.A., M.D., F.Z.S., &c., Author of
" Parrots in Captivity," " The Amateur's Aviary " ; Editor of " Notes
on Cage Birds," &c., &c. With COLOURED PLATES. *In cloth
gilt, price 5s.* " A prettier present for anyone who is fond of these
household pets it would be difficult to find."—*Stock-keeper.*

BOAT BUILDING AND SAILING, PRACTICAL.
Containing Full Instructions for Designing and Building Punts, Skiffs,
Canoes, Sailing Boats, &c. Particulars of the most Suitable Sailing
Boats and Yachts for Amateurs, and Instructions for their Proper
Handling. Fully Illustrated with Designs and Working Diagrams.
By ADRIAN NEISON, C.E., DIXON KEMP, A.I.N.A., and G.
CHRISTOPHER DAVIES. *In one vol., cloth gilt, price 7s. 6d.* " A
capital manual. . . . All is clearly and· concisely explained."—*The
Graphic.*

BOAT BUILDING FOR AMATEURS, PRACTICAL.
Containing Full Instructions for Designing and Building Punts, Skiffs,
Canoes, Sailing Boats, &c. Fully Illustrated with Working Diagrams.
By ADRIAN NEISON, C.E. New Edition, Revised and Enlarged, by
DIXON KEMP, Author of " Yacht Designing," " A Manual of Yacht
and Boat Sailing," &c. *In cloth gilt, price 2s. 6d.* " A capital
manual. . . . All is clearly and concisely explained."—*The Graphic.*

BOAT SAILING FOR AMATEURS. Containing Par-
ticulars of the most Suitable Sailing Boats and Yachts for Amateurs,
and Instructions for their Proper Handling, &c. Illustrated with
numerous Diagrams. By G. CHRISTOPHER DAVIES. Second Edition,
Revised and Enlarged, and with several New Plans of Yachts. *In
cloth gilt, price 5s.* " We know of no better companion for the
young yachtsman."—*Sporting Chronicle.*

BOOKBINDING FOR AMATEURS: Being Descriptions
of the various Tools and Appliances Required, and Minute Instructions
for their Effective Use. By W. J. E. CRANE. Illustrated with 156
Engravings. *In cloth gilt, price 2s. 6d.* " A handy manual for the
study of an interesting and important art."—*The Graphic.*

BROADS, THE LAND OF THE. By E. R. SUFFLING.
" A capital guide to the angler, the yachtsman, or the artist."—
Scotsman.

ILLUSTRATED EDITION.—The most Complete Guide to
the whole of the District—embracing the Broads and their Water-
ways of Norfolk and Suffolk—that has yet been published, as it
contains more practical and reliable information than is to be found
elsewhere respecting Yachting, Fishing, Places of Interest, Archæological Remains, Natural Features of the Country, the Birds and
Fishes found there, the Customs of the Natives, and other points
concerning which Tourists desire to know. A good Map of the
Broads, Rivers, Chief Roads, and Places named, *printed in four
colours*, accompanies the work. *Price 2s. 6d.*

CHEAP EDITION.—A Cheap Edition of a reliable Guide to the Norfolk Broads, which would meet the requirements of the general Public, having been called for, the *First* Edition of the above Book has been issued in this form, but it has been embellished with some Plates of Characteristic Sketches taken on the spot by the well-known artist of Fishing and Waterside Subjects, Mr. J. TEMPLE. A good and *clear* Map, in black and white, is also given. In Illustrated Cover, printed in colours, *price* 1s.

BULBS AND BULB CULTURE : Being Descriptions, both Historical and Botanical, of the principal Bulbs and Bulbous Plants grown in this Country, and their chief Varieties ; with Full and Practical Instructions for their Successful Cultivation both In and Out of Doors. Illustrated. By D. T. FISH. *In cloth gilt, in one vol.,* 465*pp., price* 5s. "One of the best and most trustworthy books on bulb culture that have been put before the public."— *Gardeners' Chronicle.*

BUTTERFLIES AND MOTHS, COLLECTING: Being Directions for Capturing, Killing, and Preserving Lepidoptera and their Larvæ. Illustrated. Reprinted, with Additions, from "Practical Taxidermy." By MONTAGU BROWNE, Author of "Practical Taxidermy." *In paper, price* 1s. "One of the handiest little helps yet published."—*Excelsior.*

CACTUS CULTURE FOR AMATEURS : Being Descriptions of the various Cactuses grown in this country ; with Full and Practical Instructions for their Successful Cultivation. By W. WATSON, of the Royal Botanic Gardens, Kew. Profusely Illustrated. *In cloth gilt, price* 5s.

CAGE BIRDS, BRITISH. Containing Full Directions for Successfully Breeding, Rearing, and Managing the various British Birds that can be kept in Confinement. Illustrated with COLOURED PLATES and numerous finely cut Wood Engravings. By R. L. WALLACE. *In cloth gilt, price* 10s. 6d.*; also in Monthly Parts, price* 7d. "Is calculated to be most useful."—*The Field.*

CAGE BIRDS, DISEASES OF : Their Cause, Symptoms, and Treatment. A Handbook which should be in the hands of everyone who keeps a Bird, as successful Treatment of Ailments depends on knowing what to do, and *doing it promptly.* By Dr. W. T. GREENE, F.Z.S. *In paper, price* 1s. "No lover of birds should fail to possess himself or herself of the book."—*Nottingham Daily Guardian.*

CAGE BIRDS, FOREIGN. Containing Full Directions for Successfully Breeding, Rearing, and Managing the various Beautiful Cage Birds imported into this country. Beautifully Illustrated. By C. W. GEDNEY. *In cloth gilt, in two vols., price* 8s. 6d.*; in extra cloth gilt, gilt edges, in one vol., price* 9s. 6d. "Full of information on every point."—*Public Opinion.*

PARROTS, PARRAKEETS, COCKATOOS, LORIES, and MACAWS : Their Varieties, Breeding, and Management. Illustrated. *(Forming Vol. I. of "Foreign Cage Birds.") In cloth gilt, price* 3s. 6d.

WAXBILLS, FINCHES, WEAVERS, ORIOLES, and other Small Foreign Aviary Birds : Their Varieties, Breeding, and Management. Beautifully Illustrated. *(Forming Vol. II. of " Foreign Cage Birds.") In cloth gilt, price 5s.*

CANARY BOOK.
Containing Full Directions for the Breeding, Rearing, and Management of all Varieties of Canaries and Canary Mules, the Promotion and Management of Canary Societies and Exhibitions, and all other matters connected with this Fancy. By ROBERT L. WALLACE. Second Edition, Enlarged and Revised, with many new Illustrations of Prize Birds, Cages, &c. *In cloth gilt, price 5s.; with* SPECIAL COLOURED PLATES, *price 6s. 6d.; also in Monthly Parts, price 7d.* "This very comprehensive work . . . . which is one of a most practical character . . . . may be safely consulted by all canary fanciers."—*The Field.*

GENERAL MANAGEMENT OF CANARIES. Including Cages and Cage-making, Breeding, Managing, Mule Breeding, Diseases and their Treatment, Moulting, Rats and Mice, &c. Illustrated. *(Forming Section I. of the " Canary Book.") In cloth, price 2s. 6d.*

EXHIBITION CANARIES. Containing Full Particulars of all the different Varieties, their Points of Excellence, Preparing Birds for Exhibition, Formation and Management of Canary Societies and Exhibitions. Illustrated. *(Forming Section II. of the " Canary Book.") In cloth, price 2s. 6d.*

CARD TRICKS, BOOK OF,
for Drawing-room and Stage Entertainments ; with an Exposure of Tricks as practised by Card Sharpers and Swindlers. Numerous Illustrations. By Prof. R. KUNARD. *Illustrated Wrapper, price 2s. 6d.*

CARPENTRY AND JOINERY FOR AMATEURS.
Contains Full Descriptions of the various Tools Required in the above Arts, together with Practical Instructions for their Use. By the Author of " Turning for Amateurs," &c. *In cloth gilt, price 2s. 6d.* " The best of the book consists of practical instructions."—*Iron.*

CHURCH EMBROIDERY:
Its Early History and Manner of Working ; Materials Used and Stitches Employed ; Raised and Flat Couching, Appliqué, &c., &c., including Church Work over Cardboard. A practical handbook for Church Workers. Illustrated. *In paper, price 1s.* " It cannot fail to be useful and appreciated."—*Weldon's Ladies' Journal.*

CHURCH FESTIVAL DECORATIONS.
Comprising Directions and Designs for the Suitable Decoration of Churches for Christmas, Easter, Whitsuntide, and Harvest. Illustrated. A useful book for the Clergy and their Lay Assistants. *In paper, price 1s.* " Much valuable and practical information."—*Sylvia's Home Journal.*

COFFEE STALL MANAGEMENT, PRACTICAL
HINTS ON, and other Temperance Work for the Laity. *In paper, price 1s.* " A most valuable guide."—*The Queen.*

∴ All Books Post Free.

COINS, A GUIDE TO ENGLISH PATTERN, in Gold, Silver, Copper, and Pewter, from Edward I. to Victoria, with their Value. By the REV. G. F. CROWTHER, M.A., Member of the Numismatic Society of London. Illustrated. *In silver cloth, with gilt facsimiles of Coins, price* 5s.

COINS OF GREAT BRITAIN AND IRELAND, A GUIDE TO THE, in Gold, Silver, and Copper, from the Earliest Period to the Present Time, with their Value. By the late Colonel W. STEWART THORBURN. Of immense value to collectors and dealers. 27 Plates in Gold, Silver, and Copper, and Gold and Silver Coins in *raised facsimile. In Monthly Parts, price* 7d., *or complete in gold cloth, with silver facsimiles of Coins, price* 7s. 6d. "Such a book as this has never before been placed within the reach of the ordinary collector. . . . . A model of careful and accurate work."—*The Queen.*

COLLIE, THE. A Monograph on the History, Points, and Breeding of the Scotch Collie. By HUGH DALZIEL. Illustrated. *Demy 8vo, price* 1s.; *cloth,* 2s.

COLUMBARIUM, MOORE'S. Reprinted Verbatim from the original Edition of 1735, with a Brief Notice of the Author. By W. B. TEGETMEIER, F.Z.S., Member of the British Ornithologists' Union. *Price* 1s.

COOKERY FOR AMATEURS; or, French Dishes for English Homes of all Classes. Includes Simple Cookery, Middle-class Cookery, Superior Cookery, Cookery for Invalids, and Breakfast and Luncheon Cookery. By MADAME VALÉRIE. Second Edition. *In paper, price* 1s. "Is admirably suited to its purpose."—*The Broad Arrow.*

CUCUMBER CULTURE FOR AMATEURS. Including also Melons, Vegetable Marrows, and Gourds. Illustrated. By W. J. MAY. *In paper, price* 1s. "Before entering on the cultivation of cucumbers, melons, marrows, or gourds, we would recommend to their perusal Mr. May's handbook."—*Dublin Evening Mail.*

DAIRY FARMING, PRACTICAL. A Short Treatise on the Profitable Management of a Dairy Farm. Illustrated. By G. SEAWARD WITCOMBE. *In paper, price* 1s. 6d. "A mass of interesting material."—*The Field.*

DEGREES, A GUIDE TO, in Arts, Science, Literature, Law, Music, and Divinity, in the United Kingdom, the Colonies, the Continent, and the United States. By E. WOOTON, Author of "A Guide to the Medical Profession," &c. *In cloth, price* 15s. "Is a complete storehouse of educational information."—*The Graphic.*

DOGS, BREAKING AND TRAINING: Being Concise Directions for the proper Education of Dogs, both for the Field and for Companions. Second Edition. By "PATHFINDER." With Chapters by HUGH DALZIEL on Work of Special Breeds; Trail or Drag Hounds; Training Bloodhounds; Defenders and Watch Dogs;

Sheep Dogs—Stock Tenders ; Life Savers—Water Dogs ; Vermin
Destroyers ; House Manners ; Behaviour Out of Doors. Illustrated.
In cloth gilt, price 6s. 6d. "We strongly recommend a perusal of
it to all who have to do with young dogs, whether for sport or as
companions."—*Farmers' Gazette.*

DOGS, BRITISH : Their Varieties, History, Characteristics,
Breeding, Management and Exhibition. By HUGH DALZIEL,
Author of "The Diseases of Dogs," "The Diseases of Horses," &c.;
assisted by Eminent Fanciers. NEW EDITION, Revised and
Enlarged. Illustrated with First-class COLOURED PLATES and
full-page Engravings of Dogs of the Day. This will be the fullest
and most recent work on the various breeds of dogs kept in England;
and, as its Author is one of the first living authorities on the subject,
its accuracy can be relied upon. Demy 8vo. In two Volumes ;
Vol. I. Now Ready, *price* 10s. 6d.; *also in Monthly Parts, price* 7d.
"This admirable work . . . . is packed full of curious, interesting,
and useful information."—*The Country Gentleman.*

    DOGS USED IN FIELD SPORTS (*Forming Vol. I. of "British
Dogs"*). Containing particulars of the following, among other
Breeds: Greyhound, Irish Wolfhound, Bloodhound, Foxhound,
Harrier, Basset, Dachshund, Pointer, Setters, Spaniels, and
Retrievers. SEVEN COLOURED PLATES and 21 full-page Engravings.
In cloth gilt, price 10s. 6d.

DOGS, DISEASES OF : Their Pathology, Diagnosis, and
Treatment ; to which is added a complete Dictionary of Canine
Materia Medica ; Modes of Administering Medicines ; Treatment in
cases of Poisoning, and the Value of Disinfectants. For the use of
Amateurs. By HUGH DALZIEL, Author of "British Dogs," &c.
New, Revised, and greatly Enlarged Edition. *In paper, price* 1s. ;
in cloth gilt, 2s. "Will enable anybody who keeps a dog to deal
with cases of ordinary indisposition or injury."—*The Scotsman.*

DUCKS AND GEESE : Their Characteristics, Points, and
Management. The only book on the subject of Domestic Water-
fowl and their Proper Treatment. By Various Breeders. Splendidly
Illustrated. *In paper, price* 1s. 6d. "A very desirable little work."—
The Queen.

EXHIBITION ACCOUNT BOOKS. For use at all Dog,
Poultry, Rabbit, and Cage Bird Shows. In Four Books, comprising :
I. Minute Book ; II. Cash Book ; III. Entries Book ; IV. Ledger.
With Full Directions, and Illustrative Examples for Working them.
N.B.—The Set of Four Books is kept in Three Series: No. 1,
for Show of 500 Entries, 5s. the Set ; No. 2, for 1000 Entries, 7s. 6d.
the Set ; and No. 3, for 1500 Entries, 12s. 6d. the Set. Larger
sizes in proportion. The books can be had separate. MINUTE
BOOK—No. 1, 1s. ; No. 2, 1s. 3d. ; No. 3, 2s. CASH BOOK—
No. 1, 2s. ; No. 2, 2s. 6d. ; No. 3, 4s. ENTRIES BOOK—No. 1,
2s. ; No. 2, 2s. 6d. ; No. 3, 4s. Ledger—No. 1, 2s. ; No. 2, 2s. 6d. ;
No. 3, 4s. . "Just what are wanted, for a set of these books will save
a vast amount of labour and trouble."—*The Stock-keeper.*

FANCY WORK SERIES, ARTISTIC. A Series of Illustrated Manuals on Artistic and Popular Fancy Work of various kinds. Each number is complete in itself, and issued at the uniform *price* of 6d. Now ready—(1) MACRAMÉ LACE (Second Edition); (2) PATCHWORK; (3) TATTING; (4) CREWEL WORK; (5) APPLIQUÉ; (6) FANCY NETTING. "Will prove a valuable acquisition to the student of art needlework."—*The Englishwoman's Review.*

FERNS, CHOICE BRITISH. Descriptive of the most beautiful Variations from the common form, and their Culture. By C. T. DRUERY, F.L.S. Very accurate PLATES, and other Illustrations. *In cloth gilt, price* 2s. 6d.

FERRETS AND FERRETING. Containing Instructions for the Breeding, Management, and Working of Ferrets. Second Edition, Re-written and greatly Enlarged. Illustrated. *In paper, price* 6d.

FERTILITY OF EGGS CERTIFICATE. These are Forms of Guarantee given by the Sellers to the Buyers of Eggs for Hatching, undertaking to refund value of any unfertile eggs, or to replace them with good ones. *In books, with counterfoils, price* 6d.

FIREWORK-MAKING FOR AMATEURS. A most complete, accurate, and easily understood work on Making both Simple and High-class Fireworks. By Dr. W. H. BROWNE, M.A. *Price* 2s. 6d.

FISHERMAN, PRACTICAL. Dealing with the Natural History, the Legendary Lore, the Capture of British Freshwater Fish, and Tackle and Tackle Making. Beautifully Illustrated. By J. H. KEENE. *In cloth gilt, gilt edges, price* 10s. 6d. "It is by a thoroughly practical angler. . . . Will form a valuable addition to the angler's library."—*Fishing Gazette.*

FOREIGN BIRDS, AMATEUR'S AVIARY OF ; or, How to Keep and Breed Foreign Birds with Pleasure and Profit in England. Illustrated. By W. T. GREENE, M.D., M.A., F.Z.S., F.S.S., &c., Author of "Parrots in Captivity," &c. *In cloth gilt, price* 3s. 6d. "Is worthy of a hearty welcome from all breeders and keepers of foreign birds."—*Live Stock Journal.*

GAME AND GAME SHOOTING, NOTES ON. Miscellaneous Observations on Birds and Animals, and on the Sport they afford for the Gun in Great Britain, including Grouse, Partridges, Pheasants, Hares, Rabbits, Quails, Woodcocks, Snipe, and Rooks. By J. J MANLEY, M.A., Author of "Notes on Fish and Fishing." Illustrated. *In cloth gilt, 400pp., price* 7s. 6d. "A thoroughly practical as well as very interesting book."—*The Graphic.*

GAME PRESERVING, PRACTICAL. Containing the fullest Directions for Rearing and Preserving both Winged and Ground Game, and Destroying Vermin ; with other Information of Value to the Game Preserver. Illustrated. By WILLIAM CARNEGIE. *In cloth gilt, demy 8vo, price* 21s. "Mr. Carnegie gives a great

variety of useful information as to game and game preserving. . . .
We are glad to repeat that the volume contains much useful information, with many valuable suggestions. . . . . The instructions as to
pheasant rearing are sound, and nearly exhaustive."—*The Times.*
"It is practical, straightforward, and always lucid. The chapters on
poaching and poachers, both human and animal, are particularly to
the point, and amusing withal."—*The World.*

GARDENING, DICTIONARY OF. A Practical Encyclo-
pædia of Horticulture, for Amateurs and Professionals. Illustrated
with upwards of 2000 Engravings. Edited by G. NICHOLSON,
Curator of the Royal Botanic Gardens, Kew; assisted by Prof.
Trail, M.D., Rev. P. W. Myles, M.A., B. W. Hemsley, A.L.S.,
W. Watson, J. Garrett, and other Specialists. *In 4 vols., large
post 4to.* Vol. I., A to E, 552pp., 743 Illustrations; Vol. II.,
F to O, 544pp., 811 Illustrations; Vol. III., P to S, 537pp., 564
Illustrations. Vol. IV., T to Z, and Supplement of Pronouncing
Dictionary, Indices to Plants for Special Purposes, &c. Illustrations.
Price 15s. each. Also in Monthly Parts, price 1s. "This important
undertaking."—*Daily Telegraph.* "The most complete work of its
kind."—*Daily News.* "The fullest information is given, and the
illustrations, which are exceedingly numerous, are first rate."—*The
World.*

GARDEN PESTS AND THEIR ERADICATION.
Containing Practical Instructions for the Amateur to overcome the
Enemies of the Garden. With numerous Illustrations. *In paper,
price 1s.* "It is just the sort of book one would refer to in emer-
gency."—*The Florist and Pomologist.*

GOAT, BOOK OF THE. Containing Full Particulars of the
various Breeds of Goats, and their Profitable Management. With
many Plates. By H. STEPHEN HOLMES PEGLER. Third Edition,
Revised, Enlarged, and with additional Illustrations and Coloured
Frontispiece. *In cloth gilt, price 4s 6d.* "The best book we know
on the subject."—*Chambers's Journal.*

GOAT-KEEPING FOR AMATEURS: Being the Practical Management of Goats for Milking Purposes. Abridged from
"The Book of the Goat," by H. S. HOLMES PEGLER. Illustrated.
In paper, price 1s. "We can conceive of no better book for anyone
commencing to keep these valuable animals."—*Fanciers' Gazette.*

GREENHOUSE MANAGEMENT FOR AMATEURS.
Descriptions of the best Greenhouses and Frames, with Instructions
for Building them, particulars of the various methods of Heating, Illus-
trated Descriptions of the most suitable Plants, with general and
special Cultural Directions, and all necessary information for the
Guidance of the Amateur. Second Edition, Revised and Enlarged.
Magnificently Illustrated. By W. J. MAY. *In cloth gilt, price 5s.*
"Ought to be in the hands of everybody."—*The Queen.*

GREYHOUND, THE. A Monograph on the History, Points,
Breeding, Rearing, Training, and Running of the Greyhound. By
HUGH DALZIEL. With Coloured Frontispiece. *In cloth gilt, demy*

8vo, price 2s. 6d. "As a rule, no authors are more egotistic than those who write on subjects connected with sport, but Mr. Dalziel is a brilliant exception. . . . Mr. Dalziel's summary of the points of a Greyhound is admirable, and young coursers would do well to learn it by heart. . . . The chapter on Breeding is one of the most · interesting in the book."—*Saturday Review.*

GUINEA PIG, THE, for Food, Fur, and Fancy.

Illustrated with Coloured Frontispiece and Engravings. An exhaustive book on the Varieties of the Guinea Pig, or Cavy, and their Management for Pleasure or Profit. By C. CUMBERLAND, F.Z.S. *In cloth gilt, price 2s. 6d.* "Of great interest and practical value."—*Nottingham Daily Express.*

HANDWRITING, CHARACTER INDICATED BY.

With Illustrations in Support of the Theories advanced taken from Autograph Letters of Statesmen, Lawyers, Soldiers, Ecclesiastics, Authors, Poets, Musicians, Actors, and other persons. Second Edition, Revised and Enlarged. By R. BAUGHAN. *In cloth gilt, price 2s. 6d.* "An amusing little book."—*Public Opinion.*

HARDY PERENNIALS and Old-fashioned Garden Flowers.

Descriptions, alphabetically arranged, of the most desirable Plants for Borders, Rockeries, and · Shrubberies, including Foliage as well as Flowering Plants. Profusely Illustrated. By J. WOOD. *In cloth, price 5s.* "Seems particularly useful."—*Athenæum.*

HONITON LACE BOOK.

Containing Full and Practical Instructions for Making Honiton Lace. With numerous Illustrations. *In cloth gilt, price 3s. 6d.* "We have seldom seen a book of this class better got up."—*Bell's Weekly Messenger.*

HORSE IN SICKNESS, THE, and How to Treat Him.

Being the result of twenty-five years' experience amongst Cab and Omnibus Horses. By JOHN COCKRAM. *Price 6d.* "An excellent little book."—*The Morning Post.*

HORSE-KEEPING FOR AMATEURS.

A Practical Manual on the Management of Horses, for the guidance of those who keep them for their personal use. By FOX RUSSELL. *Price 1s.* "This well-written record of intelligent observation upon horses."—*Live Stock Journal.*

HORSES, DISEASES OF : Their Pathology, Diagnosis, and

Treatment ; to which is added a complete Dictionary of Equine Materia Medica. For the use of Amateurs. By HUGH DALZIEL. *In paper, price 1s.* "Should be in the hands of every horse owner."—*Sporting Chronicle.*

INDIAN OUTFITS AND ESTABLISHMENTS.

A Practical Guide for Persons about to Reside in India ; detailing the Articles which should be taken out, and the Requirements of Home Life and Management there. By an ANGLO-INDIAN. *In cloth, price*

2s. 6d. "Is thoroughly healthy in tone, and practical."—*Saturday Review.*

JOURNALISM, PRACTICAL : How to Enter Thereon and Succeed. A Manual for Beginners and Amateurs. A book for all who think of "writing for the Press." By JOHN DAWSON. *In cloth gilt, price* 2s. 6d. "A very practical and sensible little book."—*Spectator.*

KENNEL DIARY. A Register for Owners, Breeders, and Exhibitors of Dogs, wherein they can keep full particulars of their Studs in a convenient and comprehensive manner. It contains, in addition to a complete Gestation Table for the Year : 1, Index Diary ; 2, Owner's Diary ; 3, Breeder's Diary ; 4, Diary of Pups ; 5, Stud Diary ; 6, Exhibition Diary ; 7, General Diary ; 8, Pedigree Diary ; 9, Receipts ; 10, Expenditure ; 11, General Balance Sheet. *In cloth, with Pockets for Certificates, price* 3s. 6d. "The editor has left little room for improvement."—*Live Stock Journal.*

LEGAL PROFESSION, A GUIDE TO THE. A Practical Treatise on the various Methods of Entering either Branch of the Legal Profession ; also a Course of Study for each of the Examinations, and selected Papers of Questions ; forming a Complete Guide to every Department of Legal Preparation. By J. H. SLATER, Barrister-at-Law, of the Middle Temple. *Price* 7s. 6d. "Anyone who, before entering on either branch of the profession, desires information to determine which branch it shall be, will find a great deal here that will assist him."—*The Law Student's Journal.*

LIBRARY MANUAL, THE. A Guide to the Formation of a Library and the Valuation of Rare and Standard Books. By J. H. SLATER, Barrister-at-Law, Author of "A Guide to the Legal Profession." Second Edition. *In cloth,* 112*pp., price* 2s. 6d. "A most excellent and useful handbook."—*Public Opinion.*

LILY OF THE VALLEY : All About It, and How to Grow It ; Forced Indoors and Out of Doors, in Various Ways. By WILLIAM ROBERTS. *In paper covers, price* 6d. "Lovers of these beautiful flowers will welcome this edition."—*Paper and Printing Trades' Journal.*

MARKET GARDENING, PROFITABLE. Adapted for the use of all Growers and Gardeners. By WILLIAM EARLEY, Author of "High-class Kitchen Gardening," &c. *In cloth, price* 2s. "Labour greatly assisted by a perusal of this work."—*North British Agriculturist.*

MEDITERRANEAN WINTER RESORTS. A Practical Handbook to the Principal Health and Pleasure Resorts on the Shores of the Mediterranean. By E. A. R. BALL. With a Map and 20 Illustrations. *Fcap. 8vo, price* 3s. 6d.

MICE, FANCY : Their Varieties, Management, and Breedin Re-issue, with Criticisms and Notes by DR. CARTER BLAKE, Illustrated. *In paper, price* 6d. "Goes thoroughly into the subject.' —*Cambridge Chronicle.*

MIRROR PAINTING IN THE ITALIAN STYLE.
A Practical Manual of Instruction for Amateurs. This highly decorative art has become very popular, but the execution is not always worthy of the design, in consequence of want of knowledge on the part of the artist ; this book will supply the deficiency. By Mrs. Sharp-Ayres. *Price 1s.*

MODEL YACHTS AND BOATS : Their Designing, Making,
and Sailing. Illustrated with 118 Designs and Working Diagrams. A splendid book for boys and others interested in making and rigging toy boats for sailing. It is the best book on the subject now published. By J. du V. Grosvenor. *In leatherette, price 5s.* " We can safely commend the volume."—*The Graphic.*

MONKEYS, NOTES ON PET, and How to Manage Them.
Profusely Illustrated. By Arthur Patterson. *Cloth gilt, price 2s. 6d.* " It will be acceptable to those who desire the practical information it contains."—*The Field.*

MUSHROOM CULTURE FOR AMATEURS. With
Full Directions for Successful Growth in Houses, Sheds, Cellars, and Pots, on Shelves, and Out of Doors. Illustrated. By W. J. May, Author of " Vine Culture for Amateurs," " Vegetable Culture for Amateurs," " Cucumber Culture for Amateurs." *In paper, price 1s.* " This excellent little book gives every direction necessary." —*Daily Bristol Times and Mirror.*

NATURAL HISTORY SKETCHES among the Car-
nivora — Wild and Domesticated ; with Observations on their Habits and Mental Faculties. By Arthur Nicols, F.G.S., F.R.G.S., Author of " Zoological Notes," " The Puzzle of Life." Illustrated by J. T. Nettleship, C. E. Brittan, and T. W. Wood. *In cloth gilt, price 5s.* " This little volume is full of interest."— *Nature.*

NEEDLEWORK, DICTIONARY OF. An Encyclopædia
of Artistic, Plain, and Fancy Needlework ; Plain, practical, complete, and magnificently Illustrated. By S. F. A. Caulfeild and B. C. Saward. Accepted by H.M. the Queen, H.R.H. the Princess of Wales, H.R.H. the Duchess of Edinburgh, H.R.H. the Duchess of Connaught, and H.R.H. the Duchess of Albany. Dedicated by special permission to H.R.H. Princess Louise, Marchioness of Lorne. *In demy 4to, 528pp., 829 Illustrations, extra cloth gilt, plain edges, cushioned bevelled boards, price 21s. ; with COLOURED PLATES, elegant satin brocade cloth binding, and coloured edges, 31s. 6d.* " This very complete and rather luxurious volume is a thorough encyclopædia of artistic, plain, and fancy needlework. . . After being submitted to the severe test of feminine criticism, the ' Dictionary' emerges triumphant. . . . The volume as a whole deserves no small commendation."—*The Standard.* " This volume, one of the handsomest of its kind, is illustrated in the best sense of the term. . . . It is useful and concise—in fact, it is exactly what it professes to be. . . . This book has endured the severest test at our command with rare success."—*The Athenæum.*

ORCHIDS FOR AMATEURS. Containing Descriptions of Orchids suited to the requirements of the Amateur, with full Instructions for their successful Cultivation. With numerous beautiful Illustrations. By JAMES BRITTEN, F.L.S., and W. H. GOWER. *In cloth gilt, price 7s. 6d.* A New and Enlarged Edition, *in demy 8vo, with COLOURED PLATES,* in the Press. "The joint work of a competent botanist . . . . and a successful cultivator with the experience of a quarter of a century."—*Gardener's Chronicle.*

PAINTING, DECORATIVE. A Practical Handbook on Painting and Etching upon Textiles, Pottery, Porcelain, Paper, Vellum, Leather, Glass, Wood, Stone, Metals, and Plaster, for the Decoration of our Homes. By B. C. SAWARD. *In the new "Renaissance" binding, price 7s. 6d.* "Spared no pains to give useful information as to the various processes of decorative painting."—*Academy.*

PAINTING ON CHINA, ALL ABOUT. With Twelve Descriptive Lessons. The object of this little book is to teach, by easy, Progressive Lessons, all that a beginner requires to know about China Painting. By Mrs. CONYERS MORRELL. Second Edition. *In paper, price 9d.*

PARROTS, THE SPEAKING. A Scientific Manual on the Art of Keeping and Breeding the principal Talking Parrots in Confinement. By Dr. KARL RUSS, Author of "The Foreign Aviary Birds," "Manual for Bird Fanciers," &c. Illustrated with COLOURED PLATES. *In .cloth gilt, price 6s. 6d.; also in Monthly Parts, price 7d.* "Here is all that can be desired ; the directions how to feed and how to keep foreign birds in health are given by the greatest authority living."—*Public Opinion.*

PATIENCE, GAMES OF, for one or more Players. A very clearly-written and well-illustrated Book of Instructions on How to Play no less than thirty-four different Games of Patience. By Miss WHITMORE JONES. Illustrated. *Price 1s.* "Will be welcome to many (invalids, brain-workers, and others) in search of quiet recreation. The instructions are clear, and the illustrative diagrams quite to the purpose."—*Pictorial World.*

PERSPECTIVE, THE ESSENTIALS OF. With numerous Illustrations drawn by the Author. By L. W. MILLER, Principal of the School of Industrial Art of the Pennsylvania Museum, Philadelphia. This book is such a manual as has long been desired for the guidance of art students and for self-instruction. It contains as much information about the science of Perspective as the artist or draughtsman ever has occasion to make use ·of, except under the most unusual conditions. The point of view throughout is that of the artist rather than the merely scientific theory of the art. The instructions are clearly set forth, free from all unessential or merely theoretical discussion, and the principles are vividly enforced by a large number of attractive drawings by the author, which illustrate every phase of his teachings. *Price 6s. 6d.* "The study of the science is presented in an interesting and attractive form, and the book is well got up."—*Myra's Journal.*

PHEASANT-KEEPING FOR AMATEURS. A Practical Handbook on the Breeding, Rearing, and General Management of Fancy Pheasants in Confinement. By GEO. HORNE. Illustrated with Diagrams of the necessary Pens, Aviaries, &c., and a Coloured Frontispiece and many full-page Engravings of the chief Varieties of Pheasants, drawn from life by A. F. LYDON. *Price* 3s. 6d.

PHOTOGRAPHY, PRACTICAL : Being the Science and Art of Photography, both Wet Collodion and the various Dry Plate Processes. Developed for Amateurs and Beginners. Illustrated. By O. E. WHEELER. *In cloth gilt, price* 4s. "Alike valuable to the beginner and the practised photographer."—*Photographic News.*

PIANOFORTES, TUNING AND REPAIRING. The Amateur's Guide to the Practical Management of a Piano without the intervention of a Professional. By CHARLES BABBINGTON. *In paper, price* 6d. "A very useful little book."—*Sylvia's Home Journal.*

PICTURE FRAME MAKING FOR AMATEURS. Being Practical Instructions in the Making of various kinds of Frames for Paintings, Drawings, Photographs, and Engravings. Illustrated. By the Author of "Carpentry and Joinery," &c. Cheap Edition, *in paper, price* 1s. "The book is thoroughly exhaustive." —*The Building World.*

PIG, BOOK OF THE. Containing the Selection, Breeding, Feeding, and Management of the Pig ; the Treatment of its Diseases ; the Curing and Preserving of Hams, Bacon, and other Pork Foods ; and other information appertaining to Pork Farming. By Professor JAMES LONG. Fully Illustrated with Portraits of Prize Pigs, by HARRISON WEIR and other Artists, Plans of Model Piggeries, &c. *In cloth gilt, price* 10s. 6d.; *also in Monthly Parts, price* 7d. "This is assuredly a publication to be proud of. It goes a good deal further than any book on the subject which has been issued before, and, without being infallible, is well informed, well illustrated, and well written."—*The Field.*

PIG-KEEPING FOR AMATEURS. A Practical Guide to the Profitable Management of Pigs. By G. GILBERT ("Gurth"). *In paper, price* 1s. "Not merely a good deal of useful and practical information, but many bits of homely folk-lore."—*Spectator.*

PIGEONS, FANCY. Containing Full Directions for the Breeding and Management of Fancy Pigeons, and Descriptions of every known Variety, together with all other information of interest or use to Pigeon Fanciers. Third Edition, bringing the subject down to the present time. 18 COLOURED PLATES, and 22 other full-page Illustrations. By J. C. LYELL. *Cloth gilt, price* 10s. 6d.; *also in Monthly Parts, price* 7d. "No fancier, in our judgment, should be without a copy of the work."—*The Stock-keeper.*

PLAYS FOR CHILDREN, SIX. Written specially for Representation by Children, and Designed to Interest both Actors and Audience. With Instructions for Impromptu Scenery, Costumes and Effects, and the Airs of the Various Songs. By CHAS. HARRISON, Author of "Amateur Theatricals and Tableaux Vivants." *Price 1s.* " We can heartily commend these six plays."—*Ladies' Journal.*

POTTERY AND PORCELAIN, ENGLISH. A Manual for Collectors : Being a Concise Account of the Development of the Potter's Art in England. Profusely Illustrated with Marks, Monograms, and Engravings of Characteristic Specimens. New Edition. *In cloth gilt, price 3s. 6d.* " The collector will find the work invaluable."—*Broad Arrow.*

POULTRY AILMENTS AND THEIR TREAT-MENT. A Book for the Use of all Poultry-keepers, describing the Causes, Symptoms, and Cure of Diseases affecting Domestic Fowl. By D. J. THOMPSON GRAY. *In paper boards, price 1s.* "We cannot too strongly advise all poultry-keepers to get a copy of this book, for it is the cheapest shilling's-worth we have seen for a long time."—*Farm and Home.*

POULTRY FOR PRIZES AND PROFIT. Contains : Breeding Poultry for Prizes, Exhibition Poultry, and Management of the Poultry Yard. Handsomely Illustrated. New Edition, Revised and Enlarged. By Professor JAMES LONG. *In cloth gilt, price 3s. 6d.* " Should be in the hands of all breeders of poultry."—*The Stock-keeper.*

PRINTING FOR AMATEURS. A Practical Guide to the Art of Printing ; containing Descriptions of Presses and Materials, together with Details of the Processes Employed ; to which is added a Glossary of Technical Terms. Illustrated. By P. E. RAYNOR. *In paper, price 1s.* " Concise and comprehensive."—*The Figaro.*

PRUNING, GRAFTING, AND BUDDING FRUIT TREES. Illustrated with 93 Diagrams. A book which can be followed with advantage by amateur fruit growers. By D. T. FISH. *In paper, price 1s.* " One of the few gardening books that will suit everybody."—*Gardener's Magazine.*

RABBIT, BOOK OF THE. A Complete Work on Breeding and Rearing all Varieties of Fancy Rabbits, giving their History, Variations, Uses, Points, Selection, Mating, Management, &c., &c. NEW EDITION, Revised and Enlarged. Edited by KEMPSTER W. KNIGHT. Illustrated with Coloured and other Plates. *One handsome vol., price 15s. (in the Press); also in Monthly Parts price 7d.*

RABBITS FOR PRIZES AND PROFIT. Containing Full Directions for the Proper Management of Fancy Rabbits in Health and Disease, for Pets or the Market, and Descriptions of every known Variety, with Instructions for Breeding good specimens. Illustrated. By the late CHARLES RAYSON. *In cloth gilt, price 2s. 6d.* " We have often had occasion to recommend this work."—*The Field.*

GENERAL MANAGEMENT OF RABBITS. Including Hutches, Breeding, Feeding, Diseases and their Treatment, Rabbit Coverts, &c.

Fully Illustrated. (*Forming Part I. of "Rabbits for Prizes and Profit."*) *In paper, price* 1s.

EXHIBITION RABBITS. Being descriptions of all Varieties of Fancy Rabbits, their Points of Excellence, and how to obtain them. Illustrated. (*Forming Part II. of "Rabbits for Prizes and Profit."*) *In paper, price* 1s.

REPOUSSÉ WORK FOR AMATEURS: Being the Art
of Ornamenting Thin Metal with Raised Figures. By L. L. HASLOPE. Illustrated. *In cloth gilt, price* 2s. 6d. "It is thoroughly practical, is well illustrated, and contains the information that beginners require."—*Saturday Review.*

ROSE BUDDING. Containing Full Instructions for the Suc-
cessful Performance of this interesting Operation. Illustrated Amateurs will find the information here given of great assistance. By D. T. FISH. *In paper, price* 6d. "Full, practical . . . . and contains many valuable hints."—*Garden.*

ROSES FOR AMATEURS. A Practical Guide to the
Selection and Cultivation of the best Roses, both for Exhibition or mere Pleasure, by that large section of the Gardening World, the Amateur Lover of Roses. Illustrated. By the REV. J. HONYWOOD D'OMBRAIN, Hon. Sec. of the National Rose Society. *Price* 1s.

ST. BERNARD, THE. A Monograph on the History,
Points, Breeding and Rearing of the St. Bernard. By HUGH DALZIEL. Illustrated. *Demy 8vo, price* 2s. 6d.; *cloth,* 3s. 6d.

SEA-FISHING FOR AMATEURS. A Book of Practical
Instructions on the Best Methods of Sea-Fishing from the Shore, Boats, or Jetties, with a very useful List of Fishing Stations, the Fish to be caught there, and the Best Seasons. By FRANK HUDSON. Illustrated. *Crown 8vo, price* 1s.

SEASIDE WATERING PLACES. A Description of
nearly 200 Holiday Resorts on the Coasts of England and Wales, the Channel Islands, and the Isle of Man, including the gayest and most quiet places, giving full particulars of them and their attractions, and all other information likely to assist persons in selecting places in which to spend their Holidays according to their individual tastes ; with BUSINESS DIRECTORY of Tradesmen, arranged in order of the Towns. Sixth Edition, with Illustrations. *In cloth, price* 2s. 6d. "The information it gives is of a decidedly practical and reliable nature."—*The Spectator.*

SHEET METAL, WORKING IN: Being Practical In-
structions for Making and Mending Small Articles in Tin, Copper, Iron, Zinc, and Brass. Illustrated. Third Edition. By the Author of "Turning for Amateurs," &c. *In paper, price* 6d. "Every possible information is given."—*The Reliquary.*

SHORTHAND, ON GURNEY'S SYSTEM (IM-
PROVED), LESSONS IN : Being Instruction in the Art of Short-hand Writing as used in the Service of the two Houses of Parliament.

By R. E. MILLER, of Dublin University; formerly Parliamentary Reporter; Fellow of the Shorthand Society. *In paper, price 1s.* "A very entertaining and able little book."—*Literary World.*

SHORTHAND SYSTEMS; WHICH IS THE BEST?

Being a Discussion, by various English Authors and Experts, on the Merits and Demerits of Taylor's, Gurney's, Pitman's, Everett's, Janes', Pocknell's, Peachey's, Guest's, Williams', Odell's, and Redfern's Systems, with Illustrative Examples. Edited by THOMAS ANDERSON, Author of "History of Shorthand," &c. This is a book which ought to be carefully read by every person who is about to take up the study of shorthand. *In paper, price 1s.* "Is certain to be very much appreciated."—*The Derby Mercury.*

SICK NURSING AT HOME:

Being Plain Directions and Hints for the Proper Nursing of Sick Persons, and the Home Treatment of Diseases and Accidents in case of Sudden Emergencies. By S. F. A. CAULFEILD. *In paper, price 1s.; in cloth, price 1s. 6d.* "A copy ought to be in every nursery."—*Society.*

SITTING HEN RECORD, THE.

Forming a Convenient Record of all Eggs Set, and supplying, in a handy and concise form, Labels which can be readily attached to or above the Nest-boxes, showing at a glance the Number of Eggs under the Hen, the Variety, and when they should be brought off. *Price—50 Forms, 6d.; 100 Forms, 1s.* "Every breeder should provide himself with this useful little record."—*Poultry.*

SKATING CARDS:

A Series of Cards, of convenient size *for Use on the Ice,* containing Clear Instructions and Diagrams for Learning the whole Art of Figure Skating. One of the cards, containing the figure to be learnt, is held in the hand whilst skating, so that the directions are read and acted on simultaneously. *Tinted cards, gilt edges, round corners, inclosed in strong leather pocket book, price 3s. 6d.; or in extra calf, satin lined (for presentation), price 5s. 6d.* "An ingenious method . . . and the instructions are brief and clear."—*The Queen.*

SLEIGHT OF HAND.

A Practical Manual of Legerdemain for Amateurs and Others. New Edition, Revised and Enlarged. Profusely Illustrated. By EDWIN SACHS. *In cloth gilt, price 6s. 6d.* "No one interested in conjuring should be without this work."—*Saturday Review.*

TAXIDERMY, PRACTICAL.

A Manual of Instruction to the Amateur in Collecting, Preserving, and Setting-up Natural History Specimens of all kinds. Fully Illustrated with Engravings of Tools, Examples, and Working Diagrams. By MONTAGU BROWNE, F.Z.S., Curator of Leicester Museum. New and Enlarged Edition. *In cloth gilt, price 7s. 6d.* "Throughout the volume is essentially practical."—*Daily Telegraph.*

THEATRICALS AND TABLEAUX VIVANTS FOR AMATEURS.

Giving Full Directions as to Stage Arrangements, "Making-up," Costumes, and Acting. With Numerous Illustrations.

By CHAS. HARRISON. *In cloth gilt, price* 2s. 6d. "Will be found invaluable."—*Court Journal.*

TOUR IN THE STATES AND CANADA. Out and Home in Six Weeks. By THOMAS GREENWOOD. Illustrated. *In cloth gilt, price* 2s. 6d. "We can confidently recommend this book."—*The Literary World.*

TOURIST'S ROUTE MAP of England and Wales, The. Third Edition, thoroughly Revised. Shows clearly all the Main, and most of the Cross, Roads, and the Distances between the Chief Towns, as well as the Mileage from London. In addition to this, Routes of *Thirty of the most Interesting Tours* are printed in red. The Map is mounted on linen, so as not to tear, and is inclosed in a strong cloth case ; it is thus in a convenient form for the pocket, and will not suffer from ordinary fair wear and tear, as is the case with most maps. This is, without doubt, the fullest, most accurate, handiest, and cheapest tourist's map in the market. *In cloth, price* 1s. " Reliable and accurate ; . . . an admirable companion to tourists and cyclists."—*The Tourist and Traveller.*

TOYMAKING FOR AMATEURS. Containing Instructions for the Home Construction of Simple Wooden Toys, and of others that are Moved or Driven by Weights, Clockwork, Steam, Electricity, &c. Illustrated. By JAMES LUKIN, B.A., Author of " Turning for Amateurs," &c. *In cloth gilt, price* 4s. " A capital book for boys."—*Dispatch.*

TRAPPING, PRACTICAL : Being some Papers on Traps and Trapping for Vermin, with a Chapter on General Bird Trapping and Snaring. By W. CARNEGIE. *In paper, price* 1s. "Cleverly written and illustrated."—*Sportsman.*

TURNING FOR AMATEURS : Being Descriptions of the Lathe and its Attachments and Tools, with Minute Instructions for their Effective Use on Wood, Metal, Ivory, and other Materials. New Edition, Revised and Enlarged. By JAMES LUKIN, B.A. Author of " The Lathe and its Uses," &c. Illustrated with 144 Engravings. *In cloth gilt, price* 2s. 6d. " Gives the amateur copious descriptions of tools and methods of working."—*The Builder.*

UPPER THAMES, THE ; From Richmond to Oxford. A Guide for Boating Men, Anglers, Picnic Parties, and all Pleasure-seekers on the River. Arranged on an entirely New Plan. Illustrated. *In paper, price* 1s. " One of the most useful handbooks to the River yet published."—*The Graphic.*

VEGETABLE CULTURE FOR AMATEURS. Concise Directions for the Cultivation of Vegetables so as to insure Good Crops in Small Gardens ; with Lists of the Best Varieties of each Sort. By W. J. MAY. *In paper, price* 1s. " None more simple and practically useful."—*The British Mail.*

VINE CULTURE FOR AMATEURS : Being Plain Directions for the Successful Growing of Grapes with the Means and

Appliances usually at the command of Amateurs. Illustrated. Grapes are so generally grown in villa greenhouses that this book cannot fail to be of great service to many persons. By W. J. MAY. *In paper, price 1s.* "Plain and practical."—*The Queen.*

VIOLIN, EASY LEGATO STUDIES FOR THE, for Home Students.

A Supplement to "The Practical Violin School for Home Students." By J. M. FLEMING. *In demy 4to, cloth gilt, price 3s. 6d.* "We can cordially commend this work to the attention of teachers as well as students."—*The Graphic.*

VIOLIN SCHOOL, PRACTICAL, for Home Students.

A Practical Book of Instructions and Exercises in Violin Playing, for the use of Amateurs, Self-learners, Teachers, and others. By J. M. FLEMING, Author of "Old Violins and their Makers." 1 *vol., demy 4to, cloth gilt, price 7s. 6d.; also in Monthly Parts (including as Supplement "Easy Legato Studies"), price 7d.* "Can be heartily commended to students who wish to lay a solid foundation for good and artistic playing."—*Musical Standard.*

WATERING PLACES OF FRANCE, NORTHERN.

A Guide for English People to the Holiday Resorts on the Coasts of the French Netherlands, Picardy, Normandy, and Brittany. By ROSA BAUGHAN, Author of "Winter Havens in the Sunny South," &c. *In paper, price 2s.* "We have pleasure in recommending this work."—*Cook's Excursionist.*

WINTER HAVENS IN THE SUNNY SOUTH.

A Complete Handbook to the Riviera, with a Notice of the New Station, Alassio. Splendidly Illustrated. BY ROSA BAUGHAN, Author of "The Northern Watering Places of France." *In cloth gilt, price 2s. 6d.* "It is a model 'guide,' and supplies a want."—*The Field.*

WOOD CARVING FOR AMATEURS.

Containing Descriptions of all the requisite Tools, and Full Instructions for their Use in producing different varieties of Carvings. Illustrated. A book of very complete instructions for the amateur wood carver. *In paper, price 1s.* "Will be found of great interest."—*Illustrated Carpenter and Builder.*

ZOOLOGICAL NOTES on the Structure, Affinities, Habits,

and Faculties of Snakes, Marsupials, and Birds ; with Adventures among, and Anecdotes of, them. By ARTHUR NICOLS, F.G.S., F.R.G.S., Author of "Natural History Sketches." *In walnut or sycamore, 8vo, price 7s. 6d.* From PROFESSOR RUSKIN.—"I have just opened your proofs, and am entirely delighted by the glance at them. . . . The engraving of the cobra—Mr. Babbage's—is the only true drawing of it I ever saw."

Books on the following subjects are in the Press.

THE AQUARIUM. This will be a thoroughly practical book on both the Fresh‑water and Marine Aquarium, and will be embellished with a great number of Original Illustrations of Weeds, Fish, Crustaceous Insects, &c., suitable for being kept in confinement. In every respect this work will be the most reliable of any yet published on the subject. The two Divisions — the Fresh‑water Aquarium and the Marine Aquarium—will be issued separately for the convenience of those who are interested in only one branch of the subject.

MODERN MAGIC. A Book of Conjuring for Amateurs. Well Illustrated. By PROF. R. KUNARD, Author of "The Book of Card Tricks."

COLLECTOR'S EDITION OF THE "BOOK OF THE ALL‑ROUND ANGLER." Printed on large antique paper, rough edges. Bound in Roxburghe. Only 200 copies issued, each being numbered and signed by the Author. *Price to subscribers,* 21s.

SKAT. A Book of Instructions on Playing the New Fashionable Game of Cards, which is described by those who know it as "the Acme of all Card Games." *Price* 1s.

POKER. A Practical Book of Playing this Fascinating Game with Success. *Price* 1s.

A Few Recipes for Household Use.

TO MAKE A RICH PLUM CAKE.—Take half-a-pound of butter and half-a-pound of white sifted sugar, beat these with the hand well together to a cream ; add four eggs, one at a time, and well beat each one with the butter and sugar; lightly mix in one pound of flour, previously mixed with one tea-spoonful of BORWICK'S GOLD MEDAL BAKING POWDER, then lightly mix with the whole half-a-pound of sultanas ; bake at once thoroughly, in a quick oven.

TO MAKE A GOOD PLAIN CAKE.—Mix well together one pound of flour, two full teaspoonfuls of BORWICK'S GOLD MEDAL BAKING POWDER, a little salt and spice, and a quarter-of-a-pound of sugar; rub in a quarter-of-a-pound of butter, add six ounces of sultanas, two ounces of currants, and one ounce of candied peel ; moisten the whole with two eggs and half-a-teacupful of milk, previously beaten together; bake in a quick oven very thoroughly.

BORWICK'S BAKING POWDER.

If BORWICK'S is not the best in the world, why has it gained 5 gold medals,

Any housewife will answer : Because it makes the best bread, the lightest pastry, and most tempting cakes and puddings. Tell your grocer you must have BORWICK'S.

TO MAKE BREAD.—To every pound of flour add a *heaped-up tea-spoonful* of BORWICK'S GOLD MEDAL BAKING POWDER, with a little salt, and *thoroughly mix* while in a dry state, then pour on gradually about half-a-pint of *cold* water, or milk and water, mixing quickly but thoroughly into a dough of the usual consistence, taking care not to knead it more than is necessary to mix it perfectly; make it into *small* loaves, which must be *immediately* put into a *quick* oven.

PUFF PASTE.—Mix one pound of flour with a teaspoonful of BORWICK'S GOLD MEDAL BAKING POWDER, then cut half-a-pound of butter into slices, roll it in thin sheets on some of your flour, wet up the rest with about a quarter-of-a-pint of water, see that it is about as stiff as your butter, roll it to a thin sheet, cover it with your sheets of butter, double it in a three double ; do the same five times ; it is then fit for use, or it may stand an hour covered over to keep the air from it.

Tell your Grocers you must have BORWICK'S.

www.ingramcontent.com/pod-product-compliance
Lightning Source LLC
Chambersburg PA
CBHW030352270326
41926CB00009B/1077